THE INTERNATIONAL M&A STRATEGIES
OF CHINESE COMPANIES

GLOBAL EXPANSION

THE CHINESE WAY

WEIRU CHEN, YUAN DING, KLAUS MEYER,
GAO WANG & KATHERINE XIN

Published by
LID Publishing Limited
The Record Hall, Studio 204,
16-16a Baldwins Gardens,
London EC1N 7RJ, UK

524 Broadway, 11th Floor, Suite 08-120,
New York, NY 10012, US

info@lidpublishing.com
www.lidpublishing.com

A member of:

www.businesspublishersroundtable.com

Printed in P.R China by Beijing Congreat Printing Co., Ltd
ISBN: 978-1-911498-72-8

Cover and page design: Caroline Li

THE INTERNATIONAL M&A STRATEGIES
OF CHINESE COMPANIES

GLOBAL EXPANSION

THE CHINESE WAY

**WEIRU CHEN, YUAN DING, KLAUS MEYER,
GAO WANG & KATHERINE XIN**

LONDON   MONTERREY
MADRID   SHANGHAI
MEXICO CITY   BOGOTA
NEW YORK   BUENOS AIRES
BARCELONA   SAN FRANCISCO

CONTENTS

PREFACE

In *Global Expansion, The Chinese Way*, we aim to offer insights to everyone interested in Chinese companies' approaches to internationalization. The book consists of three main parts: Strategy, Finance and Integration.

The Strategy section covers two chapters. It illustrates the motivations, approaches and modes of operation of Chinese companies going global. Supported by real-world case studies, we show that while most Western companies seek to exploit competitive advantages, achieve market growth and strive for synergies in global markets, Chinese enterprises aim to compensate for their competitive weaknesses and enhance their competitive advantages in the Chinese market. As the domestic market is the most important and attractive target for Chinese firms, we propose a three-stage model to illustrate the innovative path to globalization taken by Chinese companies: they first obtain resources and capabilities globally, then apply their newly acquired knowledge to the local market, and finally, expand to other overseas markets once they have gained a position of leadership in China.

The Finance section covers four chapters. Focusing on the principles of overseas mergers and acquisitions (M&A), we discuss the challenges that Chinese companies face in evaluating the resources and capabilities of target companies and explore some common problems in conducting due diligence. Throughout the process, decision makers need to pay careful attention to planning in order to assess their own capability in acquiring these resources and evaluating their value. One of the core issues faced by Chinese firms going global is to identify and remove risks, which should be taken into account beforehand by decision makers.

The Integration section covers two chapters. It uses case studies to analyse the post-merger integration model adopted by Chinese companies. Given the differences in motivation and paths to globalization between Chinese and Western companies, the typical post-merger integration model used by Western companies may not be suitable for Chinese purposes. We find that Chinese companies are more inclined to adopt a 'Light Touch' strategy after cross-border M&As. This strategy is best suited to enterprises in emerging economies which acquire those in developed countries, as the top management teams in developing countries are not yet fully equipped with the capabilities in management, manufacturing and marketing required in developed countries.

ACKNOWLEDGMENT

Throughout the process of writing this book, many individuals from the China Europe International Business School (CEIBS) have taken time out to help us out. We'd like to give a special thanks to our research assistants, Shiqi Xu, Lily Zhang, and Jim Zhong, from the Centre for the Globalization of Chinese Companies, for actively participating in the preparations, revisions and contributions for this book.

INTRODUCTION

Since the liberalization of its economy in the 1980s, China has become increasingly integrated into the global economy and has moved from the periphery to the centre of the international system. Chinese enterprises are in the news – devouring natural resources, soaking up investment, expanding their overseas footprint and broadening the country's global media exposure and cultural presence. Having experienced net capital inflows for more than 30 years, by 2006 China had accumulated the world's largest foreign exchange reserves, overtaking Japan; it became the world's second largest economy by 2010 (after the United States), and its economy is expected to surpass that of the US by 2025.

China's global expansion did not occur by happenstance. It grew out of government policies launched at the famous Third Plenary Session of the 11th Central Committee in December 1978 to engage in 'reform and opening'. Throughout the 1980s, China 'invited the world in' and took its first small steps on the world stage. Initially, Chinese internationalization was largely in one direction, as China received foreign investment and enhanced its economic strength by introducing advanced technologies from overseas. By the early 1990s, with China's economy developing rapidly, a conscious policy was launched to encourage Chinese enterprises to 'go out'. The primary purpose was not to pursue geographic expansion, but to use overseas investments to enhance Chinese competitiveness and improve firms' capabilities.

Thus, from the dawn of the 21st century, many Chinese enterprises believed that globalization represented the best opportunity to accelerate their growth. As a result, China's outward foreign direct investment (FDI) rose 17-fold from 2000 to 2007. Even during the global financial crisis, China's outward FDI flows continued to grow at an annual rate of 45%, from $26.5 billion US in 2007 to $56.5 billion in 2009. In 2012, when the debt crisis spread and global FDI declined by 17% compared with the previous year, China's outward FDI reached $87.8 billion, with a high growth rate of 17.6%, making China one of the world's three largest outward investors for the first time.[1]

Moreover, the Belt and Road Initiative (BRI), an economic and diplomatic programme launched in 2013 and reaffirmed in 2016 by President Xi Jinping, aims to further encourage China's global trade and investment.[2] The BRI involves China underwriting roughly $150 billion a year of infrastructure investment in countries along the old Silk Road linking China with Europe. By 2017, 74 countries and international organizations had signed up for this initiative.[3] The BRI facilitates the globalization process for Chinese firms in member countries. Thus, in 2016, China's outward FDI deal making exploded: with 438 FDI projects, Chinese enterprises stunned the world with a record $246 billion of announced outbound takeovers.[4] Although China's cross-border purchases plunged sharply in 2017, mainly due to tighter capital controls imposed by the Chinese government,[5] the trend of Chinese enterprises 'going out' appears irreversible.

In the rapid rise of foreign investment, we observe five major trends in terms of investment industries and destinations.

TREND 1: Cross-border mergers and acquisitions (M&As) have overtaken greenfield investments[6] and become an important way for Chinese companies to invest abroad. Between 2004 and 2013, the number of transactions showed steady growth. From 2004 to 2007, the number of cross-border M&As in China showed a rising trend despite fluctuations, with major deals especially in resource industries. By 2008, as the financial crisis created a rare opportunity for Chinese investors to buy high-quality assets at low prices in hard-hit Western economies, cross-border M&As rose steadily: the value of overseas M&As surged to $30.2 billion, increasing by 479% from $6.3 billion in 2007. Until 2016, the total value of cross-border M&As fluctuated, but grew at an average rate of 12.5%.

The high growth rate can mainly be attributed to two causes. Firstly, state-owned enterprises (SOEs) accelerated their global quest for resources. For instance, PetroChina, China National Grid and COFCO (China's largest food manufacturer) acquired natural resources and related businesses in Africa, Peru and Italy. Secondly, the determination of Chinese companies to gain access to brands, technology and management experience through cross-border M&A has become particularly prominent. For example, Fosun Group advanced its "model of China's impetus plus global resources" to acquire companies in financial, entertainment and other sectors; Industrial and Commercial Bank of China (ICBC) became a shareholder of South Africa's Standard Bank; while Lenovo acquired Motorola's mobile phone business for $2.91 billion.

TREND 2: Acquisition targets have become more diverse, with rapid growth in information technology and service industries. Chinese companies made overseas acquisitions in 28 industries between 2005 and 2014. In addition to traditional investment sectors such as energy resources, manufacturing, finance, construction and transportation, recent acquisitions also targeted aerospace, utilities, entertainment, healthcare, food, accommodation and other industries. In this way, China's economy is gradually shifting away from relying solely on its own development, towards the use of external resources, industrial restructuring and upgrading. In terms of M&A, the energy and mineral industry remained at the top from 2012 to the third quarter of 2014, with a total deal size of $57.137 billion, accounting for 55.3% of total M&A, followed by the real estate industry, with a deal size of $10.211 billion, accounting for 9.9%. The largest Chinese investment projects reflect this diversity: the oil corporation CNOOC acquired oil exploration company Nexen in Canada in 2012 for $15.1 billion; Shuanghui Group invested $7.1 billion in 2013 to acquire Smithfields, an American food processing company; and in 2016 ChemChina acquired animal feed and biotechnology company Syngenta in Switzerland for $43 billion.

Chinese overseas investors are increasingly aiming for high-tech industries with high value-added operations. The volume of investments in new industries is small as yet but rapidly growing. With the rise of the digital economy, more companies are willing to invest in internet, optoelectronic and other overseas industries to gain advanced technologies and improve their own operational scale. In 2016, while the manufacturing sector attracted the most outward FDI flows – 14.8% of the total amount – healthcare, education, information technologies and communications, and entertainment are the five sectors that achieved the highest growth rates, respectively 480.9%, 356.8%, 239.1%, 173.6%, and 121.4%.[7] Information transmission, software and information technology services, real estate, electricity, gas and water production and supply also showed rapid growth, but among these, high-tech industries in the United States and Germany were the first choice for most Chinese enterprises. As of 2016, high-tech investment in Germany and the US accounted for 83.1% of China's total overseas direct investment in high-tech industries.[8] More than 50% of Chinese companies were focused on three areas: IT equipment, software and IT services, and auto parts. This shows that Chinese enterprises engaged in diverse fields in their overseas M&A, with an emphasis on combining corporate strategic objectives and overseas markets, the aim being to build up a global business operation gradually, beginning by acquiring resources.

TREND 3: Cross-border M&A and outbound investment mainly focus on developing countries or surrounding regions. In 2016, Chinese companies invested in 742 overseas projects, valued in total at $107.2 billion.[9] The top five most popular investment destinations were: Hong Kong (China), the United States, the Cayman Islands, the British Virgin Islands and Australia. While the majority of Chinese enterprises invested in other Asian countries, China's outward FDI in advanced economies also experienced rapid growth. In 2008, investments in Asian countries reached a peak, at 77.9% of the total flows that year. In 2016, Asia accounted for 66.4% of China's outward FDI.[10] In terms of the number of M&As, Asia's share has been declining since 2006 – from 64.2% to 34.2% in 2012. In contrast, China's FDIs in North America and Europe account for only 10.4% and 5.4% of the total FDI capital respectively. Investment in each of these two regions was increasing at a rate of 89.9% and 50.2%. Of the two, the United States was the top destination, in both M&A activity and deal size. From 2012 to the third quarter of 2014, Chinese companies completed 78 M&A deals in the United States, accounting for 20.3% of the year's overall investments. This shows that Chinese enterprises prefer to invest in developed regions with a view to integrating global resources in a more sophisticated manner, based on their own strategic objectives.

TREND 4: Private enterprises are leading participants in the recent wave of M&As. Historically, China's SOEs have been the leaders in outward investment, both in the number and value of M&As. However, in recent years, the number of private enterprises involved in overseas investments has been growing fast. In 2006, SOEs represented 80.1% of China's outward FDI, but their share dropped to 50.8% in 2012, and by 2016, SOEs accounted for only 5.6% of all outward investors from China.[11] Private enterprises, in contrast, represented 2.2% of total China's outward FDI in 2012, and by 2016 this figure had increased to 26.2%. Furthermore, 3,000 private enterprises accounted for 60% of the enterprises 'going out' in China's manufacturing industry, and the United States and Europe are major M&A markets for private enterprises. For example, in the United States, China's private enterprises accounted for 76% of the total overseas investment capital and 90% of the total number of projects. Thus, private enterprises have not yet become the main drivers of China's overseas investment, but they are making the most of their flexibility, faster decision-making, efficiency, low overseas public profile and strong negotiation skills. Given the rapid growth rate of private investment, private companies are likely to become leaders of China's outward investment in the future.

TREND 5: Enhancing brand awareness and promoting technology are key motivations for investing overseas. According to the *Survey on Current Conditions and Intention of Outbound Investment by Chinese Enterprises* conducted by the China Council for the Promotion of International Trade (CCPIT), the importance of enhancing brand awareness is rising as a motivation for investment. In a study of enterprise brand management, SOEs paid more attention to building brand awareness than non-SOEs.[12] At the same time, the survey data shows that more than half the enterprises admitted their weaknesses in brand-building capacity and hoped that the government would help promote their brands at the policy level. Therefore, a key feature of Chinese firms' cross-border M&A strategies is the belief that overseas acquisitions can help to enhance the domestic brand image.

In the past, Chinese managers often focused on cost reduction and price competition in the domestic market. Yet nowadays, almost every CEO wants to establish the company's brand. Differentiating one's product through brand building is now seen as an effective way to increase profit margins and to avoid the intensive price wars of the past. However, establishing a well-known brand takes years of effort, while it can be destroyed overnight. So it is with technology: large Chinese enterprises are investing more in research and development than ever before, yet innovation processes are relatively slow and face high uncertainty.

Thus, 22% of investors surveyed by the Economist Intelligence Unit said that acquiring brands and technology would be the main direction of their future overseas investment.[13]

Chinese outward FDI: Opportunities and challenges

Despite rapid development of China's overseas investments, China is still in a relatively early stage compared with developed countries such as the United States and Japan. As the world's second largest economy, in 2016 China's outward FDI flow ranked second among countries in the world.[14] Since China started its overseas investment relatively late, the scale of its outward investment stock is far below that of the United States, Japan and other developed countries, only accounting for 4.9% of outward FDI stock in the world.[15] Thus, China's overseas investment stock is only 20.1% of that of US companies, though it is closing in on other countries. It already amounts to 88.7% of the United Kingdom's stock of outward FDI, 93.8% of Germany's and 91.5% of Japan's.[16]

To accelerate this catch-up with global leaders, the Chinese government is creating conditions that aim to help Chinese companies to implement 'going out' strategies. In particular, such policies aim to exploit three major development opportunities:

Firstly, economic reforms of 'opening up' and 'going out' are pushed to new heights. The Third Plenary Session of the 19th Central Committee of the Communist Party of China (CPC) emphasized the need to "give equal emphasis to 'bringing in' and 'going global', follow the principle of achieving shared growth through discussion and collaboration, and increase openness and cooperation in building innovation capacity."[17] With these efforts, the Chinese government hopes to make new ground in opening China further through links running east and west, across land and sea. As part of the BRI, China aims to import products and services valued at more than $1.5 trillion over five years.[18] To encourage 'going out', departments in charge of outward FDI have expedited reform of the investment approval system. The latest revision of the *Catalogue of Investment Projects Approved by the Government (2016 Version)* eased restrictions on overseas FDI. Chinese companies' autonomy in going-out strategies was expected to be significantly enhanced as a result.

Secondly, the Belt and Road Initiative drives infrastructure construction in both developed and emerging economies. President Xi Jinping mentioned at the 19th Party Congress that:

> "The government will pursue BRI as a priority; and the purpose is to promote 'policy, infrastructure, trade, financial and people-to-people connectivity and thus build a new platform for international cooperation to create new drivers of shared development'."

To achieve this goal, annual investments of about $150 billion are envisaged for the next decade.[19] Since many Chinese enterprises target emerging countries when going global, China's government plans to invest $9 billion annually to help other developing countries and regions to build infrastructure over the next five years.[20]

Thirdly, China promotes regional trade liberalization and facilitates intraregional investment. By November 2017, China had signed 15 free trade agreements with 23 countries and regional blocs, including the Association of Southeast Asian Nations (ASEAN), Singapore, Pakistan, New Zealand, Chile, Peru, Costa Rica, Iceland and Switzerland.[21] China has completed substantive negotiations with South Korea and Australia for a potential China and South Korea Free Trade Area and for a Sino-Australian free trade agreement, and started the sixth round of negotiations for the establishment of a Sino-Japanese-Korean free trade area. Negotiations on investment agreements between China, the United States and Central Europe are also moving ahead. Bilateral and multilateral free-trade areas (FTAs), acting as institutional arrangements to further deepen economic and trade cooperation, will greatly facilitate FDI and push bilateral and multilateral investment and cooperation to a higher level, while promoting bilateral or multilateral trade liberalization and economic and trade development. Exploiting the voids left by the United States abandoning multilateral trade agreements, China is pursuing opportunities to lead the creation of new trade and investment networks.

In the context of globalization, Chinese enterprises have reached remarkable achievements over the past decade. Yet, arguably, the past decade was only the prologue for the globalization of Chinese enterprises. Although substantial progress has been made in the structure and quality of outward investment, when compared to multinational companies from developed countries, Chinese companies lag behind in overall strength, resources and experience. Thus, Chinese enterprises can expect more challenges in their 'going out' process. At the enterprise level, we note challenges in particular in three areas.

Firstly, many enterprises do not have a clear international strategy. Many companies do not have clearly articulated goals, or a strategic plan supporting their 'going out'. Some companies are not even aware of industry trends outside China, and hence struggle to fit their own strategy into global metatrends. Unclear strategy leads to uninformed moves towards internationalization.

Secondly, small and medium-sized enterprises (SMEs) have narrow financing channels and face high financing costs for outward FDI. Most large SOEs and private enterprises are listed companies, which makes it easier for them to seek financing. However, in terms of international operations, most SMEs generally have difficulty in getting finance because of the structure of the domestic financial markets. A related problem is their high financing costs, which contribute to SMEs' lack of competitiveness in the international investment process.

Thirdly, cross-cultural integration is weak and there is a lack of international talent. Chinese enterprises implementing direct overseas investment need to respect host countries' culture and customs, and address cultural differences by considering the company's overall interests. In addition, an important aspect of business globalization is the availability of international talent. Our analysis of the employees and employee recruitment processes of Chinese companies engaged in overseas investment indicates that a large proportion of employees consists of expatriate staff from China; hence, there is much progress to be made with respect to employee localization.

Without doubt, there will be many more Chinese companies 'going out'. In the face of the challenges outlined above, however, we must consider these questions: why do they want to globalize? What is the difference between their path towards globalization and that of established enterprises in Europe and America? For Chinese enterprises, what role will the Chinese market play with respect to the international market? What risks and crises have Chinese companies encountered in their globalization? Does their globalization create value? What lessons have they learnt through organizational integration after mergers and acquisitions?

PART I

STRATEGY

CHAPTER 1

GLOBAL EXPANSION: CHINESE APPROACHES

1.1 Global expansion and traditional multinational enterprises

Companies have been setting up subsidiaries abroad since at least the late 19th century, when many firms started cross-border operations after colonization by Britain and other Western countries. International business scholars have been studying these companies since the middle of the 20th century, aiming to explain the expansion of multinational enterprises (MNEs) both between advanced economies, and from advanced economies into emerging economies. Though rival theories abound, for our purposes it suffices to consider two leading perspectives, namely the 'eclectic paradigm' of British economist John Dunning, and the 'internationalization process model' associated in particular with Swedish scholars Jan-Erik Vahlne and Jan Johanson.

John Dunning integrated leading theoretical perspectives from industrial organization, internalization theory and location theory to create the eclectic paradigm. This paradigm stipulates that companies will establish their own overseas production units when three conditions are met, related to Ownership advantages, Location advantages and Internalization advantages (hence this model is sometimes known as the 'OLI paradigm').[22]

- **Ownership advantages** are firm-specific resources and capabilities that are transferable to foreign locations, and enable a firm to compete in those locations where it would normally suffer from the disadvantages of being unfamiliar with local customs, rules and networks.

These ownership advantages can take many forms; the most important are technologies and brands.

- **Locational advantages** are characteristics of host countries that foreign investors can utilize to develop their business in the country. They include in particular two factors: advantages stemming from immovable endowments of a host country (such as natural resources, labour skills and transport infrastructure), and favourable conditions resulting from the country's regulatory and political systems.

- **Internalization advantages** refer to an MNE's ability to utilize its resources and capabilities internally rather than through market transactions. External markets are often subject to imperfections that lead to high transaction costs, or indeed inhibit the working of markets entirely. This holds true especially when the assets in question are intangible, such as brands and technologies, whose use is difficult to pin down comprehensively in contracts. Dunning distinguishes between structural and transactional market failure. The former is caused by trading barriers in a host country, and the latter by inefficient transaction channels or lack of access to relevant information.

The OLI paradigm explains clearly why traditional MNEs establish subsidiaries abroad. They develop distinct competitive advantages – or 'ownership advantages' in Dunning's terminology – in their home country, which then become the foundation for their international growth. These O-advantages typically take the form of tacit resources, such as a knowledge of cutting-edge technologies or the reputation of a brand. For intangible assets of this kind, markets are highly imperfect and thus firms prefer to set up their own subsidiaries to exploit them. In terms of locational advantages, a wide variety of characteristics of the host country are important. For traditional MNEs, the attraction of local markets is very important – conside the quest of Western consumer goods manufacturers for Chinese consumers. Other important resources include the workforce and local suppliers, which may or may not make it attractive to produce in the host country. The OLI paradigm, which is grounded in economic analysis, helps to explain why the global strategies of mature companies such as P&G, General Electric, McDonald's, Honda and Coca-Cola, along with most of the world's leading companies with any presence in China, follow this type of overseas investment strategy.

Yet, when it comes to MNEs from emerging economies, the OLI paradigm seems limited in its explanatory power. A core assumption is that the internationalizing firm has some competencies that are valuable in foreign markets. Yet, in the case of Chinese MNEs, what internationally competitive competencies did they have prior to going global? The technologies and brands they developed domestically were rarely if ever sufficient to compete abroad, especially in advanced economies in Europe or North America. There has been a considerable debate among scholars whether emerging-economy MNEs have ownership advantages, and if so, what the nature of these ownership advantages might be. Suggested advantages include operational competencies for labour-intensive production, political competencies in negotiating with host governments, and networking competencies that help firms to operate in contexts with imperfect or weakly enforced legal frameworks. Yet, while such competencies may explain the growth of firms from one emerging economy into another, they cannot explain the entry of Chinese companies into Europe or North America, as shown by many of the case studies we present. Some other forces must be at play, as we will explore in this book.[23]

CASE STUDY:
PROCTER & GAMBLE (P&G)

Head quartered in Cincinnati, Ohio, USA, P&G was founded in 1837 by William Procter and James Gamble. The core business of P&G was to make and sell soap and candles. Because the two founders continuously updated their products, during the American Civil War the company won contracts to supply the Union Army with soaps and candles. These military contracts not only increased P&G's profits during the war, but also introduced soldiers from all over the country to its products. By 1890, P&G offered more than 30 different types of soap and was known as the 'soap opera' in the US.

In the late 1890s, not long after its products had gained favour with domestic consumers, P&G started to export its soaps to other markets in North America and Western Europe. As demand increased, in 1915, for the first time in its history, P&G established a manufacturing facility outside the US, in Canada. In 1930, P&G became a global enterprise upon the acquisition of the Thomas Hedley Co., a soap and candle manufacturer based in England. Furthermore, following the establishment of its overseas division in 1948, P&G pursued global expansion aggressively: it entered Germany in 1960 and Japan in 1973. In 1988, P&G formed a joint venture to manufacture products in China.

It was only after it had entered foreign markets that P&G internationalized its innovation activities. In 1890 the company had established its first research lab in Cincinnati, which later became its first innovation centre in 1952; it was not until 1980 that P&G established its second innovation centre outside the US. Thus, all the products sold and distributed in global markets prior to 1980 had first been developed by P&G in its home country.

P&G exemplifies classic international business theories, and the OLI paradigm in particular: a company first develops a competitive advantage in the form of technologies and brands in its own country, then on that basis extends this ownership advantage to other countries. Its global strategy is geared towards building market share around the world after gaining a competitive advantage at home. Thus, the core question asked by international business scholars working in the tradition of John Dunning is: "How do companies attain competitive advantage in foreign countries?"

An alternative perspective, developed by Swedish scholars Jan Johanson and Jan-Erik Vahlne, is the internationalization process model. This model is concerned with the process of firms developing their international operations. Specifically, the model suggests that companies go through cycles of resource commitment and learning, which leads to learning processes concerning how to do business internationally, how to operate in a particular host country and how to manage particular types of international operations. The learning enabled by earlier commitment then creates competencies that enable firms to manage their international operations more effectively, and to make additional commitments. Thus, Johanson and Vahlne view the internationalization of firms as a gradual, iterative process that goes through multiple stages. International management knowledge is generally highly tacit, and hence it is not possible for firms to be successful around the world without investing in the development of international management competencies first.

The model has been criticized because, in this increasingly interconnected world, some firms establish highly internationalized operations only a few years after their foundation. This applies in particular to internet-based businesses and to high-technology niche manufacturers. However, careful analysis of such cases shows that firms that internationalize rapidly tend to draw on international management competencies from other sources, such as a team of founding entrepreneurs who have extensive international experience prior to setting up the company. Thus, the key message for our analysis is that firms need to develop international management competencies, which requires substantial investment in human resources, to be able to succeed in international markets – and normally that takes considerable time.[24]

Contemporary MNEs from countries such as China, India, Brazil or Russia tend to be mature enterprises in their own country, and when they embark on their international growth strategy they tend to have substantial financial resources that they can invest. They are not like the typical firm at the beginning of the internationalization process that Johanson and Vahlne had in mind when they developed their model. However, their lack of international management experience means that they are often in the early stages of learning of how to do business on the international stage. This leads some scholars to argue that the internationalization process could be a powerful tool with which to analyse companies from countries such as China.[25] Yet some Chinese MNEs are accelerating their international growth at very high speed, which challenges some of the assumptions of the internationalization process model.

Our research finds that most Chinese enterprises that have sought to go global were not top players in their sectors before they embarked upon globalization and did not have strong competitive advantages either (such as low labour costs). Besides, the Chinese market is vast and far from saturated. Consequently, classical theories are unable to explain the current situation. Chinese enterprises that globalize rarely start out with any advantage in the global market, and many did not even have absolute leadership in the domestic market when they began to invest abroad. These companies continue to adapt their strategies and gain advantages gradually as they globalize.

Chinese enterprises making overseas acquisitions may give the impression of biting off more than they can chew. Dalian Wanda Group (Wanda) is such a case. Its overseas business structure was regarded as a strategy for a small company to increase its profits. Wanda made its fortune in real estate and has expanded into the culture and entertainment sectors in recent years. However, the firm did not develop recognizable competitive advantages that could have been the basis for international growth. Wanda did not copy its domestic practices overseas; in fact, it did not really have the ability to do so. Yet it successfully acquired several real estate projects along with cinemas, notably AMC Theatres, in the United States and around the world.

CASE STUDY:
WANDA GROUP OF CHINA

Head quartered in Beijing, China, Dalian Wanda Group (Wanda) was founded in 1988 by Wang Jianlin, China's fourth-richest man according to *Forbes* in 2017. Wanda was initially engaged in property development, including residential and commercial properties. As of 2017, Wanda is the world's largest commercial properties enterprise, holding a combined 33.87 million square metres of property. The group has opened 222 Wanda Plaza projects in cities including Beijing, Shanghai, Chengdu and Kunming. Since 2005, Wanda has made forays into other sectors, away from the property market. By 2017, including commercial properties, Wanda was operating in four major areas: real estate, culture, internet and finance. The group's assets amounted to 882.64 billion yuan, with a revenue of 134.85 billion yuan in the first half of 2017.

Wanda's expansion into the culture sector started with its acquisition of US-based AMC Entertainment (AMC), the world's second-largest cinema operator, in May 2012. The acquisition was for $2.6 billion, including debt, making the deal the largest US acquisition by a Chinese private company as of 2012 and the biggest overseas acquisition in a culture industry.

After the acquisition, Wanda retained AMC's management team and invested $500 million in the company to strengthen its balance sheet. Although AMC had experienced two years of losses prior to the M&A, with the financial support from Wanda the company started to generate a profit by the end of 2012 and went public in 2013. Chairman Wang Jianlin said: "AMC was a springboard to expand Wanda's global cinema presence, as the acquisition made Wanda a truly global cinema owner in the world's two largest movie markets – the US and Canada. In the future, Wanda is committed to continuously investing in the entertainment business."[26]

Wanda then pursued several acquisitions around the world, aiming for a global leadership role (Table 1). In 2015, Wanda acquired HG Holdco, the second-largest cinema operator in Australia, for $365.7 million US, and Starplex Cinema in the US for $172 million. In 2016, the group acquired Carmichael, the fourth-largest operator in the US, for $3.5 billion; two leading European cinema groups, Odeon in the UK for $1.4 billion and Nordic Cinema in Sweden for $930 million; and Legendary Entertainment, an iconic film studio in the US, for $3.5 billion. Although Mr Wang has been purchasing major Western entertainment assets, he believes that the best long-term growth prospects for the film business lie in emerging economics such as China. Hence Wanda invested in its first megabudget film production, *The Great Wall*, in 2016, leveraging resources from its newly acquired company Legendary Entertainment and targeting mainly Chinese audiences. Although many critics suggested that "the film was not quite a success,"[27] Mr Wang remained determined to improve the quality of Wanda's films. His ambition has been to become the world's leading cinema company with a global market share of over 10%.

In addition to its cultural operations, Wanda has also pursued an aggressive expansion strategy in sports and real estate businesses. In June 2013, Wanda announced two investments in the UK: the acquisition of Sunseeker International, a luxury yacht manufacturer, for $495 million, and a $1 billion investment in building the Wanda London Hotel. In 2014, the group announced a $3.1 billion investment in urban renewal projects in the UK; acquired Edificio España, an iconic landmark building in Madrid, Spain, for $358 million (sold two years later for substantively the same price); and announced a plan to invest $900 million to build a 350-metre-high, 89-storey five-star hotel and apartment project which was expected to become the third-tallest building in Chicago. Chairman Wang Jianlin presented the Chicago project as Wanda's first step towards becoming a global property investor, with further expansion planned by investing in five-star hotels in New York, Los Angeles, San Francisco and other major US cities. In 2015, Wanda acquired Business Run Veranstaltungen in Germany and World Triathlon Corp in the US for $650 million. In 2016, the group invested in Infront Sports & Media and Propaganda GEM, both in Switzerland.

"To expand the size of the Wanda enterprise, international investment is required for expansion in some industries, especially in industries such as entertainment and sports, where the foreign market is more advanced than the Chinese one," Mr Wang explained. "This is a key reason why Wanda wishes to expand overseas. Furthermore, as the Chinese government encourages Chinese companies to distribute resources globally and to leverage the global market, Wanda pursue internationalization to capture potential opportunities and, most importantly, to mitigate risk."[28]

	REAL ESTATE	FILM	SPORTS
EUROPE	• 1 Nine Elms, London, UK (2014) • Edificio España, Madrid, Spain (2014; sold 2016)	• Odeon & UCI (UK; 100%, 2016) • Nordic Cinema Group (Sweden; 100%, 2017)	• Propaganda GEM (Switzerland, 2016) • Infront Sports & Media (Switzerland; 68.2%, 2016) • Business Run Veranstaltungen (Germany; 100%, 2015) • Atlético de Madrid (Spain; 20%, 2014) • Sunseeker (UK; 92%, 2013)
USA	• Beverly Hills project (2014) • Wanda Vista Tower, Chicago (90%, 2014)	• Dick Clark Productions (100%, 2016; not completed) • Legendary Entertainment (100%, 2016) • Carmike (100%, 2016) • AMC (100%, 2012)	• World Triathlon Corp (100%, 2015)
AUSTRALIA	• 1 Alfred St & Fairfax House, Sydney (2015) • Jewel project (2014)	• HG Holdco Pty Ltd (100%, 2015)	
OTHER		• PVR Cinemas (India; 100%, 2016)	

TABLE 1	WANDA'S GLOBAL ACQUISITION SPREE

Wanda's overseas approach differs from P&G's foreign investment strategy, as Wanda did not transfer its successful experience in China to the United States, or share resources within the group to exploit internalization advantages. The internationalization of Chinese companies is not typical, and cannot be explained by traditional theories. New theoretical thinking is required to explain Chinese companies' approach to globalization, and to inform their strategy implementation.

1.2.   Innovative internationalization strategies of Chinese MNEs

Chinese enterprises are different from contemporary global leaders because few of them started developing before the reform policy launched in 1978. Consequently, they are still young and their behaviour could be compared to that of young people in their early twenties. They may possess unparalleled flexibility, dexterous management, a spirit of adventure and the will to fight; however, despite their energy and vibrancy, they are still at a stage of learning and accumulation. They experienced the phase of unprecedented economic growth in the 1990s and early 2000s, and encountered globally operating multinationals in their own country as partners and/or competitors. The internationalization of Chinese enterprises then became a natural extension of their domestic catch-up. However, as latecomers to international business, Chinese enterprises need to work even harder to catch up with their Western counterparts in respect of both technology and international management knowledge. Most Chinese enterprises still lacked internationally competitive capabilities. For these reasons, the path that Chinese enterprises choose for internationalization differs from the traditional path of Western companies, which have focused on exploiting capabilities first developed in their home countries.

Our observations of the internationalization of Chinese enterprises suggest that they follow an innovative three-stage path (Figure 1).

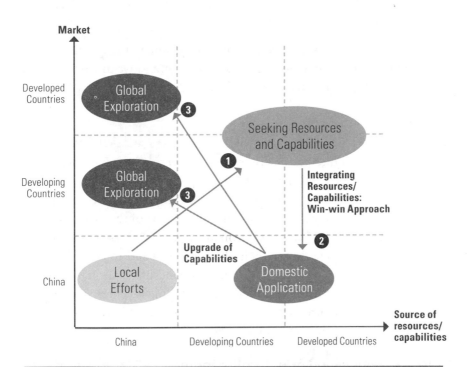

FIGURE 1 CHINESE ENTERPRISES' INNOVATIVE THREE-STAGE PATH TO INTERNATIONALIZATION

In short, we find that Chinese enterprises tend to accumulate business experience and develop firm specific advantages in China before expanding globally; this process is known as 'local efforts'. Local efforts lay the foundation for later international development, and are thus the starting point of Chinese enterprises' approach to internationalization. Then, in the first step of the three-stage path, Chinese companies obtain resources and capabilities in the global markets, mostly via overseas M&As, to compensate for their own competitive weaknesses. Next, Chinese companies apply these newly acquired resources and capabilities in local markets (stage 2). By integrating their newly acquired resources and capabilities with local features, Chinese companies start to catch up with international standards and to develop their own competitive advantages. Once these Chinese enterprises have succeeded in China, they can take the third step: to explore and expand in global markets by leveraging their own competitive advantages and local benefits.

21

Our observations indicate that the Chinese enterprises' approach to internationalization is a process of acquiring, integrating, applying and upgrading resources and capabilities. Thus, the innovative three-stage path outlined in Figure 1 is also a path of 'upgrade of capabilities'.

1.3 Acquisition of resources and capabilities

As latecomers to international business, Chinese enterprises face many challenges from domestic and foreign competitors, not only in the global market but also in their home market. Since most Chinese enterprises view China, their home market, as an integral part of the global market, the primary feature of the internationalization of Chinese enterprises is the desire to compensate for their shortcomings and to establish their own core competitiveness in China and beyond by acquiring resources and capabilities in the overseas market. Most Chinese enterprises aim to obtain three types of resources and capabilities abroad, namely: natural resources, brands, and technological capabilities.

1.3.1 Acquisition of natural resources

Although China is rich in resources and land, the 1.3 billion population also needs a lot of resources for its economic development. Take iron ore, for example: As the world's largest steel producer, China produces more than the world's other top ten steel-producing countries combined. However, China's steel industry relies heavily on imported iron ore, due to both the low supply and the poor quality of iron ore in China. In 2015, China imported 953 million tonnes of iron ore, accounting for 65.1% of global supply. However, the supply of iron ore is controlled by a few leading multinational mining corporations such as Vale SA (Brazil), BHP Billiton (Australia), and Rio Tinto Group (UK), which puts China's iron and steel enterprises at a disadvantage in the iron ore market. And there are other industries where China needs natural resources such as copper, oil and uranium, and where Chinese enterprises face similar situations.

Thus, with the encouragement of the government's 'going out' policy, Chinese energy and resource enterprises have joined the global competition for energy, mineral resources, metal minerals, non-metallic minerals and other resources. Early attempts were not always successful: for example, in June 2005 the China National Offshore Oil Corporation (CNOOC) announced a $18.5-billion bid for Union Oil Company of California

(Unocal), but withdrew the offer after encountering opposition from local regulators. However, many later bids were successful, especially during the financial crisis when asset values were depressed. In 2006, CITIC Group acquired the oil and gas resources of Kazakhstan JSC; in 2008, Shougang – one of China's biggest steel companies – acquired mining assets in Australia; Zhuzhou CRRC Times Electric Co., Ltd. acquired Canada's listed company Dynex; Sinopec Group invested RMB13 billion to take over Canadian oil company Tanganyika Oil Company Ltd. (TYK); Aluminum Corporation of China Limited (Chinalco) became the single largest shareholder of the British-Australian Rio Tinto Mining Group, the world's second-largest iron ore supplier, through mergers and acquisitions; Sinochem Group acquired Australia's Soco Yemen Pty. Ltd.; in 2009, China Minmetals Corporation bought the mining assets of OZ Minerals, including five mines located in Western Australia, Tasmania and Queensland, along with other assets for mine exploration and production; Zijin Mining Group acquired a stake in Australia's Indophil Gold; and Wuhan Iron and Steel Group (WISCO) acquired a 19.9% stake in the Canadian mining company Consolidated Thompson.

The largest acquisition in the natural resource sector – and at the time the largest acquisition by a Chinese MNE overall – was the acquisition of Nexen in Canada for US$15.1 billion in 2012. Nexen was heavily involved in oil sands exploration in Alberta, and held other oil exploration assets in, for example, the Gulf of Mexico and the North Sea. The deal was controversial in Canada because the idea of a foreign multinational owning natural resources underground did not appeal to many Canadian voters. However, CNOOC went through the formal approval process under Canadian law, which requires proof of a positive net benefit for Canada in the case of major foreign acquisitions, and attained regulatory approval from the Canadian authorities. Unfortunately, the oil price collapsed after 2012 and oil sands exploration, a relatively expensive source of energy, became unprofitable. What with a pipeline burst in 2015 and a factory explosion in 2016, the Nexen acquisition has yet to be turned into a success story for Chinese investment.

In 2014, many Chinese companies began another round of acquisitions targeting energy resources, particularly in Africa, where regulatory approval was often less difficult to obtain. For example, the China National Nuclear Corporation (CNNC) acquired a considerable stake in one of Africa's largest uranium mines in Namibia, at a cost of nearly $200 million.

Meanwhile, the China National Gold Group Corporation entered final negotiations to acquire a copper mine in the Congo. "They have returned selectively,"[29] said Michael Rawlinson, Global Co-Head of Mining and Metals at Barclays Investment Bank. "SOEs and a few exceptional private enterprises are sending a clear message, that they are open to African business, especially in areas of natural resources," said Rajat Kohli, Global Head of Mining and Metals at Standard Bank (South Africa).

CASE STUDY:
EVERGREEN HOLDING GROUP (EHG)
ACQUIRES POTASH COMPANY MAGINDUSTRIES

Liang Xiaolei, founder of the Evergreen Holding Group (EHG), fully embraced the government's 'going out' policy. EHG was founded in 1995, and developed into a diversified conglomerate involved in shipbuilding, marine engineering, resources and logistics. It aimed to become an industrial investment holding group based in China with operations across the world. As an entrepreneur struggling in the light industry sector for many years, Liang Xiaolei said, "The little money you have worked so hard for will evaporate completely in a single moment when the price of copper or PVC changes. We have no margin, and no say." This vulnerability to world market prices for critical inputs became the driving force for EHG's overseas investment strategy.

EHG became aware of an opportunity in the potash industry. Distribution of potash resources in the world is extremely uneven, and demand (consumption) and production sites are highly mismatched. According to the US Geological Survey, proven potash reserves are about 8.457 billion tonnes worldwide, which can support more than 240 years of mining at the current production rate. Canada ranks first, accounting for 52.0% of world reserves, followed by Russia (21.3%), Belarus (8.9%) and Germany (8.4%). These four countries together previously accounted for 90.6% of the world's total reserves. Africa also had substantive reserves, but they were not yet well explored. On the other hand, the main consumers of potash were China, India and other countries in Southeast Asia, which together accounted for 42% of total potash supply. It was predicted that China's potash consumption and import demand would continue to grow over the next decade.

As EHG was exploring opportunities in the potash industry, they were looking for a "natural-born beauty," that is, one of the world's top five or top three projects. Liang Xiaolei was convinced that "only high-quality assets can bring high returns," and such projects also tended to gain central government support in China. After investigating a few projects, EHG narrowed its focus on the Canadian company MagIndustries Corp., which had a potash development project in the Republic of Congo (ROC, also known as Congo-Brazzaville).

MagIndustries was founded in 1997 and listed on the Toronto Stock Exchange (TSE) in 2009. The company was operating two principal businesses: minerals and forestry. Its mineral exploration focused on the 600,000-tonne Mengo potash mine, for which it had obtained mining permission in Congo. The mine required C$1 billion investment to finance construction. MagIndustries originally intended to raise more money through an equity issue, but, during the financial crisis of 2008, the company's prominence declined and its market value fell from C$800 million to C$100 million. To cope with the financial squeeze, MagIndustries considered the introduction of strategic investors. In 2009 and 2010, MagIndustries discussed its own acquisition with two state-owned Chinese enterprises, Sinohydro Corp. and China National Complete Plant Import & Export Company Ltd. However, in the end, these both walked away without a deal. Finally, MagIndustries Corp. met with EHG, which decided to acquire 76% of the company for C$115 million, while maintaining a minority listing on the TSE. The price of ¢25 per share seemed a bargain; only few years earlier the shares had traded at C$3.50. By acquiring Canada's MagIndustries, EHG gained nearly 600,000 tonnes of potash production capacity. In an era of growing world market demand, Liang Xiaolei's decision enabled EHG to develop competitive advantages based on the control of scarce natural resources.

However, world market prices for potash declined sharply in 2013 when Russia's Uralkali withdrew from a marketing collaboration with its Belorussian partners. The shares of potash mining companies around the world declined over the following months, making new exploration projects in high-risk areas less attractive. Moreover, in 2015, MagIndustries became embroiled in a major corruption scandal under the Canadian Corruption of Foreign Public Officials Act. It was accused of having paid bribes in Congo since 2012 and, as a listed Canadian company, the investigation fell under Canadian jurisdiction. MagIndustries failed to complete an independent investigation on behalf of EHG, which had already revealed that MagIndustries or its subsidiaries, supposedly under direct instructions, had made cash payments to Congolese officials and even built a villa for one official. Sadly, such incidents are unhelpful for Chinese private companies aiming to build their reputation in the Western world.[30]

1.3.2 Acquisition of brands

A brand reflects the reputation and the public's awareness of an enterprise and its products, after sales service and cultural values. Successful brands attract consumers, establish brand loyalty, raise company awareness, and thereby help maintain the profitability of the enterprise. Foreign investors have introduced their renowned brands into the Chinese market, and have achieved substantial market shares, especially in premium and luxury segments. Their products dominate Chinese markets for automobiles, consumer goods and many other product categories. A brand represents the performance and value of the product, and most consumers favour brands with which they are familiar. Brand value thus is thus an important means to enhance the competitiveness of an enterprise. Therefore, for Chinese companies to succeed in global markets and against international competition, a reputable brand is both a prerequisite and a trump card. Without a breakthrough in brand development, it will be very difficult to survive in international markets. Even in domestic markets, brands are important not only to compete with other local businesses, but also to face fierce international competition.

However, the development, marketing and operation of a brand remain major challenges for Chinese enterprises in both domestic and international markets, for at least two reasons. First, China is still developing, and consumers and even enterprises tend to misunderstand what brands are about. Stacie Adams, Global Director of Branding & Communications at Guangxi Liugong Machinery Co., Ltd, said in an interview:

"Chinese consumers and entrepreneurs often associate brand with advertising. They think that a brand is just the product of successful advertising. In fact, any enterprise brand combines product characteristics, corporate culture, and service quality. A brand is not limited to a product or a service; the brand should penetrate every step of business operations. However, Chinese consumers do not seem to understand the connotation of branding, and entrepreneurs have no idea about brand structure."[31]

The value of a brand is created over long periods of time and over many interactions between the consumer and the brand – the most important element is for the consumer to experience personally the reliability of the product and the quality of the service.

Secondly, Chinese enterprises still face the 'made in China' challenge. Most of the Chinese companies now aiming for global expansion started in the late 1980s by cooperating with enterprises from other countries as original equipment manufacturer (OEM) partners or as distributors. Low labour costs and preferential policies to attract foreign investment made China (especially the Pearl River Delta region) an ideal destination for companies from around the world to offshore the labour-intensive parts of their industrial supply chains. At that time, China's south eastern coastal economy developed rapidly thanks to low labour costs, land-use costs and taxes. For example, TCL was established as a joint venture with Hong Kong manufacturers to produce cassette tapes. In 1984, Haier began to produce refrigerators for German manufacturer Liebherr Group. Lenovo Group Ltd (then Legend) started as an OEM for AST Computers with a contract of HK$30 million to manufacture computer components. Thus, products 'made in China' spread all over the world, as China became 'the world's factory'. However, a side-effect of this was that during this time, Chinese enterprises have attained a reputation for 'cheap' products, even when they have achieved international standards for product and service quality. Three decades later, 'made in China' is still haunted by the 'cheap' label.

For these reasons, Chinese enterprises find it hard to market their own brands in mainstream Western markets. Even in China, they often find it difficult to compete with foreign competitors and their brands. As a result, most Chinese enterprises are still operating as secondary manufacturers focusing on cost-efficiency as their main competitive advantage. This lack of recognized brands is a major obstacle for Chinese enterprises, which try to compensate for this disadvantage by internationalization.

1.3.2.1   Global brands for Chinese markets

The key to understanding branding in China is the concept of trust. Trust in a brand is accumulated by commitments that a business makes to its customers. "Trust means that when I decide to go to get a sandwich at Subway, I know exactly what it's going to taste like. Whether I am in the US or in China, Tokyo or Shanghai, it will always taste the same." So says Stacie Adams, Global Director of Branding & Communications at Guangxi Liugong Machinery Co., Ltd. "Trust means that when I get on a tram in Germany, I know that no matter how bad the weather is, the tram will take me safely to my destination."[32]

The bridge of trust between Chinese enterprises and Chinese consumers has historically often been weak. With incidents such as the 2008 milk contamination scandal involving Sanlu Group, Chinese consumers flinch at the sight of domestic products, especially in areas where safety or prestige are important. An increasing number of Chinese enterprises are committed to providing consumers with reliable products and assured services, and scandals are becoming fewer. However, the trust deficiency continues to result in significantly lower prices for domestic products, even when they achieve similar levels of quality to imported goods. To overcome this trust deficiency, some ambitious companies use foreign-made products and other foreign associations to enhance their brand, as illustrated by Bright Dairy & Food's experience.

CASE STUDY:
BRIGHT DAIRY & FOOD ACQUIRES SYNLAIT MILK IN NEW ZEALAND

Founded in 1911, Bright Dairy & Food Co., Ltd (Bright) developed its core business in the production and sale of a variety of dairy products. One hundred years later, Bright had become a diversified listed company with a combination of state, foreign and domestic private investors. The Bright Group had become one of China's largest dairy producers, and Bright Dairy was one of China's high-end brands. However, as with many other Chinese dairy brands, Bright's brand image was challenged by media and consumers in 2008 during the melamine scandal.

The scandal broke when many babies, who had been fed a powdered milk formula produced by Sanlu Group, were found to be suffering from kidney stones. Samples of the formula showed the presence of melamine – commonly known as ESB Protein Powder – an organic compound used as a chemical additive. Sanlu was using melamine to artificially inflate the protein content of its dairy products. As of September 2008, about 40,000 infants were hospitalized after ingesting dairy products containing melamine. The incident naturally raised tremendous concerns about the safety of dairy products. When China's General Administration of Quality Supervision, Inspection and Quarantine (AQSIQ) released its report on the test results of domestic dairy product manufacturers, Bright was blacklisted as one of the producers whose products contained melamine. The scandal dealt a near-fatal blow to the reputations of Chinese dairy producers, including Bright Dairy. Consumers opted to buy expensive imported milk powder, rather than more affordable products produced in China. The incident cast a shadow over Bright's brand, which had been carefully built up over generations.

To regain consumer trust, and to restore its high-quality image, Bright set its sights on Synlait Milk in New Zealand as a potential partner. Synlait had been established in 2005 to exploit New Zealand's agricultural resources and to produce milk products for global markets. However, it was hit hard by the financial crisis, which increased financing costs, and by falling global prices for milk powder. As a new company, Synlait had not yet formed a stable customer base, but relied heavily on spot sales and was unable to obtain long-term contracts to stabilize its cash flow. The resulting financial stress made for an interesting acquisition opportunity.

In May 2010, a delegation from Bright Dairy toured New Zealand in search of opportunities for business cooperation. The delegation briefly visited Synlait Milk, and was impressed by Synlait as a potential partner. The delegation reported back to Guo Benheng, President of Bright Dairy in Shanghai. Bright was not the only company with an interest in Synlait Milk, but it was one of the best-prepared. Bright had thoroughly researched Synlait before formally approaching them. Six months later, in October 2010, Bright Dairy announced a deal to acquire a 51% stake in Synlait Milk for US$52.9 million.

As a newly established company, Synlait Milk did not yet have a significant brand in New Zealand. What attracted Bright was not so much Synlait's branding, but the brand perception of New Zealand dairy in general. New Zealand attached great importance to its dairy industry's organization, quality and safety management, its technological R&D and promotion, and its focus on environmental protection and prevention of industrial pollution. As a result, dairy products from New Zealand enjoy a reputation for high quality worldwide.

Soon after the acquisition, Bright Dairy introduced the Synlait brand to the Chinese market, establishing a high-end dairy product line imported from New Zealand, branded with its foreign name. This country of origin of the Synlait brand image helped Bright Dairy to rebuild consumer trust for its products and enhance its own competitiveness in China. Thus, by acquiring and introducing a foreign brand, Bright alleviated the disadvantages of its own domestic Chinese market and consolidated its leading position in the domestic market for milk formula.

A year after the acquisition, Bright Dairy helped Synlait to expand its dairy production from 50,000 to 100,000 tonnes per year with a second milk powder processing plant capable of producing high-specification powdered milk formula. In 2013, Synlait went public on the New Zealand stock exchange and raised US$53 million, reducing Bright Dairy's stake from 51% to 39%. Furthermore, Synlait acquired a 100% stake in Auckland-based New Zealand Dairy Company for $39.8 million in 2017 to increase its blending and canning capacity. John Penno, Synlait's managing director and CEO, said:

"This acquisition will allow us to meet current demand as well as provide some room to grow with our customers' needs; and we will seek certification from New Zealand and Chinese authorities for the plant to get export registration."

The acquisition of Synlait was the first of Bright Dairy's many cross-border M&As. As Synlait proved to be a success, Bright Dairy has pursued its globalization strategy aggressively since 2011. The company acquired Manassen Foods Australia for US$516 million in 2011; Weetabix Food Company, a UK-based breakfast cereal maker, for $1.94 billion, also in 2011 (later sold); Israel's largest dairy company, Tnuva, for $2.4 billion in 2014; and Silver Fern Farms in New Zealand for US$191 million in 2017. As a result of its overseas acquisitions and expansions, as of the first half of 2017, Bright Dairy generated revenue of 2 billion Chinese yuan (US$300 million) outside China, nearly 20% of its total sales.[33]

1.3.1.2　Brands for global markets

Outside China, the challenges facing Chinese brands are even more marked by the image of cheap 'made in China' products. In the 2010s, many Chinese enterprises are no longer the cheap assembly lines of the 1980s, and they have become keenly aware of the importance of quality. Even enterprises that started as OEM manufacturers are now looking to move from operating factories to managing higher-value activities in global value chains. However, reputation evolves slowly, and it will take time for Chinese manufacturers to enhance their reputation.

Faced with this negative country-of-origin image, many Chinese companies view the acquisition of an international brand as a shortcut to enter global markets, and to attain a larger share of the value added. With international brands, Chinese enterprises can overcome the negative 'made in China' image. By acquiring firms that own reputable brands, Chinese investors obtain not only the brand but the team managing the brand, which helps to compensate for Chinese firms' lack of expertise in brand management. Therefore, acquisition of a brand and associated technologies can be an effective way for Chinese enterprises to overcome competitive disadvantages and develop competitive advantages. The acquisition of FLEX (Germany) by the Chervon Group illustrates this strategy.

CASE STUDY:
CHERVON INC. ACQUIRES GERMANY'S FLEX

Peter Pan (Pan Longquan) founded Chervon Holdings Ltd in 1993 in China's historical capital Nanjing as an OEM exporter of power tools. Over the last two decades, Chervon has upgraded its business model through expansion, innovation and branding. The company set up a testing laboratory and employed quality control engineers to ensure that it met its founder's stringent quality requirements. Mr Pan soon discovered that almost all power tools made in China were knock-offs. Nevertheless, he pressed on and built Chervon's own plant in 1997 as a springboard to transform the company from OEM to original design manufacturer (ODM). As an ODM, Chervon developed its own lithium-ion (Li-ion) battery technology, laying the groundwork for extending its product line. The OEM and ODM businesses delivered a significant boost to Chervon's R&D, manufacturing and industrial design capabilities.

In 2003, Mr Pan embarked on an original brand manufacturer (OBM) strategy by creating two own brands: DEVON for the professional market and X-TRON for the DIY market. Despite some early successes with these brands, OEM/ODM orders continued to account for the bulk of Chervon's business. Mr Pan then set his sights on FLEX, a German power tool company, with a view to exporting the DEVON brand's success in China to overseas markets.

Founded in 1922, FLEX was a high-end brand in the power tool industry, especially in Europe. In 2004, it was bought out by financial investors, after which it had a difficult decade when its strategic development stalled. Chervon became FLEX's exclusive OEM in China based on the quality of its products. As FLEX was required to disclose financial data in accordance with the OEM agreement, Mr Pan discovered that the German company faced three serious challenges. Firstly, its strategy of focusing exclusively on the premium segment limited its growth potential. As Mr Pan explained:

"FLEX insisted on presenting itself as a brand for top-class power tools; however, though such niche targeting earned it a name as a well-established brand, it handicapped its development. All markets are similar to a pyramid shape; at the peak you can get only the smallest piece of the big pie."

Secondly, FLEX faced a crisis of confidence. As the financial investors prioritized return on investment rather than strategic development, their business decisions tended to focus on rather short-term horizons. Thirdly, without its own production facilities, FLEX was dependent on other firms for the manufacture of its products.

Despite these difficulties, FLEX created opportunities for Chervon to enter overseas markets. With OEM, ODM and OBM models, Chervon had developed strong production, manufacturing and R&D capabilities. The main obstacle to competing internationally was the lack of a globally recognized brand name. Mr Pan recalled:

"The US and European markets were tough for Chinese professional-grade power tools to break into, as it seemed impossible to lure loyal local users away with other brands. Thus, Chervon found it rather difficult to tap into the Western mainstream market with DEVON. Without a strong brand presence in Europe and the US, a Chinese power tool manufacturer wouldn't have a chance to get into the local professional users' market. It was FLEX that brought us this opening."

Thus, a combination of Chervon and FLEX promised to be a good strategic fit. Mr Pan concluded:

"We are the largest OEM in the power tool industry, and many customers were our acquisition targets. In the end, we chose FLEX, partly because we could face up to failure if the acquisition deal went sour."

In September 2013, FLEX was put on the block for auction. Chervon set up an international panel of experts: financial consultants and auditors from Britain's PwC, acquisition advisors from German strategy consultants Roland Berger and business lawyers from Germany's largest law firm. Prior to the acquisition, financial consultants prepared the transaction process, which entailed understanding Chervon's stance in terms of negotiations, acquisition price and long-term strategic goals. During the acquisition, lawyers translated the agreed terms into legal terminology for the contract, to defend against unwitting violations of the law, and resumed negotiations. After the acquisition, strategic advisors converted the acquisition agreement into a feasible integration programme. This third-party team shepherded Chervon through the acquisition and integration. Chervon beat a dozen competitors in bidding for FLEX and in October 2013 officially announced its takeover of the German company.

Although FLEX was a well-known brand in Europe, especially in the German-speaking area, the brand was little known in China. Soon after the deal was completed, Chervon introduced FLEX product lines into the Chinese market and the two companies started to co-develop Li-ion battery-powered tools. Chervon had been working on the technology for about a decade, while FLEX's existing product lines did not cover Li-ion battery products. Thus, in 2015, the two companies jointly introduced more than ten types of Li-ion battery-powered tools in both Chinese and European markets. In 2014, Chervon launched the world's first Li-ion battery-powered garden tools in North America under its own brand EGO. As FLEX extended its product line, the company was repositioned to target the European mass market to boost sales. With the help of Chervon, FLEX saw its profits rise by 50% from 2013 to 2015.

Chervon continued its acquisition spree with smaller-scale projects. In 2015, it acquired Calmdura, a German high-tech start-up company that develops eco-friendly technologies. As the products of Calmdura have found favour with governments and the public sector in German-speaking countries, Calmdura could offer EGO more opportunities to expand in Europe. Furthermore, in 2016, Chervon acquired the North American power tool brand SKIL from Bosch. "Given that SKIL has been a highly recognized power tool brand for 90 years, it is an excellent complement to our existing brand portfolio," said Mr Pan. "With SKIL on board, I am looking forward to continuing to grow and develop our global branding business."[34]

1.3.3 Acquisition of cutting-edge technologies

Technological competencies are the abilities of enterprises to create technology-based products using unique product designs, patented technologies and human resources in, for example, R&D departments. They enable the creation of scarce and unique products, and thus are an important foundation for competitiveness. The systematic development and exploitation of technological competencies is a critical success factor for enterprises to successfully innovate products, and thus establish and maintain competitive advantage. Until recently, very few Chinese enterprises had internationally competitive technological competencies.

Despite its reputation as the world's factory, China has long remained in labour-intensive and low value-added segments of global industry product chains. As illustrated by the Chervon case, prior to the acquisition of FLEX, it only controlled a small part of the value added in the value chain. Consider for example the manufacturing of mobile phones: China exported more than 1 billion mobile phones in 2012, accounting for nearly 80% of the global market, yet captured less than 1% of global profits.[35] The first reason for this small share in profits is the low-end positioning of Chinese manufacturing where OEM products and even counterfeit products still account for a large share of the output, while key technologies and major equipment in some important areas heavily depend on imports. For instance, 85% of manufacturing equipment for integrated circuit chips, 80% of petrochemical processing equipment and 70% of manufacturing equipment in the automotive industry and CNC machine tools are imported.[36]

The second reason is the lack of independent R&D capability in China, especially for fundamental innovations such as CPUs and operating systems for IT products, core processors for electronic products, or software products. The lack of technological competencies has limited independent innovation by Chinese enterprises in the 20th century (notwithstanding that in the pre-industrial world, China had actually innovated many products long before Europe did). This technology deficiency takes two forms. Firstly, China has significant deficiencies in basic R&D. Even Huawei, one of most innovative enterprises in China, has invested very little in basic research. As Ren Zhengfei, President of Huawei, stated in 2011: "After 18 years of hard work, so far, Huawei has no original invention for any product." Secondly, China faces a shortage of high-end technical engineers, which inhibits companies' ambitions in developing R&D. Duan Dunhou, Vice-Chairman of the All-China Federation of Trade Unions (ACFTU), argued that Chinese enterprises faced an embarrassing situation, in the sense that "equipment is easy to get, but talent is hard to find." According to a survey conducted by ACFTU in 2012, 52.7% of the workforce was educated at Specialized Secondary Schools and their equivalents or below, while up to 76% of employees held only junior middle-school diplomas or were even unskilled workers. Only 34.6% of the workforce had received skills training since their last employment. [37]

This lack of technological competencies in the form of R&D units and technical personnel limited Chinese enterprises' international competitiveness. Thus, for many Chinese companies, the quest for technology became a major driver for outward investment as they sought to enhance their technological capabilities through overseas acquisitions and other overseas activities. For Chervon (discussed above) the quest for technology was probably as important as their quest for an international brand, while Beijing Four Dimensions further illustrates the challenges involved.

CASE STUDY:
BEIJING FOUR DIMENSIONS ACQUIRES JOHNSON SECURITY (UK)

Beijing Four Dimensions Inc. Co. (FD) was founded by Dr Wang Yan in 1989. It started as a car dealer for imported brands in China, and soon expanded to agricultural and real estate businesses (around 2008, FD exited from real estate and other non-core businesses). In 1996, Dr Wang Yan spotted a business opportunity in cash-in-transit (CIT) vehicles, recognizing a substantial demand in China at that time for converted and armoured vehicles.

Unlike general-purpose transport vehicles, CIT vehicles are highly regulated for security reasons, and several factors have to be taken into consideration, including the model size, chassis type, subdivision, external appearance, protection level, bullet and explosion resistance, internal restrictions and emergency systems. To manufacture a vehicle that would meet these standards in every respect, and would adhere to all appropriate parameters such as chassis construction, capacity and load, was not an easy task. Importing complete CIT vehicles was not an option, due to extremely high transport costs for armoured and modified vehicles. In addition, according to documents from China's Ministry of Public Security, the financial industry is banned from using imported security vehicles in order to protect state-owned manufacturers. Thus, professional security escort companies had limited choices for high-end CIT vehicles made in China.

While significant changes have taken place on the customer side in the interests of better product quality, attempts at improving technical quality on the supplier side faltered. Some security companies tried to solve the problem by hiring foreign experts, but these experts brought only limited knowledge in narrowly defined areas; they were not all that helpful in subjects that needed intensive and meticulous work, such as technical processes, production costs and quality control. China's CIT vehicles industry therefore remained fairly low-level. At that time, overseas mergers and acquisitions were not yet popular. However, FD recognized the prospects of a joint venture with an overseas enterprise, and chose Johnson Security Equipment Co., Ltd, a British manufacturer of CIT vehicles, as their acquisition target.

In 1959, when James Edward Johnson founded Johnson & Sons, the company was engaged in processing metal plates. In 1965, Johnson entered the CIT vehicles industry and later emerged as the market leader in Europe. Johnson's average annual sales reached £14 million, accounting for 85% of the market share in the UK and nearly 50% in Ireland. In 1997, Johnson's CIT vehicles were certified by the European Security Transport Association (ESTA) as the only security vehicles that met the standards of that organization. However, the company gradually began to decline after the second generation of the Johnson family took over. Around 1995, Johnson was actively looking for alternative opportunities for succession when a lifeline emerged from China.

FD and Johnson Security established a joint venture in 1997 to bring Johnson's technology to China. Johnson dispatched several of its British engineers from the UK to be stationed in Beijing, and correspondingly, FD sent Chinese personnel to the UK to learn about production processes and operations management. In consequence, FD-Johnson's production technology and capabilities improved significantly. Backed by Johnson's cutting-edge technology, FD-Johnson quickly became a symbol of quality in China. The first production run established a reputation for rigorous production and excellent quality, and soon FD-Johnson became the market leader for CIT vehicles in China.

In May 1999, FD-Johnson officially began operations, selling 30 CIT vehicles in that year. The joint venture hit the take-off point for the industry in China, and sales grew rapidly: after 80 CIT vehicles in 2000, sales increased to 134 in 2001, making FD-Johnson the market leader in China. Leading security and escort companies such as VPower Finance Security Ltd (Shenzhen) and Qingdao Finance Security and Escort Ltd became FD's clients. In 2006, with a total of 170 employees, FD-Johnson sold 718 vehicles, representing total sales of 298 million yuan. In 2007, FD-Johnson accounted for 61% market share in the professional security escort vehicles market, which accounts for about a quarter of the overall CIT vehicles market.

In 2003, Johnson Security experienced a sharp decline in orders due to the loss of a key client. Its annual sales fell to £9.7 million and heavy losses brought the company to the brink of bankruptcy. FD saw this as an opportunity and acquired equity in Johnson Security, eventually becoming its main owner, holding 63.07%. In June 2007, FD purchased the remaining 36.90% stake, completing a 100% acquisition of Johnson Security.

In this way FD greatly enhanced its competitiveness in China's domestic market and gained market share, first through a joint venture and later through a reverse takeover of the joint-venture partner. As a local entrepreneur, Wang Yan saw the benefits and changes to be brought to his enterprise by internationalization. This case study highlights how internationalization helped FD to take the lead and gain technological advantages. Two decades ago, China's market for CIT vehicles was still in its nascent stage, and outdated technology constrained the company's development. Acquisition of Johnson Security made it possible for FD to get a head start on its domestic peers in technology, and expand the market.

1.4　Application to the Chinese market

Our research found that most Chinese enterprises aim to utilize resources, brands and technologies they have acquired from overseas to enhance their position in the Chinese market. Most Chinese companies that invest in internationalization still regard the Chinese market – their domestic market – as a crucial part of their strategy. China's vast market continues to have considerable potential for growth, even with the relative slowdown in recent years. Thus, no enterprise can afford to exclude China from its internationalization plans, regardless of which industry or region it is starting from. In fact, China is the largest growth market for many Western companies too. Whether it is fast-food chains like KFC or luxury goods groups such as LVMH, China's markets are a key part of their strategic vision, and play an important role in these companies' financial reports.

Wall Street analysts even evaluate global companies on their performance in China, so, for a local business from China, naturally there is no reason to turn a blind eye to China's own market.

However, Chinese enterprises need time to digest and make full use of the resources and capabilities that they acquire overseas, and thus to develop their own unique competitive advantages. For Chinese enterprises, acquiring resources and capabilities helps offset a competitive disadvantage, yet the development of competitive advantages requires enterprises to combine *distinctive* local resources with the global market. As Tom Doctoroff, author of *What Chinese Want*, says:

> "If Chinese companies want to succeed in world markets, they need to retain their Chinese characteristics, which means that even if they acquire foreign companies, they still need to retain Chinese management. For Chinese enterprises, successful internationalization must begin from China – there is no shortcut."[38]

Thus, success in the Chinese market is an important path for Chinese enterprises to develop competitive advantages, which in the long run may also promote internationalization.

Therefore, when Chinese enterprises devise their internationalization strategies, they consider China as part of the global market. If the Chinese market is the best choice with respect to potential and profitability, then China will naturally be the priority. Internationalization does not imply abandoning China. We call this process 'reverse upgrading': Chinese enterprises re-enter domestic markets for their own development after gaining access to overseas brands, technology and capabilities. In our case research, we have come across many success stories arising from such strategies. An increasing number of mature enterprises combine resources they have obtained overseas with the product and service offerings for their customers in China, as illustrated by the case of ICBC.

CASE STUDY:
ICBC AND STANDARD BANK (SOUTH AFRICA)

Industrial and Commercial Bank of China (ICBC), established in 1983, is one of the most prominent commercial banks in China. In 1992, it started internationalizing by organic growth through the establishment of branches. From 2000 onwards, ICBC engaged in a series of M&A activities apart from bank branch establishment; acquisitions included Union Bank of Hong Kong in 2000, Fortis Bank Asia (a branch of a leading Belgian bank) in 2003, and a 90% stake in Indonesia's PT Bank Halim in 2006. ICBC's international plans are inseparable from its clear internationalization strategy. "ICBC is determined to internationalize," said Gu Shu, Vice-President of ICBC. "This is a very important conviction to guarantee continuous implementation of our strategy." [39]

About 2005, ICBC cast an eye on the African continent for two reasons. Firstly, a growing number of Chinese companies were landing on the continent to do business. Deloitte Consulting estimated that in 2013, Chinese enterprises were undertaking 12% of large infrastructure projects in Africa, particularly rail and port-related projects. China has provided substantial funding for projects in East Africa, and was the top investor-nation in East African projects. Chinese construction companies such as China State Construction Engineering (CSCEC), China Civil Engineering Construction Corporation (CCECC), Power Construction Corporation of China (Powerchina) and China South Locomotive & Rolling Stock Corp. (CSR) have led several projects in Africa. It is an important market for Chinese infrastructure and construction companies. Secondly, Africa had abundant natural and mineral resources, and some African economies were showing dynamic economic growth. Although the African market was very promising, major obstacles and restrictions arose due to the continent's vast landscape, capricious political environment, language and cultural barriers, as well as regulatory restrictions.

When ICBC began to look for feasible cooperation targets in Africa, it was looking for an international bank rooted in Africa and influential there, one that would be familiar with a variety of African markets. Standard Bank of South Africa, which was showing an interest in working with Chinese banks, came to ICBC's attention. In May 2007, ICBC Chairman Jiang Jianqing visited Standard Bank for a lecture after the World Bank's annual meeting, and spent a whole day with Standard Bank's CEO, Jacko Maree, to discuss cooperation between the two banks. "We are Africa's largest bank. ICBC is not just China's but also the world's largest bank. We agreed that we should explore in-depth strategic cooperation, instead of stake holding, so that we can refer customers to each other," Maree recalled. "We soon stopped the discussion and began to proceed with more substantive matters: strategic cooperation and shareholdings."

Subsequently, the two parties jointly drafted a Strategic Cooperation Agreement for review and approval by their respective boards of directors. The agreement mainly depicts the potential benefits that both parties stand to gain through strategic cooperation. In March 2008, ICBC acquired an approximately 20% stake in Standard Bank Group for US$5.5 billion, and became its single largest shareholder. At the time, this transaction was the largest single outbound investment ever by a Chinese company, and the largest inbound investment in South Africa. With a 20% cross-holding stake, ICBC and Standard Bank became strategic partners.

Through Standard Bank's branch network across Africa, ICBC was able to serve Chinese companies operating in those countries. China Power, China Communication Technology (CCT) and China Investment Corporation (CIC) have since become both ICBC and Standard Bank's customers in Africa. In China, these companies are ICBC's customers. By partnering with Standard Bank, ICBC can support its domestic customers to expand their African operations, specifically by helping to financing projects. Standard Bank, with its in-depth understanding of various African countries and of local African enterprises, was able to provide Chinese firms with a full range of business consultation services.

Through Standard Bank, ICBC gained a better understanding of Africa's political, economic and legal context, which provided a basis to serve Chinese-funded enterprises in Africa and to enhance

ICBC's syndicated business. Thanks to the cooperation with Standard Bank, ICBC also enhanced its cross-border Chinese currency (renminbi) business. ICBC's cross-border asset settlement can now provide prompt transactions through the link between its US dollar clearing centre in New York and Standard Bank of South Africa.

Standard Bank refocused on Africa, pursuing market leadership in the African market. Under ICBC's influence, Standard Bank downsized the scope of its own business, selling its bank branches in Turkey, Argentina, Russia and other locations between 2009 and 2010, and steadily improved its operating performance. Its representative office in Beijing is dedicated to consulting-related business.

Now that ICBC offered financial support to Chinese enterprises, an increasing number of Chinese companies decided to expand into Africa and Europe. Jiang Jianqing, then chairman of ICBC (since 2016 a finance professor at China Europe International Business School (CEIBS)), said:

"The large amount of commodities trading and the consequential needs for hedging resulting from the development of the Chinese economy, more particularly Chinese enterprises, as well as financial reforms such as the deregulation of interest rates and foreign exchange rates, along with the two-way opening-up of capital markets, have posed new demands for the transformation of the service capabilities and business model of Chinese banks."[40]

Thus, in 2011, ICBC purchased the majority of Standard Bank's shareholding in Argentina for $600 million,[41] and in 2014 it acquired a 60% of share of Standard Bank's UK subsidiary to further leverage Standard Bank's global market businesses platform. ICBC paid $770 million for the transaction.

By 2017, ICBC had become one of China's primary financial engines in global markets, with the most widespread network in Belt and Road Initiative (BRI) countries. The bank is deeply involved in projects, infrastructure, financing and manufacturing activities in member countries of BRI. President Xi Jinping emphasized the importance of BRI at the 19th Congress, saying, "ICBC is expected to expand globally, with the footprint of Chinese enterprises and Chinese economy."

We can clearly see Chinese elements in ICBC's international growth strategy. ICBC bypassed the problems of regulatory obstacles and cultural differences by partnering with a local bank. It succeeded in conducting business in Africa despite these barriers, and obtained the capability to operate in Africa. While Standard Bank (South Africa) is expanding its business in Africa, ICBC's newly gained capability to operate in Africa is closely linked to development of Chinese investments. The smooth post-acquisition cooperation between Standard Bank and ICBC, and the steadily improving performance of both companies in Africa, can be attributed to the combination of international finance capabilities and Chinese market knowledge and networks.

In many other cases, the capabilities acquired abroad relate more closely to product development and technologies, as in the case of H&H (also known as Biostime), China's main supplier of high-end milk powder. It provides a good example of operations in the domestic Chinese market that combine overseas resources and domestic market insights.

CASE STUDY:
H&H (BIOSTIME) ACQUIRES FRENCH MILK PRODUCER LALLEMAND

Health and Happiness International Holdings Limited (H&H, also known as Biostime) is a local Chinese company producing and selling infant goods. It was founded in 1999 in Guangzhou by entrepreneur Mr Luo Fei, who had studied biological engineering and specialized in biological fermentation research. After graduating in 1990, Mr Luo started his first B2B business, trading imported biological raw materials by matching manufacturers' needs for raw materials to the supply of suitable foreign products. While searching for business opportunities, the potential value of probiotic products occurred to him. However, the concept of probiotic products was as yet unknown to most Chinese consumers. Although yogurt is known to be rich in probiotics, such products were rarely sold as individual health products.

As an expert in biological products, Luo Fei saw his opportunity. He believed that probiotic products would be widely recognized by the market. There had been domestic suppliers of such products, but Mr. Luo was concerned about their quality, so he began to seek suppliers abroad. In 2010, he came across the French company Lallemand, France's largest manufacturer of probiotics. For their part, Lallemand were very optimistic about the Chinese market. The two companies complemented each other perfectly. Together they decided that Lallemand would manufacture probiotic products in France that would then be sold in China under the Biostime brand by H&H.

By 2006, the probiotics business had developed well. H&H then decided to broaden its product range to include children's nutrition-related products, specifically infant formula. About that time, Lallemand introduced H&H to a French milk powder business, Laiterie de Montaigu (Montaigu Dairy). Luo Fei recalled the situation:

"We had established a good reputation in France because of the probiotics business, so we extended to a second product – milk powder, as we benefited from cooperation between the supplier and manufacturer. Lallemand introduced us to the dairy enterprises because they knew us well – knew our credibility, and our trustworthiness when it came to cooperation. Lallemand played a very important role. The French milk company knew that we were a trustworthy company, therefore they were willing to cooperate with us."

To maintain its high quality and high-end image, H&H always uses 100% imported milk from overseas sources. Milk is processed into powdered form in France, and then transported to China in complete packages. H&H initiated research with its French suppliers to develop suitable products for Chinese consumers. They spent two years on research to identify consumers' pain points. As a result, in 2008 H&H began to sell milk powder that was 100% imported from France. The melamine milk contamination scandal broke out just a month after Biostime's product launch. As consumers were suddenly willing to pay a higher price for better-quality products, Biostime products imported from France became instantly popular.

By 2010, H&H had grown rapidly in China, with annual sales increasing from 40% to 60%. However, an obstacle arose when the original milk supplier, Montaigu, hit a production bottleneck and was unable to keep pace with H&H's development. H&H had to look for new suppliers of high-quality milk in Europe. In early 2010, H&H signed up two new suppliers, ISM (France) and Arla Foods (Denmark). In addition, Mr Luo signed a cooperation framework agreement with ISM in July 2013, by which H&H agreed to acquire a 20% stake in ISM for about €20 million.

To expand ISM's milk production, H&H agreed to build a new infant formula production and packaging facility, increasing ISM's manufacturing capacity to 50,000 tonnes per year by 2016, and committed itself to purchasing at least 18,000 tonnes of finished products annually.[42] Luo Fei said at the time: "Looking forward to the future, H&H needs to secure sufficient and sustainable supply of high quality milk source from Europe to upgrade its infant formula process technology and innovative formulas."[43] As a result of this investment, H&H Biostime became a high-end milk powder brand, ranked fifth among milk powder brands in 2014.

To diversify its product lines, in 2015 Biostime acquired an 83% stake in Australian vitamin maker Swisse Wellness Group for $989 million.[44] Swisse is Australia's top provider of vitamins, herbal and mineral supplements. Due to the regulations of China's Food and Drug Administration, many of Swisse's products could not be directly imported to the Chinese market. However, many Chinese were already purchasing their products via Taobao, a popular online shopping platform that allows enterprises to sell products directly to consumers. Prior to the acquisition, about a third of Swisse's revenue was generated by online sales from China. The acquisition would allowed Biostime to capture the growing demand of Chinese consumers for health products.

In 2017, Biostime established a research centre at Campus Biotech Innovation Park in Geneva, Switzerland.[45] This research centre was to focus on gut microbiota, probiotics and anti-infective agents, as well as on personalized nutrition and breast milk. It was expected to access and leverage academic expertise in Europe, and thus to enhance Biostime's competitive position in China.

H&H's innovations combined the first two steps of the three-phase path of internationalization for Chinese enterprises: acquisition of resources and application to the Chinese market. From the time Lallemand and H&H began cooperating on R&D in probiotics in 2010, a steady stream of French dairy resources and technology has been introduced into China by H&H. The results of introducing overseas resources and integrating the Chinese market are significant: not only are reliable and assured high-quality dairy products being supplied to consumers but, in pursuit of quality, the Chinese company's own market value has also been lifted. Thus, if it were not for good milk from French sources, H&H could not have achieved its market position in China, nor would ISM have enjoyed its steady sales growth.

In conclusion, the innovative path of Chinese internationalization creates win-win opportunities for all parties. H&H and the FD-Johnson acquisition discussed earlier are good examples of this strategy. The main difference is that FD acquired technology abroad, whereas H&H acquired a combination of technological and natural resources. Moreover, FD brought advanced technology to the Chinese market, provided Chinese consumers with high-quality CIT vehicles and thereby enhanced its competitiveness in the market, while Johnson Security grasped the opportunity of cooperation with FD because of huge demand in the Chinese market. In later chapters we will encounter several similar cases.

1.5   International market penetration

After building strong domestic market positions with the support of overseas resources, some Chinese entrepreneurs aim for a higher goal: international market leadership. Among market-oriented Chinese outward investors aiming to sell their products abroad, we found that most initially prioritize developing countries, for two reasons. First, based on their experience in Chinese markets, Chinese enterprises are familiar with challenges such as rapid economic development, volatile market demand, incomplete market institutions and periodic government intervention. They consider such conditions a 'home-game'. Secondly, developing countries, especially those in Asia, are culturally similar to China. Thus, Chinese companies are more likely to be able to accumulate international experience in these markets. It is only at later stages, and after having accumulated some experience in developing markets, that Chinese companies choose to expand into developed-country markets where their foreignness is more of a liability. Haier is an example.

CASE STUDY:
HAIER ACQUIRES GE APPLIANCES

Haier Group, China's biggest manufacturer of household appliances, agreed to acquire General Electric (GE)'s home appliance unit in an all-cash deal for US$5.58 billion in 2016. Some critics raised concerns that Haier would fail to realize synergies with GE Appliances, one of the most well-established GE brands. However, Haier's management team was confident of its capabilities in international business.

Haier established its first overseas direct investment in 1996 in Indonesia, a joint venture with Japan's Sapporo Ltd. The following year, Haier set up joint ventures in the Philippines, Malaysia and the former Yugoslavia. These operations helped Haier to train an internationally experienced talent pool, which would later play an important role in implementing Haier's international strategies. After its first experiences in developing countries, Haier made a greenfield investment in a developed-country market for the first time in 1999, and this time it was a factory in the United States. This experience in international markets laid the foundation for the GE acquisition. "We have been venturing in international markets for 20 years," said Zhang Ruimin, CEO of Haier. "Throughout the years, we have accumulated a lot of experience that can facilitate our acquisition, and even the integration plan, with GE Appliances." However, although Haier had gradually become known in international markets, the company had captured only 2% of the home appliance market in the US.

In 2008, GE decided to sell its home appliances business. GE Chairman and CEO Jeff Immelt said the company's exit from its appliances and credit businesses was key to its transformation into a "simpler, more competitive company". He added: "Sale of GE Appliances is another step in the company's portfolio transformation and its mission to become the world's leading digital industry company." Haier had been an active bidder in the initial sales negotiations. Electrolux from Sweden initially emerged as the successful bidder in an all-cash deal for $3.3 billion, but the US competition authorities intervened because a combined GE Appliances-Electrolux company would have attained a dominant market share. In consequence, GE's original plans to sell to Electrolux collapsed, opening an opportunity for Haier.

In 2016, GE again started to seek a buyer for its appliance unit, which was struggling with profit growth in the low single digits, lagging behind GE's other business units. This time, Haier was prepared for the negotiations, having assembled a team of professional financial advisors, consultants and legal advisors. As Zhang Ruimin emphasized:

"We had been preparing for the acquisition for almost a year prior to the announcement date. Although many other competitors also made offers to GE Appliances, our readiness combined with our previous experience in international business, and our leadership position in the Chinese home appliance market made us a desirable candidate to GE Appliances."

Thus, in June 2016, Haier acquired the home appliance unit from GE for $5.6 billion.[46]

As part of the integration strategy, Haier promised that:

"GE Appliances will continue to be head quartered in Louisville, and operated independently under the day to day management of the current management team. Chip Blankenship, President and CEO of GE Appliances, will retain the position and also become a new Senior Vice President of the Haier Group."

Blankenship said:

"The takeover by the Chinese entity was very important for our employees and business. Haier loves appliances and shares our goals. I'm bullish on what the future holds with Haier as our parent company. Meanwhile, Haier has resources that GE Appliances needs, to offer more products in more markets, and Haier can make the company more competitive on the global stage."

After the acquisition, Haier deployed a digital-focused strategy that aimed to build and utilize a data platform and advance the connectivity of appliances based on the 'internet of things' (IOT), building on the technological advances it had developed in China.[47] Haier integrated the hardware technologies of GE Appliances with its own data platform and cloud-computing technologies. As digital technologies were improving at an unprecedented rate, Mr Zhang believed that the key to success would be to respond quickly to the dynamic environment. Therefore, to pursue the digital-focused strategy, he broke up the gigantic company with 60,000 employees into more than 1,000 business units that were to act like customer-focused start-ups.[48] Zhang Ruimin explained:

"In the past, different departments like research and development, production, and sales worked in a linear relationship. But we have broken that structure and create many small, nimble work units, which can better respond to customers' demands."

During the first nine months of 2017, the performance of GE Appliances started to turn around: profit increased by 10%.

In 2016, Haier's profit rose 12.8% over the year to 20.3 billion yuan (US$3.1 billion) while revenue increased 6.8% to 201.6 billion yuan.[49] Transaction volume on its B2B and consumer-oriented internet platforms rose 73% to 272.2 billion Chinese yuan. According to a 2016 survey by Euromonitor, Haier accounts for 10.3% of worldwide home appliance sales, making it one of the largest players globally.

Haier's internationalization strategy is conventional in that they first aimed for markets that are structurally similar, and hence where Chinese products need fewer adaptations to meet local demand; in particular, Haier offers products that are affordable to middle-income groups within relatively less advanced economies. However, Haier is unconventional in that it targeted the US market at an early stage, even if only through a niche-market strategy. Yet this niche-market strategy, combined with experience gained in developing markets, laid the foundations for a later large-scale entry through the acquisition of a major domestic player.

A special case of international market entry by a Chinese company is the information and telecoms business Huawei. It differs from many other Chinese investors going global in that it has been pursuing international customers primarily through greenfield projects rather than acquisitions. Huawei's first international customer was Hutchison Telecom from Hong Kong, who in 1997 signed a contract for fixed-line network switches and related equipment from Huawei. In the following year, Huawei set up a joint venture with Beto Company in Russia, which assembled and produced switch gears for Huawei in Russia. Subsequently, Huawei broke into Thailand, Brazil and South Africa with its own product technology and price advantage, and began to sell directly in these countries. Following its success in many developing countries, Huawei has turned to developed-country markets. In 2001, Huawei signed its first sales contracts in the Netherlands and Germany. In 2004, Huawei made further progress in Portugal. In 2005, British Telecom selected Huawei as the preferred supplier for its next-generation network. By 2015, Huawei had more than 110,000 employees globally, and two-thirds of its sales came from international markets. [50]

1.6 Conclusion

Overall, the strategies of Chinese companies have rapidly matured. In the early 2000s, many deals were undertaken by major SOEs in pursuit of natural resources, or by risk-loving entrepreneurs pursing singular opportunities. By 2010, Chinese companies had build considerable experience in negotiating deals, and in designing strategies that offered opportunities for integrating overseas resources – especially brands and technologies – with operations in China. By 2018, an increasing number of Chinese investors have accumulated not only financial but human resources that enable them to bid for foreign markets, even in Europe and North America.

Our research suggests that the predominant mode of internationalization among Chinese companies is a three-stage model. Starting from their home market, companies acquire resources and capabilities overseas through international investments to offset competitive disadvantages, and then apply these to the Chinese market. After the acquisition, Chinese enterprises aim to integrate overseas resources and to use them to attain unique competitive advantages, initially in China and eventually in global markets. The globalization of Chinese enterprises is thus a process of acquiring, integrating and applying new resources and capabilities. We call this the 'Capability Upgrade Approach'. The home market is thus a key foundation of Chinese enterprises' efforts to globalize.

Yet there remain huge variations among companies in China, not only in ownership types and strategic ambition, but in terms of international management expertise and in their ability to realistically assess and implement overseas opportunities. China is richly endowed with risk-taking entrepreneurs. Some of them are likely to succeed and build the new China. Others will fail. Such is capitalism. We hope that this book will help the reader to identify the winners.

CHAPTER 2

INNOVATIVE PATHS TO GLOBAL EXPANSION

Zhang Ruimin, CEO of Haier Group, offers stern advice to Chinese business leaders:

> "A new order of competition resulting in internationalization of domestic markets and localization of international competition has been shaped. Globalization trends require enterprises to become international. These trends are irreversible and unavoidable. Either multinationals enter China to beat us, or we fight against multinationals. The best way to deal with the challenges of multinationals is to transform yourself into a good multinational company. If you want to 'dance with the wolves', you must become a wolf yourself, or you must await your final destiny, which is to be eaten."[51]

However, Chinese enterprises that want to succeed in global competition must first clarify their own internationalization strategy and their strategic priorities.

As described in Chapter 1, the path to internationalization for Chinese enterprises typically goes through three phases that are quite different from the paths usually observed in Western companies: acquisition of resources, transfer and integration of these resources, and finally exploiting their full potential by competing in global markets. Therefore, Chinese companies face some key challenges that they need to resolve. At the first stage, before the acquisition of resources and capabilities, they need to clarify their business strategy, business models and core competencies. They need to analyse their own competitive advantage, their unique features, special resources, and their advantages and disadvantages. On that basis, they can then select the resources they need most urgently. At this juncture, enterprises need to answer three questions:

1. What kinds of resources and capabilities are required?
2. Who controls the required resources and capabilities?
3. How can these resources and capabilities be accessed?

To apply the acquired resources in China, managers of Chinese MNEs should consider the compatibility of their M&A targets with the existing organization, which is essential for the smooth transfer, application and absorption of resources and capabilities. Compatibility in culture between the organizations, and the openness of the organization to externally introduce organizational change, are especially important. Key questions at this stage include:

1. Should the two companies be managed autonomously or integrated?
2. How should the capabilities of the target firm be integrated with those of the existing organization?
3. How well do the organizational cultures match each other?
4. How can the companies manage the processes of knowledge sharing and learning between the acquirer and its target? In later chapters we will explore these questions in detail.

When it comes to pushing into global markets – with or without resources acquired abroad – firms have to develop a clear strategy for resource development and exploitation. Specifically, enterprises need to prioritize their resource needs and to design processes to impart knowledge. Before embarking on market-oriented investment abroad, critical questions include:

1. Which markets are suitable for using such resources and capabilities?
2. What resources and capabilities should enterprises prioritize, and in what order?
3. How can the enterprise's existing resources serve market needs?

In our case research, we observed not only three distinct phases of internationalization, as identified in Chapter 1 (see Figure 1), but also four distinct operation models, namely, divide and rule, reverse upgrade, strong start international growth, and traditional-path international growth (Table 2). These four operation models of Chinese enterprises each have their own characteristic features and challenges, as we will explore in this chapter. Only by fully understanding their own position on the path of internationalization, and their strategic objectives, can Chinese enterprises devise their own blueprint for the global market of the future.

STAGE	OPERATION MODELS		COMMENTS
RESOURCE AND CAPABILITY SEEKING	Divide and rule	Opportunity-oriented	Identifying, assessing and acquiring companies with attractive resources abroad
		Relevant but not integrated	
DOMESTIC APPLICATION	Reverse upgrading	Natural resources	Applying and integrating resources and capabilities acquired overseas to Chinese markets, and upgrade operations in home markets.
		Technologies	
		Brands	
GLOBAL EXPLORATION	Strong-start international growth		Integrating capabilities acquired abroad with domestic Chinese resources (e.g. cheap labour and capital costs) to compete with global players.
	Traditional-path international growth		Entering foreign markets based on capabilities developed in China (so far rare among Chinese enterprises)

TABLE 2   STAGES OF INTERNATIONALIZATION OPERATIONAL MODELS

2.1   Divide and rule

Many of the Chinese companies that we have studied developed a 'divide and rule' operational model, which retains the autonomy of the acquired firm but secures the control of the new owners. Legally, after an acquisition the acquirer and the target become part of the same organization. Yet, the divide and rule approach provides foreign subsidiaries with almost non-interfering autonomy. The subsidiaries retain their original management team, technology and market, and enjoy almost full autonomy for operational decisions. However, the divide and rule approach has only a limited impact on the parent's domestic business. As an operational model it is not a traditional integration strategy. 'Integration' usually refers to strategic and operational integration of two companies after an M&A, while divide and rule refers to no operational integration between the two companies at all, with only limited strategic coordination. The divide and rule model is most suitable for Chinese companies that have just started acquiring businesses abroad. They may still suffer from certain competitive disadvantages compared with their Western counterparts. While they are operating well domestically and have adequate funds to finance the acquisition, they often lack the experience to manage internationalization.

Some Chinese enterprises adopt the divide and rule operational model because synergies are not a key motivation for their acquisitions, and they expect few benefits from a deep integration. These investors regard overseas acquisitions primarily as a financial investment and as risk diversification. If the objective of an M&A is simply to access natural resources, then there is no need for excessive integration. Such companies usually concentrate on the return on their investment, and on generating future overseas business. For example, China Petroleum & Chemical Corporation (Sinopec) is one of the largest offshore oil and gas producers in China, and one of the world's largest independent oil and gas exploration and production groups.

From 2004, Sinopec made about 20 acquisitions over a span of 10 years, acquiring companies in various countries and territories including Russia, Canada, Switzerland, France, Spain and the United States, as well as mining assets in Nigeria, the United States, Canada and the United Kingdom. Sinopec's strategy includes an expansion of their value chain, and to that end they have obtained many upstream resources via overseas acquisitions. However, since the focus of their acquisitions is on large-scale mineral resources and mining concessions, Sinopec usually retains the employees, teams, production and management organizations of its acquired companies. An employee at Addax Oil Company in Switzerland, which was acquired by Sinopec, said in an interview:

"The Chinese side only stationed a team of 18 people. Except for the CEO, chief financial officer, and chief geologist, all foreign employees in senior positions were retained. No Chinese operation mode was implanted, and the working language is still English."[52]

Thus, except for the financial aspects of the integration, the daily operations of the two companies can be described as non-interfering.

In contrast, enterprises that lack the ability to integrate must develop related capabilities. The process of developing capabilities is also a process by which enterprises learn and absorb new knowledge. However, Rome was not built in a day; similarly, learning and assimilation cannot be achieved overnight. Hence, if operational integration is a strategic objective, then the acquirer needs to develop a detailed integration plan before the acquisition. Bringing in a third party, such as a consulting firm, may expedite this process.

There are two strategic directions for the divide and rule operational model. First, the 'opportunity-oriented' strategy applies to target businesses with negligible synergy to the acquirer's own core business. Acquirer and target may thus be in two completely unrelated industries. Such an enterprise is either not acting with a clear international strategy, or is merely in pursuit of a diversification strategy, perhaps to reduce financial risk exposure.

Second, the 'relevant but not fused' acquisition strategy targets businesses in related industries, but with incompatible business models or organizational cultures. The result of integrating related business operations, such as finance, marketing and sales, can enable companies to improve efficiency and reduce costs, hence 'relevant but not fused' works for enterprises that lack long-term strategic planning. However, some companies do use this operation model for strategic matching. Fosun Group is one such example.

CASE STUDY:
FOSUN GROUP ACQUIRES PORTUGUESE
INSURER CAIXA SEGUROS

Fosun Group an international conglomerate and investment company based in Shanghai, was established in 1992 and prospered during China's market-driven economic reform. In 2007, Fosun Group's parent company, Fosun International, was listed on the main board of the Hong Kong Stock Exchange. Guo Guangchang, Chairman of Fosun Group, is an admirer of US business magnate Warren Buffett, and advocates Buffett's investment philosophy. Accordingly, Fosun followed the Buffett-style business model of 'insurance and investment' – that is, using the insurance company's funds to support Fosun's investment projects, so as to achieve the goal of negative costs. Under Guo Guangchang's leadership, Fosun primarily invested in the four engines of their development model: insurance, industrial operations, investment, and capital management. They pursued a value investment philosophy to steadily promote Fosun's image of a "world-class investment group with core business in insurance and focusing on China's growth momentum". The group's main investment focus has been on industries that prospered during China's market-driven development, including consumer goods, financial services, energy resources and manufacturing upgrades.

Fosun executed its investment philosophy via overseas acquisitions, starting from its initial investment in Club Méditerranée SA (Club Med), a French holiday company, in 2010. Fosun initially acquired a 7.6% stake in Club Med for 2.1 billion Chinese yuan.[53] In 2013, Fosun began its bid for Club Med, competing with BI-Invest Group, a leading Italian long-term investment group and the largest shareholder of Club Med at the time. After a bidding war lasting about two years, in 2015 Fosun acquired Club Med for US$4.3 billion.

However, despite Fosun declaring 'insurance and investment' as its business model, as of 2010 the insurance business has accounted for less than 10% of Fosun's total assets. Fosun therefore found it difficult to raise insurance funds as sources for its investment plans. Consequently, Fosun looked overseas to expand its insurance business, and the Portuguese Caixa Seguros insurance group became an important target.

Founded in 1835, Caixa Seguros was Portugal's largest insurance company. It had insurance business in seven countries and regions, with its own insurance brands such as Fidelidade and Multicare in Portugal. In 2013, Caixa Seguros accounted for 30% of Portugal's nationwide market, with total assets of €13 billion, and net assets of €1.35 billion. The company had Portugal's largest sales network, and was the leading brand in Portugal's insurance industry.

However, Portugal was severely hit by the global financial crisis, which put pressure on both its financial system and its government's finances. In 2011, the Portuguese government committed itself to a package of economic reforms to address its debt crisis over the next three years, which included privatization of government-owned banks. Thus, Caixa Geral de Depósitos (CGD), one of Portugal's largest state-owned banks, had to increase its own core capital, and it did so by reorganizing its insurance company Caixa Seguros, offering shares in a public auction.

Fosun beat US investment fund Apollo Global Management and acquired an 80% stake in CGD's insurance division with its three wholly owned subsidiaries. The reason behind the success of this bid was that before merging with Caixa Seguros, insurance had not been Fosun's main business.

After the acquisition, Fosun retained Caixa Seguros' original management team and business model, although financial aspects had to be integrated according to laws and regulations. Caixa Seguros also retained its operational autonomy. As it had once been an SOE, the state valued the impact of the merger on employment. In this way, the merger reflected Fosun's strategy, which was the key to its success in winning the bidding process.

The divide and rule operational model made sense in this case because Fosun had expertise in investing, but not in insurance. Therefore, after the merger, the two companies continued to run their own businesses, creating a win-win outcome for both Fosun and Caixa Seguros. After the merger, the insurance business accounted for one third of the total assets of Fosun Group. In the words of Fosun's chairman, Guo Guangchang: "This is a solid step on Fosun's road to a Buffett-style development process."

Fosun has also been involved in numerous other M&A projects: from two projects in 2012 and 2013 to 14 in 2014, 17 in 2015 and four in 2016. Companies acquired by Fosun include Greek fashion accessory company Folli Follie, American filmmaker Studio 8, British travel company Thomas Cook and German private bank Hauck & Aufhäuser.[54]

2.2   Reverse upgrade

The 'reverse upgrade' operational model refers to making foreign resources serve Chinese operations. In other words, Chinese enterprises obtain resources and capabilities through acquisitions of overseas companies, and bring them back to China to upgrade their own operations in domestic markets, and thus to enhance their competitive advantage and market position. The main goal of globalization for such enterprises is the Chinese market. Companies use the reverse upgrade operation model to acquire companies in their own industry, and then to transfer technologies, teams, management processes and development capabilities from the acquired firm to China. There are three types of overseas assets used to upgrade the Chinese market: resources, technology and brands.

2.2.1   Reverse upgrade of resources

The 'reverse upgrade of resources' operational model is mostly applied in energy, minerals, food and other resource industries. Companies in such industries usually operate under relatively stable conditions and with a steady cash flow. They may enjoy a certain level of visibility in the domestic market, but rarely become leading enterprises. Their international objectives are clear, as resources are the core foundation of their competitiveness. However, resources are affected by public policy and market volatility, and hence these enterprises are subject to many external factors beyond their control. This external uncertainty often puts Chinese enterprises at a competitive disadvantage compared with leading Western multinationals.

For such enterprises, the acquisition of overseas resources is often the first step to internationalization.

In applying the reverse upgrade of resources operation model, the first step is to clarify what resources are needed, and to assess the demand for these resources in the respective domestic industry. The second step is to assess global markets and potential acquisition targets that have high-quality resources and are available at a reasonable price. As a third step, the company needs to confirm whether these resources can be used in the Chinese market. These are challenging operational tasks whose complexity is underestimated by many Chinese investors. For example, Smithfield Food Inc. in the US, which was acquired by Wanzhou International (formerly known as Shuanghui Group), is an example of a Chinese enterprise's failed attempt to apply resources gained overseas to reverse-upgrade its domestic operations.

CASE STUDY:
WANZHOU ACQUIRES SMITHFIELD FOOD INC.

Wanzhou International Holdings Ltd (known until January 2014 as Shuanghui Group), listed in Hong Kong, is one of China's largest meat processing enterprises and the controlling shareholder of China's largest listed meat company, Shuanghui Development. In 2010, Shuanghui Development had a breeding stock inventory of 310,000 pigs and slaughtered 11.42 million pigs each year to produce 2.7 million tonnes of meat. Its sales revenues were 39.3 billion yuan, with profits of 3.8 billion. Shuanghui Development was a pioneer of China's food processing industry. As early as 1994, it introduced ISO 9000 quality management systems, and put in place a quality assurance system. Its factories were ISO 9000, ISO 14001 and ISO 22000 certified, conformed to Hazard Analysis and Critical Control Points (HACCP) criteria and passed import license tests for Japan, Singapore and other countries; all of this enhanced Shuanghui's reputation for quality and brand value.

However, in March 2011, media reports pushed Shuanghui to the edge. Clenbuterol hydrochloride, also referred to simply as 'clenbuterol', is a drug used to treat bronchial asthma, chronic bronchitis, emphysema and other diseases. When added to animal feed (especially for pigs), clenbuterol acts as a growth-promoting drug, producing leaner meat with a higher muscle-to-fat ratio, which can increase the sales value of the meat. However, clenbuterol can be harmful to human health, and is thus banned in many countries (including China) as an animal feed additive. According to media reports, in the city of Mengzhou (Henan province) and other places, pig farms added the banned drug to animal feed, and this was blamed for contaminating pork at Shuanghui's factory in Jiyuan.

Although the clenbuterol scandal was resolved within two weeks of media exposure, and three clenbuterol manufacturing labs were shut down, concerns about food safety continued to worry consumers. Consumer trust in the Shuanghui brand dropped. Moreover, the price of high-quality pork in China soared after the clenbuterol scandal and Shuanghui's product costs skyrocketed. Therefore, Shuanghui began to seek an alternative supply for high-quality meat from overseas, as well as enhancing its expertise in advanced farming techniques. US meat processor Smithfield Foods thus became a target for Shuanghui.

Smithfield Foods Inc. was founded in 1936 in the state of Virginia. In the 1980s it rapidly expanded, and in 1998 the company became the largest pork processor in the US, with the largest swine stock, slaughterhouse and meat-processing plant in the world. It employed cutting-edge processing and quality control technologies, a solid management system and a professional management team. It held 30% of the US meat market and had a foothold in 12 other countries around the world. It operated three sector divisions: pork, swine, and the international business. In the 2012 fiscal year, Smithfield Foods reported net profits of US$361.3 million, and the company ranked 218 in the 2012 Fortune 500 list.

However, the 2008 financial crisis severely impacted the company. Due to falling livestock prices, Smithfield Foods suffered a net loss of $250 million in 2009, followed by a further net loss of $100 million in 2010. Consecutive years of losses created the opportunity for Shuanghui to buy Smithfield at what appeared to be an attractive price.

The acquisition process did not go smoothly. In June 2013, the merger was blocked by a majority of Smithfield Foods' shareholders, who argued that Smithfield had been undervalued in the transaction; if the meat processor was broken up and sold in parts, shareholders would realize more value. Moreover, the governor of Missouri vetoed two bills that contained clauses allowing the sale of Missouri farmland to foreigners, thus raising legal barriers to real estate-related aspects of Shuanghui's proposed merger. In July, a US non-profit organization submitted a petition to the Committee on Foreign Investment in the United States (CFIUS), asking them to veto the Shuanghui merger. By the end of July, CFIUS indicated a need for a second-phase review on the merger, and the review period was extended to 45 days.

On 6 September, this high-value merger transaction was finally approved by CFIUS, which meant that all policy barriers to this merger had been cleared; the long-winded process was completed. Smithfield Foods held a special shareholders' meeting on 24 September, which approved the deal, and patience finally paid off. Where there's a will, there's a way – or, as the Chinese say, "The Heavenly Power will not disappoint those with well-prepared minds." Shuanghui completed the 100% acquisition of Smithfield Foods, valued at about $7.1 billion including Smithfield's net debt.

Shuanghui held great expectations for the acquisition, hoping that high-quality pork from the US could be provided by Smithfield Foods and that as a result, Chinese consumers could obtain a reliable supply of trustworthy pork, allowing Shuanghuai to restore its brand image and enhance its influence in the Chinese market. Unfortunately, things did not turn out the way top management had hoped. Back in 2011, Shuanghui had come under criticism in the clenbuterol scandal. The US was one of the few countries around the world where it was legal to use clenbuterol in feeds, while in China and other countries it remained strictly prohibited. Therefore, from 2013 onwards, the Chinese authorities tightened the regulations on pork imported from the US. These restrictions undermined the cooperation between Smithfield Foods and Shuanghui, and prevented the realization of the original business model, namely to access US-raised pork through the acquisition of a leading US meat processing company.

In view of the regulatory differences, Smithfield now focused on producing meat without clenbuterol, so that the company, with the help of Shuanghui, could benefit from the growing demand in China. By 2016, Smithfield "followed through its promises to halt the use of the controversial feed additive material in half of its pork production".[55] Three of its subsidiaries produced products eligible for export to China. After the acquisition, Smithfield kept its management and its Virginia headquarters, but became a wholly owned subsidiary of Shuanghui. Larry Pope, the CEO of Smithfield, said: "We did not anticipate any changes in how we do business operationally in the US and throughout the world."[56] Wang Long, Chairman of Shuanghui, emphasized that "Smithfield would help meet the demand in China for pork by importing high-quality meat products from the US."[57]

The acquisition of Smithfield did not stop Shuanghui from continuing to buy. In 2016, the Chinese firm acquired Clougherty Packing, an American supplier of meat products, for $145 million.[58] In 2017, Shuanghui acquired Pini Group's packaged meat companies in Poland and two packaged meat manufacturers in Romania, Elit and Vericom.[59]

The case of Shanghui highlights an aspect of due diligence that is particularly relevant to the model of reverse upgrading of resources. Specifically, not all resources and products can be imported to China and not all technologies can be applied in Chinese operations, because regulatory requirements vary across countries. In the case of Smithfield Foods, Shuanghui Group failed to determine in advance whether Smithfield's pork resources could be imported to China. It appears that Shuanghui panicked due to public pressure after the clenbuterol scandal, and prematurely rushed into a foreign acquisition. They failed to appreciate the regulatory differences which allowed US pig farmers to use clenbuterol legally. The result was that Shuanghui's original business model of obtaining high-quality pork resources from Smithfield Foods for Chinese consumers was unfeasible. And thus, the attempt to use this acquisition to restore Shuanghui's reputation and brand image failed. So from a strategic point of view, Shuanghui's acquisition of Smithfield Foods has to be considered a failure.

In contrast, the earlier-mentioned case of H&H's acquisition in France illustrates a successful reverse upgrade of Chinese operations using resources gained overseas. H&H obtained milk from France, then sold it in China. High-quality formula products helped H&H to win the trust of Chinese consumers, enhanced its reputation and gave it a competitive advantage in the Chinese high-end market for formula milk. These examples suggest an important lesson regarding the failure and success of overseas acquisitions: it is vital to establish whether the resources that the enterprise seeks to obtain abroad are actually useful to the Chinese market.

2.2.2   Reverse upgrade of technology

Enterprises that follow the reverse upgrade of technology operational model are mostly in technology-driven industries such as information technology, machinery manufacturing and biomedicine. The internationalization strategy of these enterprises focuses on technology as the main basis of their competitive advantage. Thus, technological innovation is crucial to their future direction and development. There are two reasons for Chinese enterprises to adopt the reverse upgrade of technology model. First, such companies are likely to have prior experience of international cooperation in projects or of collaborative R&D; secondly, they will have relevant technical personnel matching the organizational structure in China.

Unlike natural resources, technology is generally difficult to transfer across locations and between different companies. When a Chinese company obtains overseas technology through M&A, it needs to learn how to manage and apply the technology to the local conditions in the Chinese market. Therefore, acquirers need relevant technical staff in their parent organization who can effectively engage with individuals abroad to work jointly on technology projects. Such personnel are often in short supply.

Thus, it makes sense for companies to first assess the industry and the future direction of technology before investing abroad with a view to applying the reverse upgrade model. First, scalability of technology is essential; therefore, the enterprise should appraise the maturity of the technology. Secondly, companies need to be sure of the technical capabilities of overseas teams; there should be no drastic changes in technology on or after acquisition. Thirdly, companies need to clarify that the technology can be assimilated and applied to the Chinese market. The process of adopting technology requires personnel with technological skills, collaboration between personnel and management teams, and operations and processes to conceptualize the design of an integration programme.

CASE STUDY:
SANY HEAVY INDUSTRY
ACQUIRES PUTZMEISTER (GERMANY)

Sany Heavy Industry Co., Ltd. (Sany Heavy) was founded in 1994 in Changcha by three entrepreneurs, and became successful at independent innovation. In July 2003, Sany Heavy was listed on the Shanghai Stock Exchange. As the core subsidiary of Sany Group, Sany Heavy is mainly engaged in the development, manufacture and sales of construction machinery. It achieved world records in several aspects of machinery manufacturing and thus enjoys a great reputation in the industry in China. Sany Heavy's products include machinery for concrete, excavation and road construction, including pumps, trailers, excavators and crawler cranes. It had become China's leading brand, and its concrete pumps, pump trucks and full hydraulic rollers all ranked highest in the country. Thus, Sany Heavy had grown from a little-known private enterprise to China's largest, and the world's sixth-largest, construction machinery manufacturer.

As early as 2001, Sany Heavy Industry introduced the concept of "transformation into an international business" as its mission. The internationalization strategy of Sany Heavy Industry targeted the "use of resource advantages to integrate resources in foreign countries, and to use such global resources to enhance the internationalization of Sany Heavy". The company's internationalization strategy was divided into three phases: in the first phase,

Sany Heavy would export its machines, build the brand and rapidly respond to international market trends; secondly, the firm would invest in factories and plants overseas; and in the third phase it planned to invest abroad and integrate on an international level professionals and expertise, capital, markets and other resources through foreign acquisitions.

The case of Sany Heavy Industry's acquisition of Putzmeister Holding (Germany) concerns the third phase of its internationalization. Putzmeister was one of the world's leading manufacturers of concrete pumps, along with its fellow German arch-rival Schwing. Putzmeister focused on the production of concrete-pumping equipment, and it accounted for about 40% of the global market. With more than 90% of its sales revenue coming from overseas markets, including Europe and North America, Putzmeister had captured 56.3% and 20.8% market share in Europe and North America, respectively.[60] The firm had a long history. In 1994, when Sany Heavy had just been established, Putzmeister was already a famous machinery manufacturer in Europe, and its technological leadership in the field of concrete-pumping machinery was beyond all doubt. In fact, Putzmeister had long been a role model that inspired the entrepreneurs of Sany when they developed their own concrete pumps.

However, the financial crisis severely impacted on the construction industry, and even more so the construction equipment industry, a key supplier to construction firms. Thus, Putzmeister's sales and profitability dropped sharply. In 2010 and 2011, sales were €550 million and €560 million, while their net profit margin was only 0.27% and 1.07%, respectively, well below the 12.4% historical peak of 2007.[61] Faced with a financial bottleneck, and the need to find a successor for the founder-owner who still held control in the firm, Putzmeister considered a public auction to sell the company. Other machinery manufacturing enterprises such as Zoomlion Heavy Industry Science & Technology Co. (also from Changcha) were expected to participate in the bidding. However, Sany Heavy took the initiative and proactively contacted Putzmeister's owner, expressing their intent to acquire the company.

Negotiations between the two entrepreneurs – Mr Scheuch for Putzmeister and Mr Liang for Sany – proceeded very quickly.

On 31 January 2012, Sany Heavy announced the acquisition of Putzmeister by purchasing a 90% stake, causing ripples in the industry. The acquisition marked the first takeover of a famous German enterprise by a Chinese company, and boosted the overseas M&A record of Chinese enterprises in the construction machinery industry. As "the world's largest concrete machinery manufacturer" acquired the "No. 1 concrete machinery enterprise in the world", the merger of Sany Heavy Industry and Putzmeister formed an alliance between giants, which would reshape the global competitive landscape of the construction machinery industry.

With the acquisition of Putzmeister, Sany Heavy Industry acquired the German firm's cutting-edge product technology in the field of concrete machinery, including Putzmeister's product technical standards, reliability, stability, quality control standards and processes. In addition, Sany Heavy has been able to reduce its power system emissions, improve the emissions standard of its own concrete machinery and provide better services to its clients in China. Sany Heavy has made full use of technology accessed overseas, and enhanced its position in China with more comprehensive and high-quality product lines.

Post-acquisition, the two companies operated a two-brand strategy.[62] In China, for instance, for the products that both companies had in common, Putzmeister would remove its products from the Chinese market, because Sany's already enjoyed a good reputation in that market. For complementary products, Putzmeister would benefit from Sany's distribution network to sell products that Sany does not have in its portfolio. The two-brand strategy also holds in overseas markets. As a result, sales of Putzmeister increased by nearly a third by 2016. Furthermore, since Sany strictly kept its promise to guarantee jobs until 2020, the German firm's global workforce has remained stable at 3,300. While the result of the acquisition has been satisfying so far, both companies acknowledge that "more time is needed for the integration to succeed on all levels and in all countries."[63]

2.2.3. Reverse upgrade of brands

Enterprises that adopt the reverse upgrade of brands operational model are mostly in the consumer goods, services and information technology fields. A brand affects consumers' shopping decisions and quickly promotes market development; therefore such enterprises usually are of larger size, with adequate funds. Their strategy is radical, and needs quick movement to open a new market or enhance visibility; and they prefer to raise brand prominence in both domestic and foreign markets through internationalization. Usually, such enterprises have already established a certain reputation within their industry in China, and may even be leaders in the Chinese market. Therefore, the reverse upgrade of brand operational model is suited to enterprises that have vast experience in internationalization, and in their respective industry in China.

Before deciding to apply this operational model, enterprises need first to assess the brand value of the target company, which is directly related to the purchasing price and the expected investment return on the acquisition. Secondly, they need to ensure they have sufficient market size and channel deployment to support the marketing and application of the brand in China. Finally, the effectiveness of a brand is closely related to the company's other capabilities. Brand is a soft asset, so if the firm's technology or resources are inadequate, it is difficult to maintain a brand over the long term.

CASE STUDY:
GEELY ACQUIRES VOLVO

Zhejiang Geely Holding Group was one of China's top ten automobile manufacturers. Founded in 1986 by entrepreneur Li Shufu in Taizhou, its headquarters are in the city of Hangzhou. By 2004, Geely had achieved remarkable successes in making cars, motorcycles, auto parts including engines and gearboxes, and also in higher education, interior decoration materials, tourism and real estate. It had total assets of more than 20 billion yuan.

Beginning in 2007, Geely pursued a transformative strategy: rather than engaging in a price war, it decided to reposition its core competitiveness from cost advantages to technical superiority and high-quality service. However, Geely cars had come to be seen as 'grassroots' products due to their low prices and humble brand image. Low cost and low price brought Geely generous profits, yet these elements hindered the brand from being raised to a higher level. Geely offered no high-end products that might be exported. Although the company was producing under three major brand names – Englon, Emgrand and Gleagle – its portfolio lacked a brand with an international pedigree. Volvo would be the perfect brand to complete the puzzle for Geely, and so they turned their attention to Volvo.

The famous Swedish car maker was founded in 1924 by Assar Gabrielsson and Gustav Larson. Volvo cars enjoy a high reputation for their excellent quality and performance, especially in safety systems. Volvo made safety their speciality, with the slogan: 'For Volvo, every year is a "safe year".' The American Highway Loss Data Institute (HLDI) have consistently ranked Volvo as No. 1 on their top ten safest cars list. The Volvo brand was renowned internationally as the world's safest car.

Despite the marque's solid brand reputation in Western countries, in 2006 Volvo's parent company Ford suffered a huge loss of about US$12.7 billion. Ford decided to retrench and concentrate on development of their central brand, with the slogan 'One Ford, One Team'. Volvo car sales had been declining in the preceding years after the merger with Ford. From 2005, Volvo suffered a continuous five-year loss of on average more than $1 billion annually.[64]

Geely and Ford were well matched: what one wanted to buy, the other was willing to sell. After several rounds of negotiations, Li Shufu had developed a great respect for Volvo and promised that within Volvo, an independent system of operations would be retained. Geely would not interfere with Volvo's operations and management, the executive team would stay, and a deal was made with the labour union that the factories would not be relocated and there would be no layoffs. In short, Li Shufu promised to maintain extraordinary independence for Volvo. The level of respect he showed impressed Ford, and Geely's bid was favoured. Thus, on 25 January 2011, Volvo China officially set up headquarters in Shanghai. On 28 March of that year, the Ford Motor Company (US) and Zhejiang Geely Holding Group signed an agreement for Geely's acquisition of a 100% stake in Volvo Cars in Gothenburg, Sweden, where the Volvo plant is located.

Through this acquisition, Geely gained the Volvo brand, which has helped it to enhance the company's brand prominence in the Chinese market, and has laid a strong foundation for the enterprise's future development. In 2013, Volvo made a profit. As of 2015, Geely has also been discreetly forging ahead through transformation strategies adopted in its own Chinese proprietary brands. Volvo's acquisition has accelerated the release of new models in Geely's high-end saloon range, such as Emgrand and the SC11 series. From January to May 2015, Geely sold 219,038 cars, a year-over-year increase of about 40%, and reached 49% of the 2015 annual sales target of 450,000 cars, an increase much higher than the industry-wide growth rate.[65]

In addition to Volvo, Geely acquired British electric vehicle start-up Emerald in 2014, and promised to invest at least $200 million over the next five years in the technological development of new-energy vehicles.[56] Furthermore, in 2017, Geely announced its intention to purchase a 49.9% stake in PROTON Holdings, a Malaysian-based car maker, along with a 51% controlling stake in Lotus Cars, a British company that manufactures sports and racing cars. Also in 2017, Geely announced the acquisition of Terrafugia, an American developer of flying cars, and a 30% share of Saxo Bank, a Danish technology and banking company specializing in online trading and investments.[67]

When Chinese enterprises go through reverse upgrade in China, they are outshone by the overseas companies they have acquired, whether in terms of company size or market share. Consider the three case studies previously mentioned as examples. Shuanghui Group had some recognition in China, but was not as reputable as Smithfield Foods, prior to the acquisition – Smithfield Foods' annual sales accounted for almost one third of total sales in the North American market, and its products were exported worldwide. When three entrepreneurs in Changcha were plotting the creation of what would become Sany Heavy, Putzmeister was already one of the world's leading multinational companies in its field. Similarly, Volvo started almost half a century earlier than Geely, and if it had not been for the acquisition of Volvo, Geely would still be almost unknown overseas. Since Chinese enterprises often have to bridge the gap between themselves and their overseas acquisitions, the internationalization of Chinese enterprises is sometimes referred to as a 'gluttonous snake' (idiomatically in Chinese, a greedy snake that is eager to swallow an elephant). So Chinese businesses face daunting challenges.

Furthermore, the three acquired companies discussed in this section – Smithfield, Putzmeister and Volvo – share a common feature: they were severely affected by the financial crisis of 2008, their performance plummeted, and some were caught with high external debt at a time when banks were cutting their financing lines. The acquired enterprises all faced financial problems, large and small, yet their fundamental assets remained intact in the form of technologies and/or brands that could become the basis for renewed growth once market conditions improved and the liquidity bottlenecks had been resolved.

Realizing the full potential of these assets and growing the business beyond their historical markets were the first priorities that Chinese acquirers had to address. Ahead of an acquisition, acquirers had to evaluate the strategic resources and capabilities of their potential target, including a sober assessment of its strengths and weaknesses. Moreover, the acquirer has to develop appropriate processes to be able to learn from the acquired company, define the relative positions of the post-acquisition companies, and establish channels of reporting and responsibility within both organizations. The reverse upgrade of Chinese operations requires investors to learn and absorb the advantages and characteristics of the companies they have acquired, and this learning process requires a wide range of capabilities. The rest of this book will explore the strategies that Chinese firms have developed to address these challenges.

2.3 Strong-start international growth

The strong-start model of international growth applies to enterprises that are completing the reverse upgrade of their Chinese operations. By this stage, they are able to integrate capabilities and other local resources, such as China's low labour and capital costs, to develop their own core competitiveness, and thereby contend with overseas competitors in international markets. However, creating a new enterprise that makes full use of acquired resources, technology and brands by combining them with the acquirer's own resources is a major challenge for entrepreneurs who eventually want to compete head to head with the global leaders in their industry. Integrating resources from different sources to create a unique, superior business is the key challenge for these entrepreneurs on their path to compete with their Western peers in the latter's home markets.

Chinese enterprises using this strong-start model are mostly in mature industries such as home appliances, manufacturing and consumer goods. They have accumulated experience in China, and attained competitive advantage in the domestic market. They choose the strong-start operational model to exploit the capabilities they have already developed: rich international experience and leadership in Chinese markets.

Since the process of internationalization of Chinese enterprises begins with the acquisition of resources and capabilities in overseas markets through M&A, the pace of international expansion has often been dizzying. The reason is that enterprises taken over by Chinese investors usually have more than one type of resource or capability that these investors need. Three of our case studies indicate this:

1. Shuanghui acquired the US pork producer Smithfield Foods, obtaining a source of fresh and reliable pork; but at the same time, Shuanghui also took over Smithfield's sales channels in the North American market, and their brand reputation that had been built in the industry over many years.

2. When Sany Heavy purchased Putzmeister, in addition to world-class production technology and R&D capabilities, Putzmeister's brand effect permitted Sany Heavy's entry into the European market.

3. Geely's acquisition of Volvo provided Geely not only with an international brand, but also with Volvo's production technology, thereby improving Geely's own product quality and enabling it to better compete with overseas companies.

All three enterprises, Shuanghui, Sany Heavy and Geely, sold their products abroad, and within a few years of their acquisitions, at least 50% of their global sales were generated outside China. This proves that acquisitions of overseas enterprises are an effective means of internationalizing the sales of Chinese enterprises. The best-known case of such a strategy is Lenovo Group's acquisition of IBM's PC business.

CASE STUDY:
LENOVO GROUP

Lenovo Group was founded in 1984 by 11 computer researchers at the Chinese Academy of Sciences, and grew into a diversified conglomerate in information technology. In 1989, Yang Yuanqing (who would become Lenovo's Chairman in 2013) graduated from the University of Science and Technology of China (USTC) with a Master's degree in computer science and joined the Lenovo Group. In 1993, he was promoted to general manager of the personal computer department. He quickly perceived that rapid changes were taking place in the computer market, and realized that Lenovo would not survive unless drastic reforms were undertaken.

In response, Yang Yuanqing first decided on a low-cost strategy, and significantly reduced the selling price of Lenovo personal computers (PCs), keeping the margins razor-thin with respect to cost. Then he dissolved the direct sales team, establishing in its place a 'think big' sales network (Lenovo's original logo was literally 'think' in Chinese) consisting of hundreds of local distributors. The network was well organized and highly loyal to the group, offering a competitive advantage over the third-party distributor system commonly used by foreign brands. Thus, Lenovo's inventory turnover rate greatly improved. In 1996, Lenovo launched its first laptop using Intel Pentium chips. The previous generation of personal computers were sold at big discounts, which drove the sales surge. Lenovo replaced IBM as China's PC market leader with a 7% market share. By then, Lenovo had sold as many as

200,000 PCs, a year-on-year increase of 90%, achieving top sales in the desktop market.[68]

By 2000, Lenovo's PC market share in China was close to 30%. Management believed that further expansion of the market share would become increasingly difficult, and concluded that Lenovo needed to work out a new growth strategy. After a series of discussions, the company established new goals: "With the Internet as core, comprehensive customer orientation as principle, meet the demands of family, individuals, small, medium and large industries and enterprises." They built a diversified business along the twin axes of products and service. The principles of three business inputs – customer demand, profit potential, and synergy with existing business – drove Lenovo to diversify into a variety of products, ranging from existing fixed-line PCs and independant appliances (IAs) to wireless, portable notebooks, personal digital assistants (PDAs) and smartphones. This also included content services from integrated new 3C services to internet service provider (ISP) services, FM365 and PALM365, and from general IT services for small and medium enterprises to full IT systems services, including consulting, program integration and operations maintenance.

However, at the outset of their pursuit of this new vision, Lenovo encountered a sudden slowdown. In the second half of 2000, the internet bubble burst and the global IT industry tumbled; and in 2001, the overall turnover of China's PC market dropped by 3.2%. While the ranks of domestic competitors were continually being reduced, the advantages of internationalized foreign enterprises emerged. Lenovo's main competitors, Dell and HP, not only had larger output combined with stronger bargaining positions when sourcing parts, but could also maximize cost-effectiveness and continue to increase their investments in China, throwing money into the Chinese market utilizing profits and abundant resources drawn from other markets.

As industry growth slowed and competition intensified, profits correspondingly declined. In 2002, for example, unit sales of commercial computers in China increased by 21.7%, while sales increased by only 2.4%. Shipments of Lenovo's home computers increased by 9.5%; however, sales revenue fell by 7.8%. In addition, as Lenovo endured fierce competition in the PC market, its market share slightly declined three years in a row from 30% to 27%. Meanwhile, Dell increased its market share more than 15%.[69]

Faced with the slowdown, Yang Yuanqing had to reflect on the reasons for the failure of Lenovo's diversification strategy. Three causes were identified: first, they were not fully up to date on the rapid changes in the IT industry; secondly, Chinese companies were not fully prepared to compete with foreign enterprises, as environmental barriers were removed upon China's formal accession to the World Trade Organization (WTO) in 2001; thirdly, Lenovo was not prepared with a full range of resources, including material, personnel, energetic leadership and other resources. They had set their target too high, resulting in stretching their resources over too many projects.

At this juncture, Yang Yuanqing was reminded of a proposal that had been sent to Lenovo by IBM, wherein IBM intended to put their loss-making PC business up for sale. Yang Yuanqing, who had been concerned about Lenovo's future growth strategy, began to seriously consider how best to approach internationalization.

Founded in 1896, IBM (International Business Machines) started a strategic transformation in 1992 under the leadership of the new CEO, Louis V. Gerstner, shifting its business from hardware manufacturing and distribution to that of a service provider of turnkey solutions to high-end customers. It would henceforth concentrate on developing consulting services (including enterprise IT outsourcing) and middleware solutions (software that is typically bundled with server hardware); and it acquired Rational, a specialized systems software development management company, among others.

Although IBM had introduced the first personal computer in 1981, the rise of HP and Dell had undercut IBM's high-priced PCs. Consequently, its sales and market share had been declining, and it continued to suffer losses. In 1998, IBM's PC business lost $992 million. In 2003, with a PC business pre-tax loss of $349 million, the gross margin was 3.7%; but in the following year, with a 2004 pre-tax loss of $10 million, the gross margin was reduced to 0.1%. This showed that successive years of PC business losses had become a heavy burden on IBM.[70]

IBM was not seeking a simple asset transaction, but strategic cooperation. IBM could not completely give up its PC business, nor was it likely to be beaten by Dell and HP in its full-service business. If a long-term cooperation with Lenovo was to be forged, the prospects would improve for IBM and it could enter into Chinese markets with a first-mover advantage over its competitors. Secondly, IBM also hoped to make use of Lenovo's channel advantage in the Chinese market, and entrench a government contracting position that would help its high-end servers and IT services business to percolate through the Chinese market. Thirdly, once the strategic alliance was forged, IBM could obtain Lenovo's 'access rights' to provide IT services to Lenovo's PC business, especially in the small and medium-sized business markets which were Lenovo's speciality. Finally, IBM could convert Lenovo into a potential client for IBM's POWER microprocessors.

The deal was a tempting one for Yang Yuanqing. First, IBM's ThinkPad was a world-renowned brand. Secondly, the two companies were highly complementary, and the growth potential could not be ignored. Geographically, Lenovo was focused on the Chinese market, while IBM served customers in 138 countries. By product type, 85% of Lenovo's sales revenue was earned through PCs; 60% of IBM's sales revenue was from notebooks. With respect to customers, 80% of Lenovo customers were small businesses and individual consumers, while 57% of IBM customers were group buyers and corporations.[71] Thirdly, if the scale could be increased, the upstream bargaining position could be greatly enhanced, and the ability to control the supply chain would increase. Fourthly, the lack of core technology had always been Lenovo's weakness, and as Yang Yuanqing once said: "Lenovo's current technology is mainly on the application level, [we] have not yet mastered [our] own core technology.

To obtain core technology requires a process and, for Lenovo, this process may need three or five years." So, after several rounds of negotiations, in December 2004 Lenovo announced its acquisition of IBM's PC business.

Following this, Lenovo continued to grow rapidly worldwide by pursuing overseas M&A. For example, in 2011, Lenovo formed a joint venture with Japanese electronics company NEC Holdings to produce PCs, in which Lenovo held a 51% share and NEC held 49%.[72] The purpose of the joint venture was to boost Lenovo's sales by expanding its presence in Japan, a key market for PCs. In 2016, Lenovo acquired a further 44% share from NEC for $195 million. This acquisition made Lenovo the single biggest PC maker in Japan. An even bigger deal soon followed: in 2014, Lenovo acquired IBM's low-end server division for $2.3 billion and the handset division of Google for $3 billion.[73]

Before acquiring IBM, Lenovo sold low-cost products, and found its market position under threat from Dell's famously efficient supply chain, offering PCs at similar prices. However, on acquiring IBM's PC business, Lenovo obtained resources and capabilities, from brands to technology, as well as an international customer base and other assets. These resources and capabilities could more than offset Lenovo's competitive disadvantage, and Lenovo used them to reverse-upgrade its Chinese operations, effectively competing with Dell and other international rivals. Lenovo thus successfully defended its leading market share of 30% in the domestic PC market as of 2016. Subsequently, Lenovo was able to make a strong start into Western markets armed with the ThinkPad brand and technology, combining China's low-cost advantage and its own unique core competencies. As of 2016, Lenovo was a world leader by sales, with a global share in the PC market of 20%.

2.4   The traditional path to international growth

The traditional model of internationalization, as observed in Western enterprises, envisages firms developing capabilities at home which become the foundation for foreign direct investment projects aiming to exploit these capabilities. Moreover, as highlighted by the internationalization process model, overseas expansion involves iterative processes or learning and commitment that enable firms to build operations abroad step by step. For most multinational enterprises, the primary purpose of internationalization is to expand their market and thus to consolidate their competitive advantages. Though scholars such as John Dunning long ago recognized the possibility of 'asset-seeking' foreign direct investment, this type of FDI has largely been an exception.[74] For example, Japanese and Korean firms at early stages of their international venturing in the 1980s set up facilities in Silicon Valley with the primary aim of tapping into knowledge pools and innovation networks in the technology community in that area.

The difference, however, is that for Chinese investors asset-seeking foreign investments have taken centre stage. Very few Chinese companies have been able to develop domestic resources and capabilities that enable them to compete internationally; exceptions include Huawei in communications networks and some consumer durables manufacturers that focused initially on developing countries, such as Haier. Similarly, Shanghai-based Shanggong Group has exported its Butterfly-branded sewing machines to Africa where they attained considerable brand recognition, long ahead of its more ambitious foray into industrial sewing machines that included several acquisitions in Germany.

Indeed, for many Chinese enterprises, the catch-up process with global leaders started with domestic upgrading, and hence the process of building international management capabilities began by partnering with foreign investors and learning from these partners. This pattern of inward-outward linkages in terms of preparing to invest internationally, is illustrated by the case of Chervon, discussed in Chapter 1. Table 3 lays out the stages of Chervon's internationalization process, including three stages that took place within the firm's Chinese operations but with international customers in mind.

	BUSINESS MODEL	CAPABILITIES DEVELOPED
LOCAL CULTIVATION	OEM	Production capabilities
	ODM	Product design capabilities
	OBM (domestic)	Local brand-management capabilities
INTERNATION-ALIZATION	International brand	International brand-management capabilities (Europe)
	Multiple international brands	International brand-management capabilities (US)
	International expansion	Global operations capabilities

TABLE 3   STAGES OF CHERVON'S CAPABILITY BUILDING

Chervon started as a trading company with a good sense of quality, specializing in power tools. When its founder, Pan Longquan, found out that almost all local products were counterfeit, he established Chervon's own manufacturing plant in 1997, and transformed the company into an OEM manufacturer for leading global brands, later adding industrial design capabilities, including a design centre in North America, to become an ODM manufacturer. On the basis of the robust OEM and ODM business, Chervon developed competencies in all aspects of manufacturing, R&D and design. In 2003, Pan Longquan began to guide the strategic upgrade of the company's OBM brand, Devon. The brand quickly prospered in China, and as of 2013, ranked sixth in China's power-tool market.

However, in European and North American markets, Chervon at that time was still just an OEM manufacturer for European and US brands. In 2010, Chervon thus established an M&A team that was to draft a merger and acquisition plan with the help of a third-party consulting firm. Thanks to its extensive preparations, in 2013 Chervon successfully acquired German power-tool manufacturer FLEX. The FLEX brand opened the way into the European and American markets. In February 2017, Chervon added the SKIL brand to its portfolio, a leading power-tool brand in North America that had been owned by Bosch of Germany for many years.

Thus, before its acquisition of FLEX, Chervon had already achieved organic growth through its own value-chain upgrades (from OEM and ODM to OBM). Initially, Chervon had been cultivating business locally as a 'local factory'. While collaborating with OEM and ODM customers, Chervon accelerated its learning and set up overseas marketing and industrial design centres. These enterprises, however, were part of the process of 'learning ability and technology', rather than resources and capabilities acquired in overseas markets. FLEX was Chervon's first attempt at overseas acquisition, and of a well-known European brand at that. However, even before the acquisition of FLEX, Chervon had developed its own Devon brand, which had established a reputation and taken a leading position in China's domestic power-tool industry. Chervon did not pursue the overseas market until its own brand Devon was successful in China. Thus, Chervon did not need much support from FLEX for its Chinese market operations; the key reason for Pan Longquan to buy FLEX was to make an entry into European and American markets. Chervon's ultimate goal was not to upgrade the Chinese market, but to expand into overseas markets. Thus the acquisition of FLEX was soon followed by that of SKIL, which provided Chervon with a solid foothold in the US market (Figure 2).

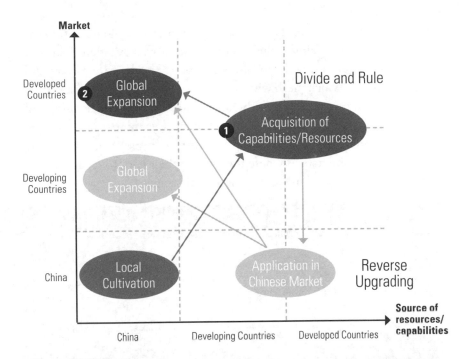

FIGURE 2   CHERVON'S INTERNATIONALIZATION PATHWAY

The Chervon case highlights the fact that Chinese enterprises that follow the traditional internationalization strategy need to have a solid foundation for operations and management, and adequate time to design and deploy their own international development. Upgrading the value chain and gradually improving the management of enterprises is just one way to assimilate; however, for most Chinese enterprises that started in the manufacturing industry, this is a 'safe and stable' choice.

2.5 Conclusion

Our case studies illustrate the motivations, approaches and operations of Chinese enterprises going global. In this chapter we have identified four operational models – divide and rule, reverse upgrade, strong start and traditional path – which mesh with the three-stage pattern of globalization for Chinese enterprises. Each of the four models has unique features and poses practical challenges for Chinese enterprises, as summarized in Table 4. Chinese enterprises can develop a footprint in global markets only when they fully understand where they are on their path to globalization, and can therefore develop a coherent global strategy.

OPERATION MODEL	DIVIDE AND RULE	REVERSE UPGRADE
STRATEGY	• Pursue investment targets that are viable in the short run and offer synergies in the long run • Core business in China will continue with little change	• Identify critical gaps in the capability portfolio of the company • Seek foreign partners that provide access to resources that help fill these gaps
CASE STUDIES IN TEXT	• Sinopec, Fosun, CIC, Wanda	• Natural resources: PetroChina, Sinopec, Shuanghui, COFCO • Technologies: BGI, Geely, H&H • Brands: Lenovo, Geely, Bright Foods, Sany
INDUSTRY	• Energy & minerals, finance, manufacturing and integrated industries	• Wide variety of industries
SCALE AND FINANCE	• Mostly large companies with sufficient funds • Good and stable main business operations	• Large and small firms with access to financial resources • Leaders in their industry in China, or with ambition to become leaders
GLOBALIZATION EXPERIENCE	• Relative lack of international experience, thus unable to integrate fast, or • Few potential synergies, thus no need to integrate fast	• Experience varies, and can become a major constraint to implementing the integration and application of the acquired resources
OPERATIONAL CHALLENGES	• Sound valuation of acquisition target and of expected return on investment (ROI) • Ensuring effective governance of the relatively autonomous subsidiary	• Assessment of the critical resources, and the global markets for them. • Reverse transfer of resources, but inhibited in some cases by regulatory barriers or gaps in human capital in the parent organization

TABLE 4   SUMMARY OF THE FOUR OPERATIONAL MODELS

STRONG START	TRADITIONAL PATH
• Acquire capabilities abroad in a high-profile move, followed by integration with existing competencies in China	• Competitive advantages in China are core for international market entry • A conventional strategy, with stepwise strategic moves and corrections
• Lenovo	• Haier, Huawei, CSSEC, Sany
• Household appliances, manufacturing and consumer goods	• Household appliances, IT and construction engineering, etc.
• Mostly large companies with sufficient funds	• Mainly large companies with sufficient funds • Companies with extensive experience in China, and strong domestic competitive advantages
• Rich international management experience • Leading players in the industry in the home country	• Possess rich experience in globalization • These companies are leading players in the industry in the home country
• Combination of overseas resources, capabilities and brands with advantages in China, so as to create a company competitive with Western counterparts	• Timely improvements in operations and strategy • Selection of appropriate markets for expansion strategy

PART II
FINANCE

CHAPTER 3

DUE DILIGENCE

This chapter is concerned with pre-acquisition due diligence in cross-border mergers and acquisitions. It does not explain how to conduct due diligence as carried out by investment banking and consulting firms. Instead, we observe the process from the perspective of a business operator, and we hope that through better design, we can take advantage of due diligence to help businesses make good decisions in cross-border M&As.

3.1   What is due diligence?

Due diligence is a comprehensive audit carried out by specialist agencies in collaboration with companies to investigate a company's historical data and documents; its management background; and its market, management, technological and financial risks. It is usually conducted before an initial public offering (IPO), merger or acquisition. Due diligence often occurs in a friendly takeover scenario, involving exclusive business negotiation rights. This gives the acquiring firm ample time to obtain management support in order to get more information, and hence be able to assess the business more comprehensively. Due diligence is conducted mainly to resolve the information asymmetry caused by the fact that target companies have reams of information that acquiring companies do not know about, and this often includes information which is for decision-making in acquisitions.

3.2   Purposes of due diligence

Due diligence can help companies assess the viability of proposed transactions. Firstly, due diligence gives a preliminarily assessment of the legitimacy of a transaction. It also investigates legal requirements in cross-border M&As, such as the scope of intellectual property rights, environmental protection obligations, potential legal costs of dismissals and redundancies, liability of repayment issues, validity of current contracts, etc.

Secondly, due diligence assesses the feasibility of the strategy and helps the acquirer to understand the current status of the target company, to determine whether the target enterprise conforms to the overall post-acquisition strategic requirements, whether the enterprise has other businesses that need to be shed, and also whether the transaction will add value to the company's core strength.

Thirdly, due diligence provides a preliminary understanding of the financial status of the target company: if it is in a financial crisis or in a poor financial situation, it is more likely to seek a merger or acquisition. If the target company's shareholder holdings are dispersed, and its major shareholders are institutional investors, then the acquisition will be easier.

The audit will analyse the quality of earnings and assets to arrive at a preliminary evaluation of the target company; any problems and issues found during the due diligence process will further increase the bargaining power of the acquiring company in negotiating the price and contract terms.

The investigation will seek an understanding of the organization and business model of the target company. This will help lay a foundation for the post-acquisition operations and integration of the group. The acquiring firm can prepare for the integration and operational plan while conducting due diligence.

The adequacy of due diligence is directly related to the integrity and authenticity of the information in the acquisition-related disclosure and declaration documents as required by relevant national laws and regulations. Accurate disclosure is mandatory not only in the country of the target company, but also in the country of the acquiring firm. Conducting due diligence helps to fulfil the relevant obligations.

3.3 Ways to conduct due diligence

Due diligence begins with public information: annual reports, disclosure of listed companies, analysts' reports, etc. Due diligence on these items is usually conducted in the early stages of large transactions, and is not applicable if the company involved is non-listed, or is a subsidiary of a listed company. This type of due diligence investigation, conducted in the initial stages, can be standardized and programmed to gain maximum information. Since the more detailed methods of investigation may be difficult to implement in practice, surveying publicly available information is the most basic method for conducting due diligence.

The senior management of the target firm may then be approached for more information. This tactic is often used in friendly takeovers, and acquiring firms can question target firms about their management and other issues arising from the investigations based on publicly available information.

On-site inspection is commonly practised in small and medium-sized transactions. It is not very common in larger transactions, especially when there is a question of confidentiality.

An intermediary agent may be commissioned by the seller to conduct due diligence investigations, especially in large transactions and where there are multiple potential buyers. Agents are relatively independent, but they only have limited liability towards the buyer. The buyer usually still needs to employ a due diligence team to review and analyse the seller's due diligence report, and to conduct a series of due diligence procedures, such as inquiring about how the seller is managing potential problems.

Since due diligence is a highly specialized area of work, it is usual to commission professional organizations, especially in the case of a small company that does not have a complete team of its own that can conduct due diligence independently. The company's decision makers can play several roles in due diligence investigations:

1. It is the board members who constitute the decision-making body in mergers and acquisitions, and not the investment banks or accounting and consulting firms that have been employed. These third-party units help the board to make decisions based on the data collected in their investigations. The fees paid to them are sunk costs, and when there is information which suggests that a deal should be suspended, then such mergers and acquisitions ideally should not continue.

2. The company's decision-makers should specify the direction and content of due diligence. Due diligence services by third-party agencies usually have standardized procedures. To suit the company's strategic purpose, its decision-makers must understand the purpose of the acquisition, and then put forward specific requirements based on this purpose, so that third-party organizations can collect information accordingly.

3. The company's decision-makers cannot put all their cards on the table with third-party agencies. The negotiation process in mergers and acquisitions is very tough and, because of the asymmetry of information, not all preset directions can be verified. Negotiations can be terminated at any time if unfavourable information is found. Also, if agencies know the preset position of the company's decision, they may develop a tendency to relax their efforts during due diligence and subsequent negotiations.

4. Some of the problems found during due diligence investigations, especially management-related issues, may not be serious enough to affect the final decision. The acquiring firm needs to address these issues after the acquisition is complete, in order to realize the value of improved management after the acquisition.

5. Finally, the company's decision-makers should actively participate in the due diligence investigations. The ideas and opinions of management teams, shareholders and stakeholders of the target firm, and key employees are not only helpful for understanding the company better but can also contribute to the integration process after acquisition. This is an indispensable activity that third-party organizations cannot replace.

In conclusion, due diligence is a process that takes a lot of effort. The knowledge and skills of professional agencies are very important in this process. However, the company's decision-makers must not hand over their power to external agencies just because a huge consulting fee has been paid.

3.4   Essentials of due diligence

Due diligence in the target enterprise generally includes surveys of its organizational structure, business management and internal reporting systems, accounting policies, management and auditor's attitudes, and other key accounting issues.

3.4.1   Organizational structure

The main goal is to investigate each facet of the target company, especially when it comes to important decisions such as the equity structure required to permit acquisition and asset sale. This also mitigates problems in the acquisition process. Secondly, it is important to pay attention to the provisions of the company, whether it has special voting rights and restrictions. Thirdly, it is necessary to review the record of shareholders and board meetings. In addition, in the case of an asset acquisition, it is necessary to obtain documents and resolutions of sale from the shareholders.

If the organizational structure of the target company is overly complex, it is necessary to delve deeper into the core of the business. Some companies will set up a positive and beneficial organizational structure on their own, such as setting up an entity in some low-tax country such as Ireland, which can serve as a legal tax shelter for the company. Such organizational structures revealed during due diligence are considered reasonable. However, some companies set up complex organizational structures for which a clear and rational explanation may not be forthcoming. These may be used to disguise hidden liabilities, or to serve as grey areas to protect the business of subsidiaries or associated companies. These are the areas that require special attention during due diligence.

It is precisely because of the limitations in the laws and regulations of certain countries where offshore companies are established, that some companies are able to disguise their core business. To understand the complex nature of these legal systems, companies can often only rely on the professional knowledge of local branches of international law firms, especially in the area of international law, to provide necessary help. It is thus important to seek explanations through communication with the management of the target company during due diligence.

3.4.2 Business management and internal reporting systems

Due diligence should focus on investigating business units of the target company. A diversified group tends to have a wide range of different investments. If the buyer is only interested in the target company's core business, then the target company may place conditions on the sale, to ensure that the acquisition is not just limited to one core business unit but extends to its other businesses as well, or even to the entire company. Firstly, these peripheral business units may not be in the interests of the buyer's strategic planning, and it may be very expensive to opt out of them; if they are not closed, the efficiency of the integration may be jeopardized. Secondly, these scattered businesses increase potential risks. A company with a large number of scattered businesses is usually not a listed company. The buyer has to initiate due diligence procedures to verify the reliability of these companies' financial data as well as the capability of the target company to control these scattered businesses, and to assess whether these business units actually have the production capability attributed to them on paper. Another point to consider is whether the target company has the ability to continue its operations while maintaining adequate control over these business units, especially after the acquisition.

Due diligence should also assess the management and internal control systems of target companies. A chaotic management system and a loose internal control system will greatly limit the reliability of the target company's statements, and make it difficult to manage the company in the future. It would be too late to construct an adequate management and internal control system after the acquisition is completed. Action needs to be taken to conduct an initial assessment on the system, to gauge whether it would reduce the risk of an acquisition and, to prepare the target company for its future management.

3.4.3 Accounting policies

3.4.3.1 Comparison with industry standards

If the target company's accounting policy and code of conduct are found to be inconsistent with industry standards, this would be a controversial issue with respect to finance. Since companies differ in business environment and scale, target companies may well have accounting policies and codes of conduct that are different from the industry standard, and this is not necessarily an issue. However, extra attention should be paid in such cases, to ensure that the company discloses accounting information which accurately reflects its financial status, operating results and cash flows. For example, if the company adopts a longer or shorter depreciation period than the industry average, the service life of its fixed assets will also be different; if it adopts a different revenue recognition method when the industry standard is the percentage-of-completion method, then the company is more radical and will anticipate more revenues by recognizing certain forms of income when signing the contract. If these problems arise, the management must be asked to explain the rationale behind its accounting policy.

3.4.3.2   Substance over form

There is a very important principle in accounting called 'substance over form'. There are certain circumstances, frameworks and financial arrangements in accounting practice that serve certain accounting purposes, and are not an issue of actual economic substance. For instance, the way some companies handle their fixed-asset accounting clearly serves to disguise their financing lease as an operating lease, so as to treat it off-balance-sheet. If this is not investigated during due diligence, post-acquisition risks are bound to emerge.

CASE STUDY:
NANJING TANKER CORPORATION

On 5 June 2014, Nanjing Tanker Corporation (NJTC) was delisted from the Shanghai Stock Exchange, as the accounting process in its final announcement had revealed a significant loss, resulting in a huge controversy.[75] NJTC operated 20 tankers, which were all off-balance-sheet leases, but in fact all 20 ships were registered in Hong Kong, and the owners of the tankers were registered under a special-purpose vehicle (SPV) with traces of them being controlled by NJTC from the Virgin Islands and Panama. These 20 tankers were mortgaged to eight banks and four syndicated agencies simultaneously, and a loan was secured by NJTC's parent company, Sinotrans & CSC. More importantly, the duration of the loan contract and the lease period of the 20 oil tankers were essentially the same. Due to the presence of an SPV and other related arrangements mentioned above, NJTC avoided disclosing the actual status of this lease to the China Securities Regulatory Commission (CSRC) and to its own shareholders. The facts in this case were exposed only after NJTC had incurred huge losses.

In fact, these tankers were specially provided for NJTC, but through a series of complex and hostile arrangements, these assets (the 20 tankers) and liabilities (syndicated mortgages) were arranged into operating leases. NJTC only needed to pay rent for these leases, and hence they were not revealed fairly on the balance sheet, and were treated as off-balance-sheet items.

3.4.4 Attitude of management and auditors

If a company frequently changes its auditors, it is important to find out why. Quite often, if the auditor detects signs of potential trouble but cannot persuade the management to rectify them, they then choose to resign to maintain their professional reputation for prudence; in such cases, the acquisition would involve enormous risks. In addition, if a company's CEO tries to hard-sell the company during due diligence, without giving sufficiently convincing explanations for the sale, one must be vigilant. If the buyer finds it hard to understand the reasons for the sale, and the seller is reluctant to give detailed explanations, then it is best to give up the acquisition. Although this may sometimes lead to a missed opportunity, it is always worthwhile looking into any past issues. We may not be able to gauge hidden risks in acquiring the company. The acquiring firm would also be at a loss what to do with the management after taking over the new company.

There may also be inconsistencies among the internal management teams, and this can be grounds for anxiety if the management and auditors, or management and shareholders, have different standpoints. This may suggest some issues with the management, though sometimes inconsistent standpoints may work better for the acquiring firm. In developed countries, for example, the ownership and management of companies are sometimes separated, so that the management team often does not have much equity and sometimes has none at all, and the team members serve only as professional managers. When a company is acquired, its management has to consider key points for its future parent company. For example, it might increase the ratio of accrued expenses to lower its profits at present, and this may allow the parent company to realize some profits in the future (there are many other similar accounting practices, which are covered in detail in later chapters). Further, after the acquisition, some staff may consider leaving the company, or the parent company might consider laying off staff. There may also be some management teams that the parent company plans to retain. When different management teams gather for a meeting, one may see a clear-cut difference between these two groups of people: those that intend to stay will have an incentive to negotiate better conditions with their prospective new employer.

CASE STUDY: EVERGREEN HOLDING GROUP'S ACQUISITION OF MAGINDUSTRIES

In 2009, Evergreen Holding Group acquired MagIndustries, a mining company listed on the Toronto Stock Exchange (TSE), with exploration rights in the Congo. If their explorations were not fruitful, the value of the company would drop. Fortunately, they found potash and, on obtaining the mining rights, the company planned to mine 600,000 tonnes annually; this required an investment of more than C$1 billion. MagIndustries originally wanted to raise funds from the stock market by issuing more equity, in order to start mining. However, it was the time of the financial crisis and the company was not performing well in the stock market; its stock price was depressed and it was not in a favourable situation to raise more money. One possible solution was to attract larger shareholders who could act as strategic investors. It was prepared for an acquisition, and it had contacted two Chinese SOEs, Sinohydro Group and China National Complete Plant Import and Export Corporation. However, due to several issues, the collaboration failed. Later, TSC Capital Ltd also expressed its intention to buy MagIndustries, and even conducted due diligence investigations, but the deal did not go through.

In this case, it is very clear that MagIndustries, management wanted to sell the company, and the reason was abundantly clear: they had mining rights but lacked the funds for development. The capital market was performing poorly, shareholder holdings were widely dispersed, and the company's management held a lot of shares and options. MagIndustries, especially its management team, had a strong desire to sell the company. In the event, Evergreen judged the risk to be acceptable: it successfully acquired MagIndustries and became its largest shareholder.

3.4.5   Key accounting items
3.4.5.1   **Valuation of goodwill**

Valuation and due diligence with respect to fixed assets are not simple matters; however, one can utilize professional means and third-party organizations to do the research. It is very difficult to conduct a standard valuation, as well as due diligence, on non-standard assets, especially intangible assets. If the company being acquired has a history of several mergers and acquisitions, it is likely that the firm enjoys sufficient goodwill, which is very important in due diligence investigations. Goodwill may be especially important in the hospitality sector.

CASE STUDY:
HUNTSWORTH

In February 2011, the board of directors of 'Company A' (from China) travelled to the UK to conduct due diligence for the acquisition of Huntsworth, a British firm specializing in public relations (PR). Company A was an upcoming star in the Chinese PR industry. Huntsworth, an international PR company, was founded in 1998 by the British PR master Peter Chadlington after the sale of Shandwick; it has a large number of international clients and has other well-known brands such as Citigate and Grayling under it. For Company A, acquiring Huntsworth would expedite its globalization process and help it become an international company. Prior to visiting the UK, Company A asked an investment bank to conduct a background check for the acquisition, and the board had high hopes for the project.

Huntsworth was registered in the UK and specialized in public relations management and marketing communications. Peter Chadlington acquired part of the shares of Huntsworth in 1998, and served as the company's CEO from 2000. His former subordinate, Michael Murphy, also came to Huntsworth to help manage the business. When Chadlington took office, Huntsworth was performing poorly and incurring huge losses; no dividend had been paid for nine consecutive years. In the first three years, Huntsworth sold shares at low prices several times to sustain itself. Peter Chadlington painstakingly managed it till 2003, and Huntsworth had a successful turnaround, pulling out from the position it had been in for the past 12 years. It issued a dividend of 0.1 pence per share, which symbolically meant a lot more than the actual face value.

The PR industry in Europe and America has a long history; current players include large international companies such as WPP, Omnicom, Publicis, IPG and so on (Table 5). These enterprises share one common factor: the history of their development is essentially a history of mergers and acquisitions, and ultimately their intangible assets (mainly in the form of goodwill) account for a very large proportion of their total assets.

FINANCIAL INDICATORS	HUNTS-WORTH	WPP	OMNICOM	PUBLICIS	IPG
Intangible assets/ total assets	82.60%	45.23%	41.33%	34.36%	25.77%
Intangible Assets/ net assets	141.39%	165.63%	225.87%	152.75%	131.23%
Current assets/ total assets	15.61%	46.24%	52.10%	60.34%	64.67%
Current liabilities/ total assets	21.60%	49.60%	56.30%	39.70%	59.20%
Current ratio	72.20%	93.23%	92.48%	152.00%	109.00%
Financial liabilities/ total liabilities	42.41%	21.78%	16.06%	17.93%	17.01%

TABLE 5   2010 FINANCIAL DATA OF 5 INTERNATIONAL PR COMPANIES

Source: Huntsworth 2010 Annual Report and Accounts, WPP 2010 Annual Report and Accounts, Omnicom Group Inc. 2010 Annual Report, Publicis 2010 Annual Report, Interpublic Group of Companies 2010 Annual Report.

It is necessary to analyse the acquisition process of each business unit (BU) and the goodwill impairment test of the acquired BU. First, it is important to investigate the operations of the acquired BU, to understand how the goodwill is formulated. Each component of the goodwill generated during the process of its past acquisitions needs to be verified, to understand how it has been generated in mergers and acquisitions.

In our case study, the acquiring firm needed to check the working papers of past acquisitions of Huntsworth, to see how it dealt with acquisitions and valuations, and the expected valuation of each BU at that point in time, as well as the value added through improvements in management. The acquiring firm could also investigate Huntsworth's working papers and cross-check to see whether the reality was consistent with the initial evaluations and expectations, in order to assess its acquisition value. Since Huntsworth had almost no other assets apart from goodwill, its core competitiveness consisted of its industry insights and bargaining power. The acquiring firm could investigate whether each BU functioned properly, which would affect the goodwill impairment test. The acquiring firm could thus understand whether Huntsworth was actually doing an impairment of the asset.

One can assess the prudence in the acquisition of Huntsworth by looking into its goodwill valuation and goodwill impairment, because these also constitute its core competitiveness. The PR industry is driven by acquisition, either defensive or offensive. Takeovers are the norm in the PR industry; therefore, in addition to doing the PR business well, a firm's abilities must reflect the companies wanting to acquire it. In the first two rows of Table 5, all the ratios of intangible assets to net assets exceed 100%. Therefore, these companies would theoretically lose most of their assets if the goodwill is gone. These are world-class PR companies and cannot be liquidated; only sustainable operations can guarantee their value.

Goodwill is the largest asset of any PR company. It must be handled properly, or else the acquisition would encounter major risks. For example, in 2001, Hewlett-Packard (HP) spent more than US$11.1 billion to acquire the British software company Autonomy, but in less than a year the British firm was reported to have engaged in fraudulent accounting activities, causing an impairment of HP's goodwill by more than US$8.8 billion. Its stock price also went down drastically, showing that goodwill management is a significant risk factor.

To sum up, in acquiring a company of this nature, the first step is to examine the quality of intangible assets in its goodwill valuation. Then one must look into the company's management, integration and coordination abilities, and assess how conservative its impairment test methodology is.

3.4.5.2 Quality of earnings

In addition to intangible assets, the quality of earnings and financial statements are also key areas to consider during due diligence activities. Many value analysis models consider net profit and other profit items such as gross margin and earnings before interest and tax (EBIT). When it comes to mergers and acquisitions, some firms set the purchase price as multiples of the net profit, and some take into account future cash-flow discounting models. Therefore, the evaluation of earnings quality is of vital importance.

The main purpose of profit smoothing is to reduce profit fluctuations. Management can influence the profit distribution in each period by changing the timing when income or costs are recorded, and this helps to generate stable and increasing cash flows. For instance, reserves may be built up in years of higher net profits and then released later when profits are lower. Manipulation of accounting estimates is a common practice. For example, adjusting the number of years over which assets are depreciated can have a huge impact on the firm's current profits. Reasonable explanations must be offered for changes in accounting estimates. Careful attention should be paid to frequent or significant changes in profits. When there is a shift in the management, companies tend to use conservative accounting policies: withdrawing a certain percentage of future liabilities or underestimating the income from certain assets in order to generate higher profits in the future. This behaviour is commonly referred to as 'taking a big bath'. These methods require extra attention during due diligence, as they directly affect the valuation and the management's operation of the financial reporting system after the acquisition.

In addition, due diligence practices may involve a series of situations specific to the target company that require ad-hoc analysis based on their specific circumstances. There were several abnormal issues in the case of Evergreen's acquisition of MagIndustries.

CASE STUDY: EVERGREEN HOLDING GROUP'S ACQUISITION OF MAGINDUSTRIES

Prior to the acquisition of MagIndustries by Evergreen Holding Group, another company, TSC Capital Ltd, had expressed its intention to acquire the company. TSC is a private equity fund that invests primarily in mining and natural resources projects. It has investments in mining industries in Africa, Asia and Europe. On 21 December 2010, MagIndustries announced that TSC had signed a letter of intent to buy it and that TSC would conduct due diligence on MagIndustries. In return, MagIndustries would offer 113,481,000 options to TSC at a price of US$0.32 per option. TSC could then exercise its right at any time within a year. However, MagIndustries was negligent when signing the acquisition agreement, and the parties failed to agree that once TSC had finished its due diligence investigation, MagIndustries would cancel the option granted to TSC. Therefore, on 11 February 2011, when TSC announced that it had concluded its due diligence on MagIndustries and was unable to acquire the company, it still retained a part of the options granted to it earlier.

Poor due diligence created a major obstacle for Evergreen, the new major shareholder in MagIndustries. Evergreen's original plan involved getting a potash mine into production as soon as possible, for which it was ready to increase investment in MagIndustries. This would inevitably require more financing.

Evergreen was faced with a dilemma at this time: if it increased investment in Mag Industries through private placement, this would send a strong signal to the market. Also, MagIndustries was a listed company with an obligation to announce any such action. With more announcements following the project's development, the company's shares would be highly sought in the market, and the share price would soon rise. At present, TSC could buy MagIndustries shares for $0.32 each and make a huge profit. However, if the stock price was lowered through artificial means, MagIndustries would be sanctioned by the Canadian Securities Regulatory Commission. If TSC waited for a year without making the investment, it would not be able to sustain itself due to high daily operating costs. The TSC options were a huge dilemma for Liang Xiao Lei, Evergreen's CEO, and the whole affair left him with sleepless nights for weeks.

Since the options of MagIndustries were widely dispersed before Evergreen's acquisition, the largest shareholder's holding was less than 6%. It was manipulated by its management executives and most of its executives had corporate options. However, the management team was probably not the same during the mining period as it was during the operation period, and there seems to have been little need to provide so many options to the executives. On the other hand, the management fees of MagIndustries had remained high for several years, and finding a way to reduce its operating costs was another difficult issue that needed to be tackled. In addition, the TSC options issue exposed a serious problem concerning the competence and diligence of MagIndustries' executives.

Before the acquisition, MagIndustries was not in good financial health; its mining project was under way, but it had no cash in hand. The plan was for Evergreen to inject funds to help the company survive. There were two ways to offer fresh money to the company: to let MagIndustries offer private placements to Evergreen to increase its equity, or to lend money to the listed company. In the first approach, as a major shareholder, Evergreen believed in the future development of MagIndustries; with the very low share price, if Evergreen could get private placements, it would be able to get more equity at a low price. However, because of the TSC options, the idea was not feasible. If Evergreen's money was injected as equity, it would send a strong signal to the market that Evergreen, a major shareholder of MagIndustries, had great confidence in that company, and later it would be obliged to publicly release certain information which might cause the stock price to rise. If TSC then exercised its options, it would make a killing from the sell-off.

However, it was impossible for Evergreen not to inject funds, as MagIndustries would be unable to continue its potash fertilizer project. This left Evergreen with no choice but to go with the second option, that is to lend money to MagIndustries. But this was not a regular loan, as Evergreen determined an exercise price and conditions whereby this loan (C\$50 million) could be converted into equity. Evergreen could set an exercise date after TSC's option exercise date so as to prevent TSC from getting a free ride on the whole deal, and this would give Evergreen more room to manoeuvre. If the stock price shot up, TSC was likely to exercise its right, but if it did so – with Evergreen's exercise date being after TSC's – Evergreen would have the right to ask MagIndustries to repay the loan. At this point MagIndustries would have received only a subscription fee from TSC, and Evergreen would walk away with the money, amounting to C\$36,313,920 (113,481,000 × 0.32). Once Evergreen took the money, MagIndustries would be left with no money again, and its stock price would fall. If it were to issue more shares, then TSC's original shares would be diluted; concerned about this lending structure arrangement, TSC would not exercise its right. Later, as planned by Evergreen, TSC did not exercise its options (which expired automatically on 21 December 2011), and by 12 March 2013, Evergreen had converted the loan into equity shares.

Once Evergreen had become the new large shareholder, the next urgent issue was the stock ownership of executives. Evergreen took a hard line on this particular issue: it put in a requirement which acted as a hurdle for MagIndustries' executives, asking them to give up their equity shares, with the aim of making all these options invalid. All executive options were cancelled in 2012. The board of directors was replaced, and the old management team was gradually phased out, with only two or three remaining in the end. Old incentive plans were first abolished, and many left MagIndustries once Evergreen had taken over. Evergreen also replaced some people internally. As the mining site was in Africa, the income and operating expenses would be mainly generated in Africa, and therefore it wanted to control the cost of its headquarters in Canada.

3.5 Conclusion

This chapter has focused on the purpose of due diligence in target companies, and has outlined the key principles of due diligence investigations and related practices. Due diligence is highly professional work, and it requires collaboration between lawyers, auditors and other professional teams. It also needs a third-party agency with the ability to provide international services. There is not space in this book to go into technical details; suffice it to say that the acquiring firm should not entrust its due diligence responsibility solely to a third party. It is better for the decision-makers of the acquiring firm to be closely involved in the due diligence process. This not only helps control the risks involved in the acquisition, but also initiates the execution of the acquisition.

CHAPTER 4

MODELS AND VALUATION

There are several viable models that Chinese enterprises can follow in their globalization process to help them gain access to quality global resources or skills. These include licensing, greenfield projects, wholly-owned subsidiaries, long-term contracting, joint ventures, strategic alliances, mergers and acquisitions. M&As may vary from a 100% buyout to a stake of 50% or even less than 20%. For different types of acquisition, the level of control, accounting processes, requirements for financial strength and management capabilities also differ.

It is better for the buyer to acquire scarce strategic resources or core capabilities through equity-based partnerships than through strategic alliances or long-term contracts. Compared to greenfield projects, equity interests contribute towards rapid growth. In this book, we assume that companies wish to acquire scarce and high-quality resources and capabilities quickly to help them in their domestic market expansions. Joint ventures and M&As are by far the quickest methods, so this book focuses on them.

4.1   Joint ventures

Joint ventures were one of the main vehicles of early foreign investment in China. In the earlier stages of foreign direct investment (FDI), China lacked capital, technology and management experience. In fact, this sort of collaboration depended on the market exchange of capital, technology and management experience. Foreign companies had a major say in decision-making and operations in any joint venture, which made it difficult for the Chinese to acquire technical skills. There have been several joint-venture companies operating long-term in China, but the core technology was still in foreign hands. Today, Chinese companies have relatively more capital, but there are still major challenges as to whether they can acquire core technology and bring their management to international standards.

CASE STUDY:
JOINT VENTURE BETWEEN TCL AND THOMSON

In Chinese enterprises' globalization process, TCL (formerly Telephone Communication Ltd) is considered a front-runner in testing international waters.[76] TCL established its leading role in China, Southeast Asia, the Middle East and Eastern Europe as well as other emerging markets. However, due to anti-dumping tariffs, lack of technical patent rights and sales network, it was hard for TCL to tap into developed markets such as the United States and Europe. In an attempt to enhance its R&D capability, and hence its patent portfolio, TCL was always looking for opportunities to enter the overseas market through M&As.

In 2004, Thomson, a French company well known for its television business, set up a joint venture with TCL called TTE, with TCL holding 67% of the shares and Thomson holding 33%.

Thomson is one of the top four consumer electronics companies, with its brands Thomson and RCA, possessing more than 34,000 patents in the television industry. It also has R&D centres in the US, France, Singapore and China. However, its television business was at that time making the greatest losses of all of its business units, and Thomson understandably was in a hurry to sell it off.

For this joint venture, both TCL and Thomson brought in all of their TV business units and assets, including Thomson's R&D centres in Europe and America. However, Thomson did not bring in its technology and patent assets, which TCL wanted most, so TCL would still have to pay for their use. The use of trademarks was free only for the first three years, and sales networks in North American and European markets were still exclusively assigned through Thomson. Thomson mainly brought its tangible assets into this deal, and this became the biggest burden for TTE, ultimately leading to factory shutouts and layoffs due to excess capacity. The legal proceedings against redundancies not only caused huge losses for TCL, but also affected its senior management and operation teams, who had to be changed frequently.

Most of Thomson's patented technology was in the field of cathode ray tube (CRT) and rear projection display systems; however, CRT technology was facing intense competition and was being phased out, while the rear projection technology was gradually being superseded by liquid-crystal displays (LCDs). In 2004, the Japan-based Sharp Corportion started its LCD production line with billions in investments, leaving TTE to plod along at an agonizingly slow pace. TTE's business operations deteriorated and it experienced enormous losses in European and US markets. In desperation, Thomson converted its TTE equity into TCL equity, and withdrew its shares after the lock-in period.

TTE then undertook a drastic overhaul of its structure in Europe, which took an immense toll on the company, including factory closures and employee redundancies. Starting from a 'borderless concentration' business model, it finally became profitable in terms of overseas earnings in 2009. It stopped selling RCA products in North America in 2010, with the aim of introducing TCL to the US market.

Given this scenario, it was difficult to predict the display screen technology trends in the market. Apart from errors of technical judgement and management issues, TCL chose the joint venture model for its M&As, and its valuation model considered only tangible assets, such as factories, R&D centres and working capital. As for the more important intangible assets including brands, patents, R&D operations and marketing, TCL did not own these, nor did it have control over its joint ventures. TCL did not have much international management experience or much of a talent pool to manage its joint venture, and this made it difficult to work with Thomson while resolving certain issues. This marriage between the two brands ended soon, after an 18-month honeymoon period.

TCL was clear that it wanted to seek a global strategy, but in practice it went in the wrong direction. The intention of the joint venture was ideally a marriage between Chinese capital and Western technology, brands, patents, etc. However, TCL failed to integrate the resources it tried to acquire into the framework of its joint venture. We have seen that the purpose of Chinese companies going global is to acquire resources or abilities, and the best form of joint venture is to combine Chinese capital with foreign technology; yet this was not the case with TCL. In addition, due diligence investigations were not done with care and precision. TCL later found that RCA's sales in North America were not as promising as they had thought initially, and TCL did not have a good understanding of French union laws and regulations, thereby immersing itself in a quagmire of lawsuits which compounded the company's suffering.

4.2   Acquisitions

Chinese companies intending to go global do not always have to acquire resources and capabilities through holdings or buy-outs. Equity can serve the same purpose through a win-win arrangement which provides a stable mechanism for collaboration between the partners. In the case of Biostime, a manufacturer of baby food and other nutritional products, we found that it could achieve the same strategic purpose in the form of an equity stake.

CASE STUDY:
BIOSTIME INC. AND ISM

Biostime's Chairman Luo Fei and the Director General of French dairy producer Isigny Sainte-Mère (ISM), Daniel Delahaye, vigorously promoted a cooperation framework agreement in July 2013. Biostime paid around €20 million for this transaction, of which €2.5 million was used to acquire shares and €17.5 million was for ISM bonds. Biostime paid €2.5 million for a 20% equity stake in ISM, whose net profit was €2.61 million at the time. Some domestic industry insiders wondered how Biostime could secure such a high-quality dairy company for such a bargain price.

In fact, things were not as simple as they seemed. ISM was essentially a rural credit cooperative, which was under the jurisdiction of French agricultural law rather than company laws. Shares of credit cooperatives could be traded only at face value. That is to say, 20% of the shares could be sold at a price of only €2.5 million euros in the future. Also, Biostime could not enjoy dividends from the credit cooperative. As compensation, non-member cooperative shareholders could only get a fixed interest rate on the shares subscribed by the cooperative shareholders, plus 2% interest. Although Biostime had 20% of the shares, it could only have 10% of the voting rights and one board seat out of a total of 15 as a non-member cooperative shareholder.

Agricultural law also stipulates that a non-member cooperative shareholder can only hold 20% of the shares, which means Biostime could only fund the €2.5 million through equity shares, and the remaining €17.5 million was through a ten-year bond subscription. It is because of the ten-year bond that the bank was able to lower the risk against the loan, and was therefore willing to lend €30 million to the firm.

This arrangement marked the first investment by non-member cooperative shareholders in the history of France. Luo Fei and Daniel Delahaye both said they saw a promising future in this cooperation and they shared common ground. Negotiations between leaders of both sides went smoothly; the biggest obstacle was the complex legal issues. Luo Fei's and Daniel Delahaye's entrepreneurial spirit made it possible to reach agreement, albeit within a complex framework.

This agreement further stipulated that a total of €50 million (plus €5 million from ISM) would be invested exclusively in the construction of a new plant. Before the new plant was operational, ISM's annual output of baby formula was about 20,000 tonnes, but with the new plant it would now increase by 30,000 to 50,000 tonnes. The factory construction was completed in early 2015, and when it began operations, 30%-40% of its production capacity was supplied to Biostime, which ensured a long-term stable supply of high-quality baby formula from ISM for the next 15 years.

Biostime experienced years of rapid development in the Chinese market, as the supply of high-quality baby formula had always been an issue of concern to Luo Fei. Working closely with ISM, a producer of quality milk products, it guaranteed a stable supply for the future. As a long-term shareholder, Biostime could increase its influence in ISM, and invest more in baby formula R&D.

In addition, Biostime firmly stood by its position of using only high-quality milk, which helped promote its French brand and the image of French quality. Having previously experienced damage to its brand image in a scandal involving bogus foreign brands, Biostime had a black mark against it, and the market was suspicious about whether it was using Chinese baby formula in its French brand. Collaborating with a highly reputed company such as ISM thus strengthened Biostime's brand image.

Its counterpart ISM also became the largest baby formula company in France by leveraging the expansion. The extra 30,000 tonnes of production capacity was designed to supply not only Biostime, but also its own clients in Europe. The expanded capacity for baby formula also required an increase in the production capacity of fresh milk, which created 100 more jobs in the village where ISM was located. More importantly, the expansion of milk production also increased the production of ISM's cheese, butter and other dairy products. For a long time, ISM's star products, cheese and butter, were in short supply because of their high quality and the quota restrictions on dairy products from the European Union. In 2015, the European Union removed the quota restriction on milk, and this allowed ISM to raise more dairy cows and invest in plant construction (it takes about two years for a cow to reach an age when it can provide milk). The €50 million brought in through the collaboration with Biostime in July 2013 helped to fund this development.

Both Biostime and ISM had a clear intention to establish deeper cooperation. For Biostime, its vision in this equity collaboration was to lock down a long-term contract with a high-quality supplier. After becoming a shareholder in ISM, Biostime could push ISM to invest more in infant formula R&D, which could not have been achieved through a long-term supplier contract.

ISM is a resource-based enterprise, and Biostime saw great value in its high-quality milk. It was not difficult to procure ISM's high-quality milk for the Chinese market and the risk was relatively low. The situation could have become more complicated if the resources that the Chinese company sought had been difficult to transfer to the acquiring firm, or if the target firm had been reluctant to transfer them. For example, some overseas brands, marketing channels, R&D professionals and other intangible assets would have been difficult to transfer to China physically, and might have even encountered a certain degree of resistance. In that situation, taking full control would have been very difficult.

Compare this example with the previous case study of ICBC. The Chinese bank wanted to invest in an African bank that had wide coverage in local markets. The Standard Bank Group obviously matched ICBC's requirements, and it was looking for opportunities to cooperate with a reliable Chinese bank. ICBC is a front-runner in overseas M&As and was the first of the top four Chinese banks to adopt global strategies, which undoubtedly fitted well with Standard Bank Group's expectations.

From a business point of view, the two banks complemented each other. In 2006, ICBC's net interest income was almost 10 times the combined transaction fee and commission income, while Standard Bank's net interest income and non-interest income accounted for 47% and 53%, respectively. Standard Bank Group's business is divided into three major sectors: private and commercial banking, corporate and investment banking, and other service sectors. Its corporate and investment banking division contributed 40% of its total profits. If ICBC was a typical commercial bank, Standard Bank Group was more like an investment bank. Worthy of note is Standard Bank Group's noble metals business: it is one of the world's top ten banks offering noble-metals-related services. As of 2006, no Chinese bank had tapped into the noble metals market.

In May 2007, at the World Bank's annual meeting, ICBC Chairman Jiang Jianqing and the CEO of Standard Bank Group, Jacko Maree, spent a whole day discussing possible collaborations between the two banks. "We are the largest bank in Africa, ICBC is the largest bank not just in China but also the world, we all think we should probe into the matter on a deeper level, and we can share our customer base not only through share holdings, but also through strategic cooperation," Maree recalled. "We soon reached the end of discussions, and started taking actions to do something more practical such as strategic collaborations and shareholdings." After that, the top management of the two banks met numerous times and drafted a strategic cooperation agreement for deliberation by their respective boards of directors. The agreement mainly listed the potential gains of the two sides in a strategic cooperation. On 25 October 2007, ICBC published a notice that it would invest US$5.46 billion to acquire a 20% stake in Standard Bank Group, which would make it Standard Bank Group's largest shareholder. Of the 20% shares, 10% were newly issued to ICBC from Standard Bank Group, amounting to US$2.75 billion. The other 10% were existing shares purchased from Standard Bank priced at 136 rand per share, which means that Standard Bank Group would have a 30% weighted average price premium within 30 days of the announcement.

The case study shows that Standard Bank Group fits perfectly into ICBC's strategy in Africa. ICBC is financially strong and a management powerhouse, but even with that, this acquisition involved only 20% of the equity, which is far from being a buy-out like the MagIndustries case in the previous chapter. There are two main differences: first, the ICBC acquisition differs from MagIndustries' acquisition by Evergreen Holdings, although generally speaking both companies were buying resources. Evergreen was acquiring tangible resources, while the bank was acquiring intangible assets, including the management from Standard Bank Group. Therefore, to avoid potential risks caused by rapid changes, ICBC wanted to adopt a softer approach and used its influence to build stronger ties, thus preventing a negative impact on Standard Bank Group. In the case of Evergreen Holdings, it was necessary to buy out MagIndustries based on its own strategic needs and planning, as the human factor played a very small role in potash mining, and tangible assets such as quality potash played the most significant role.

Secondly, MagIndustries was a listed mining company in Toronto with limited capital. Canada is one of the world's most important market bases for potash fertilizer production. With numerous production companies in the sector already, the focus of its capital market was not on potash exploration companies. In the ICBC case, the aim was to buy the largest bank in Africa, and this move by ICBC would have attracted a lot of public attention in the local market. From a diplomatic perspective, Western society is very sensitive, and Evergreen's overseas acquisition of a mining company certainly attracted attention from the *Wall Street Journal*. However, in the case of ICBC, a Chinese state-owned bank, its overseas activities would surely face even more public scrutiny. It would be a wholly different story and tough to seal the deal if the biggest Chinese bank were to buy out Africa's largest bank. In the following chapters we will talk more about the huge PR crisis ICBC encountered and its emergency action plans after it acquired 20% of the equity in Standard Bank Group.

For ICBC, 20% was the threshold to be a shareholder in the company, as only then could it get its own people on Standard Bank Group's board and create an impact; further, it was financially required to have fair value adjustment for investments of less than 20% in a listed company. If the investment was 20% of the equity, it would not require fair value adjustment. If fair value was required, the resultant volatility in the company's stock price and fluctuations in exchange rate would have had an impact on the income statement, which was a situation ICBC wanted to avoid. Standard Bank Group was not willing to have ICBC acquire 20% of its shares. ICBC strongly pushed for it and then adopted an equity method when it reached 20%. Thus the fluctuation in Standard Bank's share price would not affect ICBC's financial statements. According to the equity method, Standard Bank and ICBC had created a joint-venture enterprise, rather than just having a purely financial investment relationship, hence it made sense for them to establish strategic cooperation with each other and their affiliated companies.

ICBC's 20% stake in Standard Bank was divided into two 10% tranches: the first 10% was through newly issued shares, the new share price was set at the weighted average price of all shares of Standard Bank's traded 30 days prior to the official announcement, and the new funds were retained on Standard Bank's books. The second 10% came at a premium, and were acquired from existing shareholders based on an offer. This financial arrangement would not only serve to avoid fast capital expansion for Standard Bank, but would also serve ICBC's need to increase the capital in order to develop Standard Bank further.

4.3 Valuation of overseas mergers and acquisitions

Valuation is the most compelling and essential part of mergers and acquisitions. Even the most strategically matched acquisition could become a loss-making deal due to an overpriced premium when there is less than ideal synergy between the companies. On the other hand, if the price is low enough, there will be more space for subsequent integration and management, which is crucial for Chinese enterprises that lack experience and expert personnel for cross-border M&As.

We will not focus here on specific valuation models for corporate decision makers, but on the principles of valuation. First, we must clarify the concept that purchase price is not equal to the total acquisition cost. The purchase price is the consideration paid by the acquiring firm to the selling firm, while the acquisition cost is the cost required to maintain the pre-acquisition state of the company (not including any management improvement). The total cost of acquisition consists of three parts:

1. cost of mergers and acquisitions
2. liabilities of the selling company
3. any working capital investment and expenses required to take the target firm forward in a state of continuing operations.

4.3.1 Cost of mergers and acquisitions

Here we need to consider whether the acquisition is being done to acquire resources or capabilities. If it is resources, we need to use the liquidation method, in which the valuation process includes an assessment of all assets and resources. In the case of acquisition of capabilities, which are considered as assets for continuing operations, we are interested more in the profitability of the target company and its ability to improve its profitability (i.e. its growth strength), rather than the size of its assets. A common mistake made by domestic Chinese companies and regulators is to focus on the size of the asset, especially when it comes to tangible assets such as factories, machines and equipment. This mindset is deeply rooted in the nature of a manufacturing industry, whose traditional financial creditability is measured according to the mortgage model of bank credit or investment credit, and this attitude requires substantive changes. The transformation into a global company essentially relies on upgrading capacity. The abilities that eventually accumulate with time, often rely on intangible assets. However, when it comes to either bank loan approvals or equity financing approvals from securities regulatory bodies, we tend to overemphasize the importance of the proportion of tangible to intangible assets. Business leaders need to transform their way of thinking to see the issue through a new set of lenses, and understand that intangible assets often indicate the sustainability of a company.

As to the valuation of intangible assets, we discussed the goodwill issue in the Huntsworth case in the previous chapter. Here we will look into the total valuation of assets needed to sustain operations. We need to pay attention to three main pitfalls in the valuation of intangible assets. First, intangible assets are usually non-standard and have low liquidity, which makes the valuation process quite challenging, as it is difficult to find a perfect reference. Secondly, the valuation of intangible assets is closely related to the operating capability of the firm's owners while it is in use. For example, a company can buy the right to use the trademark of a foreign brand, but it cannot guarantee the same level of sales as before. If it possesses the ability to operate these intangible assets well, it will generate added value for management. In addition, the valuation of intangible assets is related to the ability of a company to continue its operations. If the company becomes bankrupt, the liquidation value of most intangible assets will reduce to zero. If the company can continue to operate, its intangible assets will be able to generate added value.

Business leaders also need to avoid double payment of premiums for assets. For example, if they pay the seller a price in multiples of its earnings during the initial negotiations, and later propose to acquire other brands or businesses from the current trading capital structure, then the acquiring firm has to pay again to obtain this brand. During negotiations, we usually employ two valuation methods: one is to value based on multiples of profits, and the other is to calculate intangible and tangible assets separately, using a liquidation method. In the above-mentioned case, the price is set as multiples of earnings, and paying for additional intangible assets would compound the premium.

4.3.2   Liabilities of the selling company

In fact, when it comes to the liabilities of the selling company, it is essentially a question of choosing between an asset deal or an equity deal. In an asset transaction, the acquiring firm should not take responsibility for these liabilities, which means its financial risk is reduced. However, an asset transaction takes a lot more technical effort to process. The cost of divestiture can be very high, and some assets are tied together. Forced divestiture of such assets can result in huge losses. Operation-wise, the target company may not be willing to do so, and the acquiring company may need to establish a new company to absorb these assets.

Practically, most M&As are equity deals, and these are technically easier to transact. It is not difficult to strip the core assets of the company. However, this increases the financial risk, and when the acquiring firm becomes a shareholder of the target company, it has to take on the responsibilities of a shareholder and repay the debt. This involves many issues, especially when it comes to hidden liabilities, contingent liabilities in the balance sheet, and other off-balance-sheet liabilities. These issues must be investigated in detail during the due diligence stage. Audit agencies play a vital role in due diligence investigations, and they should fully audit all possible off-balance-sheet liabilities as well as contingent liabilities. Considering all of these potential risks, we will cover details of debt repayment, and other debt issues arising after the acquisition, in the next chapter.

4.3.3   Working capital investment and expenses

The third consideration is the expenses required to propel the target firm forward, to enhance continuing operations

This is an issue often overlooked by business leaders due to many legal restrictions and regulations. The whole process of cross-border M&As takes a long time – from a few months up to a year. By the end of this process, the state of the company may be different from what it was at the beginning of the deal. If the buyer only wants to force the price down, while ignoring the fact that the target company needs funds to sustain business operations, then the selling company would be most likely to generate funds in the following ways:

1. collect receivables as soon as possible, which may lead to customer defections
2. sell inventories and delay procurement at the same time, which could lead to an inventory shortage
3. cut R&D costs, travel costs, training fees, advertising costs from the budget (the company is unlikely to be willing to use its funds to help the new owners pay for these).

If these things happen, there will be a drastic difference between the 'state of health' of the business during the due diligence process and when the deal is sealed. If business leaders intend to acquire a company that has ongoing operations, then they should focus not only on lowering the purchase price (total cost discrimination), but also look beyond to make sure the company when transferred stays intact and is in the condition originally stated in the agreement.

Precautions to avoid these incidents include checking on the working capital in the agreement and controlling changes in the working capital after the acquisition. If it is a negative change, then compensation is required after the acquisition. Further, for expenditures permitted in the budget, compensation is required for any part outstanding after the acquisition.

4.4   Conclusion

The total cost of an acquistion can still be effectively controlled and balanced, even if the acquiring firm pays more premium, as it can later take control of the working capital invested and use this to restore the target firm to a state of continuous operation. Most importantly, a careful evaluation guarantees the state of health of the acquired firm and that it will to continue to operate after the acquisition.

CHAPTER 5

FINANCIAL PLANNING

In Chapter 3 we focused on preparatory work before acquisition, considering specifically some key points and principles with respect to due diligence. Chapter 4 looked at models and valuations in overseas M&A. This chapter will concentrate on overall financial planning for M&A, with specific emphasis on post-acquisition capital chain management, and how to conduct post-acquisition financial planning to support the new company's strategic planning and management on a daily basis.

5.1   The importance of free cash flow

Theoretically, a company's value is determined by the current value of its future free cash flow. A company's free cash flow for the year refers to the remaining profit after deducting any reinvestment in that year. Reinvestment in a company includes additional net working capital and additional net capital, such as investment in fixed assets, for example. This theory gives us some insight into the value of the working capital and investment required for a company's growth, apart from making a profit.

This theory emphasizes the company's own cash flow instead of profits. It addresses such questions as whether a company's net profit and net profit rate have increased in its financial statements, and whether its inventory and accounts receivables have grown faster on the balance sheet, with heavy investment in fixed assets such as plant and machinery and increased debt. All these factors suggest that any increase in net profit is only apparent, and when it reaches a certain point, it may encounter a rupture in the capital chain.

Companies need to pay particular attention to these interrelated value-determining factors in order to maintain a certain level of growth, to determine whether reinvestment is required, and to decide whether to consider investment in working capital or in fixed assets. When investment increases, associated risks also increase, and without due attention and control, this may lead to difficulties. Many companies have gone bankrupt not because they were no longer making a profit, but because of a rupture in their capital chain resulting from overexpansion. This is more common in the 'snake-eats-elephant' type of mergers and acquisitions, whose goal is capital expansion. When a 'once in a blue moon' M&A opportunity presents itself to business decision-makers, it is possible to achieve leapfrog growth or even upgrade to the next level if only they can seize the opportunity. But if those decision-makers cannot clearly evaluate their financial strength and management ability, even a strategically sound M&A may fail due to ruptures in the capital chain.

The theory of corporate value in corporate finance reveals that we are more concerned with *future* free cash flow. In the case of overseas acquisitions, financial planning must take place before the acquisition is carried out. We need to make plans for future growth and sustainability, profitability, reinvestment (working capital and fixed assets) and risks. This will ultimately determine the profitability of the overall acquisition, how much we can invest with the desired returns, how much debt we can bear (how much we can borrow from the bank and how much we can repay), and how big the future funding gap is likely to be be.

CASE STUDY:
WH GROUP ACQUIRES SMITHFIELD FOODS

WH Group, formerly known as Henan Shuanghui Investment & Development Co., Ltd (Shuanghui Development), is a listed holding company on the Chinese stock market. It is the largest meat processing enterprise listed there. Shuanghui Development bought out the world's largest swine supplier and pork producer, Smithfield Foods (Smithfield), in 2013 for US$4.7 billion. After the transaction was completed on 26 September 2013,

Smithfield was delisted from the United States Stock Market. The deal also led to a transfer of Smithfield's US$2.4 billion debt to Shuanghui Development (renamed WH Group before the listing).

In this high-value transaction, US$319 million was self-funded, and Shuanghui Development took out a syndicated loan of $3.925 billion from the Bank of China, backed by a $882 million priority unsecured commercial paper from a shell company. As a result, the deal was completed for a $4.7 billion consideration (paid to Smithfield's original shareholder) and a $200 million transaction cost was incurred. After the transaction was completed, there was the matter of repayment of the loan. The syndicated loan from Bank of China had a tenure of no more than five years, and there were loan terms on WH Group's debt ratio and interest repayment rate; if these requirements were not met, the bank would terminate the contract immediately in advance for early repayment. Smithfield's new Chinese 'owners' (this was an equity acquisition rather than an asset acquisition) also needed to repay Smithfield's debt. WH Group had to find ways to solve all these issues.

Shuanghui Development was popular on the stock market, and had a net profit of less than $500 million in 2012. WH Group turned to the capital market to find prospective investors. In their initial public offering (IPO) they planned to issue 3.655 billion shares at a price of HK$11.25, amounting to HK$41.2 billion. The assumption was that if the proposal was accepted, the cost of the M&A would be almost covered by the capital market, and WH Group would have acquired the world's largest pork producer by selling a part of its equity.

This case study analyses the two economic entities within WH Group: Shuanghui Development and Smithfield Foods. (Shuanghui Development is a listed company, Smithfield Foods only recently delisted, so the financial data of both companies are transparent). The questions under consideration are:

1. How to repay the debt
2. How much WH Group could bid

3. What form the acquisition should take
4. How much the group should borrow for the acquisition.

Since specific terms on liabilities were unknown, and future cash flows can only be roughly estimated, this financial analysis needed to be based on past financial performance and some practical hypotheses.

The first consideration is that WH Group acquired Smithfield at US$34 per share. Smithfield's fiscal year ends in April. Based on a net profit of US$361 million for the fiscal year ending 29 April 2012, the purchase price corresponded to a price-to-earnings ratio (P/E) of 15.4. Based on a net profit of US$184 million for the fiscal year ending 29 April 2013, the P/E came to 25.

By the end of 2013, WH Group had an outstanding debt of US$7.432 billion, accounting for 52.5% of its total assets, and the ratio of debt to shareholder equity was up to 236.8%. Around US$760 million of WH Group's debt was due to mature in one year, $306 million in two years and $4.950 billion in three to five years. Assuming an annual repayment of $1.650 billion for debt with one-year maturity, and $1.416 billion for debt with a maturity of over five years, a total of $6.16 billion would need to be repaid within five years. The debt interest rates for Smithfield Foods can be obtained from its own annual report. WH Group's primary loan for the acquisition of Smithfield was US$3.925 billion from the Bank of China (due in 2018; interest rate is LIBOR +3.5% to +4.5%), assuming an average interest rate of 5%. Several possible scenarios presented themselves:

SCENARIO 1

Assuming that the acquisition of Smithfield Foods is a leveraged buyout (LBO) – meaning the total acquisition loan will be repaid by Smithfield Foods itself (WH Group's other entities would not be involved) – and assuming that Smithfield maintains an annual growth rate of 5% based on its profit in 2013, and a 3% rate of net earnings before interest and tax (NEBIT), the NEBIT of Smithfield Foods can be calculated.

Debt repayments are as shown in Table 6.

All figures are in millions of US$

	2014	2015	2016	2017	2018
WH Group debt interest estimate	392	359	345	248	152
WH Group principal due	760	306	1650	1650	1650
WH Group principal + interest	**1152**	**665**	**1995**	**1898**	**1802**
Smithfield estimated NEBIT	416	437	459	482	506
Outstanding debt	**735**	**228**	**1536**	**1416**	**1296**

TABLE 6	DEBT REPAYMENTS FOR WH GROUP (SCENARIO 1)

In this scenario, Smithfield's annual NEBIT is just about enough to repay WH Group's debt interest and a small portion of the principal.

SCENARIO 2

Still assuming that the Smithfield acquisition is an LBO – meaning that the total acquisition loan will be repaid by Smithfield itself – we now assume that WH Group has managed the merger well after the acquisition, and that Smithfield now has the same profitability as Shuanghui Development. Assuming also that Smithfield maintains an annual growth rate of 11% based on its profit in 2013, and that Shuanghui Development had a 6.5% rate of NEBIT, the net profit before interest and tax of Smithfield Foods can be calculated.

The debt repayments under this scenario are shown in Table 7.

Millions of US$

	2014	2015	2016	2017	2018
WH Group debt interest estimate	392	359	345	248	152
WH Group principal due	760	306	1650	1650	1650
WH Group principal + interest	**1152**	**665**	**1995**	**1898**	**1802**
Smithfield estimated NEBIT	954	1059	1175	1305	1448
Outstanding debt	**198**	**-394**	**820**	**594**	**354**

TABLE 7   DEBT REPAYMENTS FOR WH GROUP (SCENARIO 2)

Assuming that Smithfield's profitability matches that of Shuanghui Development, NEBIT as calculated here is more than twice that in Scenario 1. However, after covering WH Group's debt interest, there is only enough left to repay a part of the principal.

SCENARIO 3

In this scenario, the debt would be repaid using Smithfield's net profit before interest and tax as well as from a portion of Shuanghui Development's net profit before interest and tax, based on the acquisition body. The acquisition body in this case is Rotary Vortex Ltd, which directly and indirectly holds 73.26% of the shares of Shuanghui Development through Shuanghui Group. Assuming that Smithfield maintains an annual growth rate of 5% based on its profit in 2013, and a 3% rate of NEBIT, we can calculate the net profit before interest and tax of Smithfield Foods. Assuming an annual growth rate of 11%, with an average 6.5% NEBIT rate for Shuanghui Development based on its profitability in 2013, we can calculate the net profit before interest and tax of Shuanghui Development, and then multiply this by 73.26% (Table 8).

Millions of US$

	2014	2015	2016	2017	2018
WH Group debt interest estimate	392	359	345	248	152
WH Group principal due	760	306	1650	1650	1650
WH Group principal + interest	**1152**	**665**	**1995**	**1898**	**1802**
Smithfield estimated NEBIT	416	437	459	482	506
WH Group (acquisition body) estimated NEBIT	402	446	495	549	610
Shuanghui Development & Smithfield combined NEBIT	**818**	**883**	**954**	**1031**	**1116**
Outstanding debt	**334**	**-218**	**1041**	**867**	**686**

TABLE 8   DEBT REPAYMENTS FOR WH GROUP (SCENARIO 3)

If the debt is repaid using Smithfield's net profit before interest and tax, and a portion of Shuanghui Development's net profit before interest and tax, based on the acquisition body, after covering WH Group's debt interest, there is only enough left to repay part of the principal.

SCENARIO 4

If the debt is repaid using Smithfield's net profit before interest and tax as well as from a portion of Shuanghui Development's net profit before interest and tax, based on the acquisition body, and if we now assume an annual growth rate of 11%, with an average 6.5% NEBIT rate for Smithfield based on its profitability in 2013, debt repayments will be as shown in Table 9.

Millions of US$

	2014	2015	2016	2017	2018
WH Group debt interest estimate	392	359	345	248	152
WH Group principal due	760	306	1650	1650	1650
WH Group principal + interest	**1152**	**665**	**1995**	**1898**	**1802**
Smithfield estimated NEBIT	954	1059	1175	1305	1448
WH Group (acquisition body) estimated NEBIT	402	446	495	549	610
Shuanghui Development & Smithfield combined NEBIT	**1356**	**1505**	**1670**	**1854**	**2058**
Outstanding debt	**-204**	**-840**	**325**	**44**	**-256**

TABLE 9 DEBT REPAYMENTS OF WH GROUP (SCENARIO 4)

This scenario assumes that Smithfield is able to repay WH Group's debt interest and principal only if it does so using its net profit before interest and tax, and with a part of Shuanghui Development's net profit before interest and tax, based on the acquisition body. If there is no additional capital outlay, and the reliance is solely on the operation and management of the company, WH Group needs to take Smithfield to the level of Shuanghui Development to match the indicators listed in Table 9.

Business operators understand how difficult it is to improve even one decimal place beyond existing key performance indicators (KPIs), even when no effort is spared. So it was almost an impossible task to take Smithfield Foods to the level of Shuanghui Development in such a short time. It was also impossible for WH Group to clear the loan on its own; it needed to find more money. The first option was the capital market, and WH Group took this into account in its prospectus for the IPO, to raise the capital and repay the debt generated from its acquisition of Smithfield Foods.

On 23 April 2014, investor confidence was not high, and WH Group announced a reduction in its fundraising target by two thirds, while the price range also dropped to HK$8-11.25 per share. Soon thhis second plan also failed, and WH Group suspended its listing plan. On 5 August 2014, WH Group finally listed at a price of HK$6.2 per share, and eventually raised about HK$18.3 billion. On 30 September 2014, WH Group announced a new round of financing with a US$1.5 billion loan. New funds and debts from the capital market helped to temporarily relieve WH Group's anxiety about obtaining the US$4 billion syndicated loan from Bank of China.

However, in our previous analysis, we assumed all annual profits of Smithfield Foods and Shuanghui Development could be converted into cash flow to repay the debt. (We assumed zero reinvestment in working capital and fixed assets in all four scenarios.) But in fact, to maintain sustainable and steady growth, there would have to be some working capital input every year, which would mean less cash flow to repay the debt.

In ten years of development from 2004 to 2014, Shuanghui Development's sales revenue increased rapidly, and although its sales declined after the 'lean meat' scandal in 2011, a year later Shuanghui Development recovered from the damage caused by this incident and continued its rapid growth. However, according to its first three quarters' sales estimates for 2014, Shuanghui Development's sales volume were set to face further decline throughout 2014 (see Figure 4).

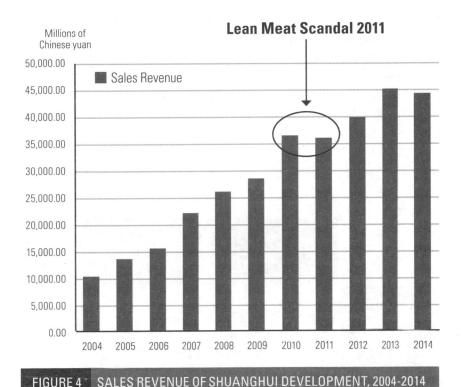

Millions of Chinese yuan

Lean Meat Scandal 2011

■ Sales Revenue

FIGURE 4 ° SALES REVENUE OF SHUANGHUI DEVELOPMENT, 2004-2014

Of course, the decline in sales suggested by the three quarterly reports could be due to a variety of reasons, including changes in the dietary habits of consumers, which may lead to lower pork consumption. But there is probably another critical reason. On 12 September 2013, as explained in the last paragraph of the Shuanghui Development board of directors' statement:

> "To repay our bank loans, Rotary Vortex Limited, Shuanghui Group and Shuanghui International will make commitments to foreign banks for overseas loan agreement, and it will use no less than 70% of its retained earnings to pay dividends to its parent company each year, after auditing the consolidated net profit attributable to the parent company, while complying with relevant laws and regulations."

In fact, for a long time to come, Shuanghui Development will continue to distribute dividends to the parent company from its outstanding profitability and cash generating-capacity, to repay liabilities generated from its acquisition of Smithfield Foods.[77]

On comparing Shuanghui Development's third-quarter reports of 2014 with those of 2013, and its ten-year averages (Figure 5), we can see that part of Shuanghui Development's high growth can be reflected in its cash flow structure. Constant reinvestment ensured the final conversion of net profit into operating cash flow. But when profits are paid out as dividends and capital left for reinvestment decreases, it becomes difficult to increase profits (as well as income growth) and cash flow from operating activities.

Hundreds of millions of Yuan

	Q3 2014	Q3 2013	Capabilities developed	Average change over the ten years to 2014
Net cash flow from operating activities (+)	**30**	31	-2.4%	+26.2%
Net cash flow from investment activities (-)	22	27	-17.4%	+30.8%
Net cash flow from financing activities (-)	35	20	+72.3%	+23.8%
Profit available for dividend, profit	**34**	16	+113.8%	+4.9%
Closing cash balance	12	25	-52.7%	+27.5%
Net profit	13	14	-8.22%	+30.6%

FIGURE 5   COMPARISON OF SHUANGHUI DEVELOPMENT'S THIRD-QUARTER REPORTS OF 2014 WITH THOSE OF 2013

5.1.1 Conclusion

In this chapter we have explored the details of the WH Group case to illustrate the importance of financial planning throughout the entire process of overseas M&As. We can see that WH Group's planning in general is in good shape. It started its IPO roadshow only half a year after the completion of the acquisition, and it quickly adjusted its IPO plan when the market response was not ideal. Although the adjusted plan failed in the end, it still managed to complete its IPO three months later, with many compromises, including a painful discount and reduced issue size, and gave up on the transfer of the old shares. After the IPO, it repaid part of its debt, the high dividend of Shuanghui Development and the US$1.5 billion bank loan; it also sold its shares in Campofrío, Europe's largest meat production company. These complicated capital operations by WH Group were required to solve its urgent debt crisis.

The union between China's largest meat product company and the world's largest pig-farming company sounded like a match made in heaven. In retrospect, we can see that the story is more about capital than strategies.[78] Although the strategic intent of this acquisition may have been misguided, nevertheless WH Group has demonstrated excellent capital operation capabilities, and was ultimately able to defuse this crisis, at least for the time being.

5.2 The capital chain problem: Planning for all eventualities

Globalization enables Chinese companies to improve their technology, branding and management through overseas mergers and acquisitions. The capital chain issue is one of the common problems for 'snake-eats-elephant' acquisitions with a high purchase price. Therefore, finding different ways of financing at the precisely the right time, in order to support corporate strategy for daily management activities, is of vital importance. The core of financial planning is to make estimates for optimistic, average and pessimistic scenarios, and to make respective plans for each so that if the pessimistic situation occurs, the company will not be caught off guard.

Companies can use appropriate financial arrangements to tackle multiple issues when it comes to financial weak points, lack of experience in managing global companies and even lack of public relations ability.

Let us look at Lenovo's acquisition of IBM's personal computer business to see how sophisticated financial operations can help a firm's globalization strategy.

CASE STUDY:
LENOVO GROUP AND IBM

THREE PRIVATE PLACEMENT AGENCIES

TPG (Texas Pacific Group) is a world-famous private equity (PE) investment firm, established in 1993, and has investments in a broad range of industries including technology, telecommunications, health care, consumer/retail, airlines, oil and gas, food and beverage, luxury goods and many other areas. As a global private equity investment agency in science and technology, TPG has invested in enterprises such as wafer manufacturers in Silicon Valley, MEMC Electronic Materials and ON Semiconductor, Seagate Technologies, etc. TPG has extensive experience in private equity investments including leveraged buyouts, minority equity investments, joint ventures, business demergers and corporate restructuring. TPG specializes in corporate acquisitions and holding investments in European and American markets, while in Asia's emerging markets it focuses on minority equity investments and becomes an important shareholder of the enterprises it has invested in.

In 1994, TPG and another private equity agency, Blum Capital, jointly established Newbridge Capital (NC), which is in fact an extension of the two companies in Asia. NC's strategic positioning is mainly in strategic financial investment, and the right of control has always been what NC fights for on the battlefield. "The purpose of gaining control is to change management of the acquired company and ultimately increase the company's value," said the new managing partner. "Acquisitions can generate profits only by creating value."[79]

Another private equity firm, GA (General Atlantic), founded in 1980, specializes in information technology, business process outsourcing (BPO) and telecommunications, and was actively investing in the United States market in the early 1990s. In 2000, when Lenovo wanted to spin off its businesses, GA offered to invest in Digital China as its second major shareholder. GA has enjoyed close cooperation with Liu Chuanzhi, the founder of Lenovo.

When news of IBM selling off its PC business broke, TPG hoped to buy it at a low price. According to media reports, TPG's initial offer was US$200 million.[80] Ma Xue Zheng (Lenovo's Senior Vice President and Chief Financial Officer at that time) did not consider TPG as a threat. She said, "Lenovo is a strategic investor, mergers and acquisitions have synergies, and we have an advantage in valuation. TPG does not have this synergistic advantage." Once the quotation had reached more than US$1 billion,[81] TPG gave up its idea of purchasing at a low price and immediately put forward a cooperation proposal to Lenovo, successfully becoming Lenovo's acquisition partner. Later, TPG led an investment of US$350 million, and Lenovo also hired its operation team. TPG's participation encouraged Lenovo, IBM and other investors greatly, giving it a much-needed vote of confidence. Not only that, Lenovo thought TPG's position in the field of technology investment in the US market would be of great help for its market expansion and sales.[82]

GA carefully evaluated the return and earnings on shares from a professional investment point of view, and provided financial analysis reports. GA's Managing Director, William O. Grabe, served as Senior Vice President of IBM, and had a detailed understanding of IBM's corporate culture, teams, technology, sales and human resources. He offered valuable guidance for Lenovo in the negotiation process: what terms should it adhere to, what issues it should let go of, what techniques to use in negotiations with IBM's upper management. After the acquisition was completed, Grabe also became a board member.

However, an investigation by the Committee on Foreign Investment in the United States (CFIUS) almost caused the acquisition to be aborted. In January 2005, three Republican senators called on the US government to extend investigations into Lenovo's acquisition, expressing concern about Chinese companies owning the technology and corporate assets of an American company after the acquisition. They were worried that the Chinese government would expand its shareholding rights in Lenovo, and cut down its price to drive American competitors out of the PC market. If this happened, the United States would be forced to rely on China for computer technology. More importantly, this would generate security issues once the market dynamics changed. Moreover, IBM had several computer-related contracts with the Federal Government, which raised fears about US national security. CFIUS decided to extend its 30-day review period to 45 days. Lenovo sought to compromise on terms such as restricting its employees from accessing IBM's list of government clients. With support from TPG Chairman Jim Coulter, Lenovo passed the review.

On 31 March 2005, Lenovo chairman Yang Yuanqing commented on the positive role of private equity firms in a press conference after the acquisition:

> "They conducted intensive research on business development, and possessed strong planning and design abilities in corporate strategy development, and they have also helped many famous companies successfully integrate their businesses. Their joining Lenovo laid a solid foundation for the company to achieve a smooth transition and steady development.[83]"

EQUITY STRUCTURE

On 30 March, 2005, Lenovo announced that TPG would invest US$350 million. Lenovo Group issued additional preferred shares and convertible common stock warrants to TPG, GA and NC, for financing the US$350 million. The investment structure is: A. 273 million convertible preferred shares, priced at HK$1,000 per share, with fixed dividend rate of 4.5% per annum, paid quarterly. Preferred stock can be converted into ordinary shares at any time and can be redeemed after 17 May, 2012; B. 237,417,474 options for free; C. Preferred shares can be converted into ordinary shares, rights can be exercised, conversion price is HK$2.725; D. TPG placed 3 people on the board of directors. TPG owns 7.1% of Lenovo Group's shares, GA holds 3.5%, and NC holds 1.8%.

Lenovo added three board seats for foreign shareholders. This created a strong international board for Lenovo Group to go global, which would benefit the company in terms of corporate branding, international vision and building experience. Lenovo introduced private equity firms onto its board as third parties, and they served as a communication bridge for both companies. For an acquiring company like Lenovo with a lack of experience in branding, strategy and management, this was a constructive tactic. If there is any disagreement, this arrangement can avoid direct confrontation between Lenovo and IBM. Liu Chuanzhi thought of it as a 'Chinese tactic.'[84]

In December 2005, private institutions played an important role in coordination and communication when CEO Stephen Ward left the company, and the transition was smooth with William Amelio taking over. Ward's departure was inevitable, but Liu Chuan Zhi was concerned that it would trigger cultural and political strife between Lenovo and IBM, and between China and the United States. To his credit, two of the PE agencies on the board played positive roles in the process, and softened the atmosphere on both sides.

When conflict arose as to whether Lenovo should cut costs, these private-equity firms were on Lenovo's side. "These PEs are all Americans, they have seen many advanced enterprises, so this conflict is no longer one of Chinese with Americans. We could also say that Lenovo initiated the cost cutting issue because Lenovo did not know much about global management," said Liu Chuanzhi. He admitted that Ward's resignation went smoothly because he and Yang Yuanqing had put a lot of effort into balancing the interests of the board of directors.[85]

The industry believes that the capital investment was an important factor that attributed to Lenovo's loss in the fiscal year 2008.[86] International private equity firms, after all, have a purpose for their financial investment, and what concerns them most are financial reports and share prices, leading to many short-term-oriented decisions at the expense of long-term strategic goals. Yang Yuanqing's dual business model missed a golden opportunity to fast-forward development, as the transformation of the IT system was not ready on time. The main reason was the cost of the system: as much as US$500 to $700 million. These expenses would be deducted from the company's profits. The PE agencies were concerned with the impact on financial reports and therefore were against the decision, which led to Lenovo's revenues having a smaller share from consumer businesses, and this brought a drastic decline after the 2008 financial crisis.

In early 2009, Liu Chuanzhi proposed to replace Amelio with Yang Yuanqing at a board meeting; however, together with the decline in its performance and its huge losses, such management changes would have been interpreted by the Western public as a move by Lenovo to become a wholly Chinese company once again. This would affect the business's clients, and the PE agencies were deeply worried. Liu Chuanzhi devoted a lot of effort to communicating and negotiating with the PE board members, hoping that they would listen to him and allow Yang Yuanqing to serve as CEO. As a result, when the management was about to be changed, the PE board members proposed Liu Chuanzhi to become Chairman of Lenovo Group. In February 2009, 'Yang-Liu' (a Chinese pun on the word 'willow') returned to the centre of power at Lenovo Group.[87]

REASSIGNMENT OF PRIVATE EQUITY AGENCIES

The three PE firms became Lenovo shareholders to further promote themselves in China through the acquisition, and to invest in the Chinese currency renminbi (RMB) while it was appreciating. With Lenovo's good business performance in the market, they were hoping to cash in as soon as possible. These were the most practical concerns of the three foreign shareholders.[88] In November 2007, TPG and the two other PE firms sold 350.46 million Lenovo shares for HK$8.16-$8.33 per share, cashing in about HK$2.859-$2.919 billion. After that, Lenovo Group's share price suffered from the subprime mortgage crisis, and showed a cumulative decline of 70% in 2008. In September 2009, the three PE firms sold about 291.5 million Lenovo shares at around HK$3.56 per share, cashing in about HK$1.4 billion. Affected by this, Lenovo shares fell by 5.7% on the same day. In February 2010, TPG sold 100.8 million Lenovo shares at a price of HK$5.35-$5.45 per share, cashing in about US$70 million. In November 2010, these three strategic investors cashed in their shares for the fourth time through bulk transactions, and converted 100 million Lenovo shares at a conversion price of HK$5.4 per share, placing 2.8% stake of Lenovo Group in the Hong Kong stock market, fully selling out all their Lenovo shares at this point. According to the analysis, after these four cash-in activities, the three institutions made a more than 200% total return on investment.[89]

It is highly likely that Lenovo will cooperate with international capital again in the future. The company will need to consider how best to manage the symbiotic relationships with international capital, and how to manage conflicts of interests with international PE agencies.

Involving overseas private equity firms increased the possibility of success for this acquisition. Specifically, these American private equity firms helped Lenovo to pass the investment review from CFIUS. With these agencies' professional skills, Lenovo improved its level of internationalization, strategic planning and management ability. For overseas M&As, especially those involving high-value transactions, overall financial planning before the deal will determine the success and subsequent integration of the acquisition.

CASE STUDY:
WANDA'S ACQUISITION OF AMC[90]

On 31 August 2012, China's Dalian Wanda Group (Wanda) acquired a 100% stake in AMC, North America's second-largest cinema chain, for US$700 million. At that time, AMC had 343 cinemas and 4,950 screens, dominating 24 of the 25 largest markets in the United States and accounting for 20% of the US box office. Seven of the ten cinemas with the highest gross profit in the country belonged to AMC. However, AMC had suffered consecutive years of losses and was heavily in debt.

Established in 1920, AMC was bought out by five famous leveraged buyout funds, including Apollo Global Management, in 2004, when the chain had a debt of US$1.5 billion. AMC achieved a turnaround in 2010, and submitted a listing application with a self-valuation of US$1.5 billion. In the same year, Wanda contacted AMC to discuss the possibility of a takeover. Wanda offered a consideration of US$1.2-1.3 billion but was rejected. However, in 2011, AMC suffered another loss, and by 2012 it was in huge financial debt, with liabilities worth US$3.6 billion, including US$1.9 billion interest-bearing debt – and its financial situation was worsening. At the same time, the funds that had invested in AMC for nearly eight years since 2004 were in a rush to exit the investment, which impeded the IPO plan. The company's sale became the best choice among its remaining options.

In August 2012, Wanda eventually bought out AMC for US$700 million, much lower than the 2010 offer. As Asia's largest cinema business, with the second-largest cinema chain in North America, Wanda Group was set to become the world's largest cinema chain. However, the North American movie market was saturated, and there were signs of decline. If Wall Street experts could not make AMC profitable, what chance would Wanda have in this acquisition?

Wanda analysed AMC's financial statements and identified two main reasons for the loss. First of all, the leveraged funds from its original shareholders were putting pressure on cost-cutting and capital expenditure, and they were not willing to invest in upgrading the cinema. Secondly, the company had a low credit rating resulting from its large leveraged funds, and the financial burden was huge. In addition, the original five AMC funds each held the same percentage of shares, so there was no controlling shareholder. The management lacked incentive mechanisms, knowing that these funds would exit from the company eventually, and was also concerned that AMC would be sold again. As a result, this nearly 100-year-old company was in hot water.

While Wanda was in negotiation with AMC shareholders, it decided to negotiate with 42 of its core management members, promising to renew a long-term contract of 4-5 years with them, and install only a chairman and a deputy finance director at AMC. It also promised that it would not sell AMC and that it would invest US$300 million to upgrade the cinemas over the next three years. Also, Wanda promised to allocate 10% of AMC's profits in the US market to reward its management. After taking over AMC, Wanda also set up a target responsibility system, assigning profit targets as responsibilities to each management team, and implemented a financial management system to strengthen financial and performance control.

After building up the confidence of AMC's management and setting up an incentive mechanism, it became easier for AMC to turn itself around. In the second year after the acquisition, AMC announced a successful turnaround: net profit had increased by US$188 million compared with its performance in 2012. According to our analysis, more than two thirds of this improvement is from increases in gross profit margins, and part of it comes from interest reductions (see Figures 6 and 7).

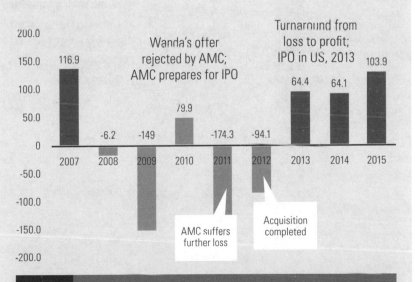

Millions of US$

FIGURE 6   AMC'S NET PROFITS, 2007-2015

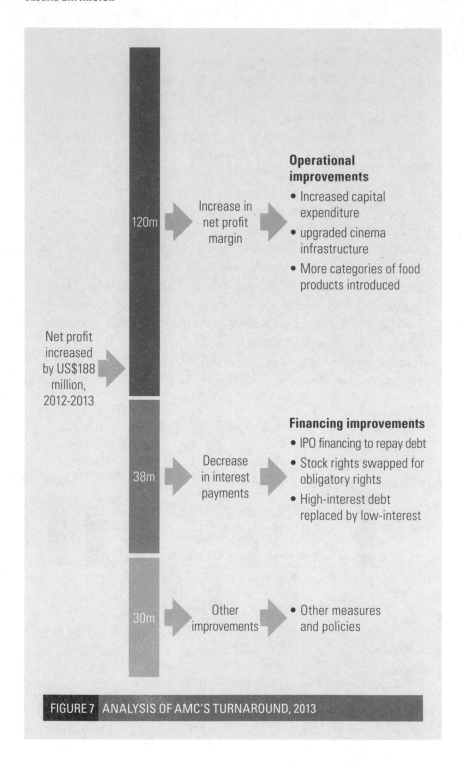

Operational improvements
- Increased capital expenditure
- upgraded cinema infrastructure
- More categories of food products introduced

120m

Increase in net profit margin

Net profit increased by US$188 million, 2012-2013

Financing improvements
- IPO financing to repay debt
- Stock rights swapped for obligatory rights
- High-interest debt replaced by low-interest

38m

Decrease in interest payments

30m

Other improvements

- Other measures and policies

FIGURE 7   ANALYSIS OF AMC'S TURNAROUND, 2013

Wanda's capital investment in AMC was effective. The cinema introduced first-class booth seats and increased prices of food and beverages. The gross profit of its catering service was almost 90% higher than that of its box office, and the increased profit from catering boosted overall gross profit. On the other hand, Wanda, as a shareholder with 100% controlling rights, possessed formidable financial strength. It was said that Wanda had a nearly US$5 billion line of credit. This eased creditors' concerns about the equity, and interest rates decreased further with the increase in AMC's credit rating. AMC's IPO raised enough funds to repay some of its debts, which further decreased the erosion of AMC's profits from interest payments.

On 18 December 2013, AMC listed on the New York Stock Exchange with a market value of US$1.938 billion. Wanda holds 78% of its shares, with a market value of $1.46 billion. By 25 November 2015, AMC had a total market value of $2.415 billion and Wanda had a market value of about $1.89 billion. A century-old, debt-ridden company had been revitalized by Wanda, using a combination of financing and incentive mechanisms.

5.2.1   Conclusion

There are various scenarios to consider when Chinese companies go global. A company attempting a 'snake-eats-elephant' type of acquisition, carrying too much debt which results in profit erosion due to interest expenses, is one such scenario. Added to this, if further issues come to light that have been overlooked in the due diligence process, further capital investment may be needed. Or the acquiring company may encounter mismanagement and cultural conflicts in the deal itself. To protect itself, the acquiring firm must conduct scenario analysis before the acquisition. It should make funding estimates for optimistic, average and pessimistic scenarios, and draw up respective plans for each scenario. It should prepare action plans so that it can respond promptly to emergency situations.

CHAPTER 6

RISK PREVENTION AND CONTROL IN OVERSEAS M&AS

Previous chapters have provided an introduction to the management of strategic and financial risks in the globalization process of Chinese enterprises. Part III will look at human capital risks, cultural risks, etc., and how to formulate plans to avoid and tackle these risks. However, the globalization of Chinese enterprises encounters many unique risks associated with unexpected incidents, and these risks are often interlinked. For example, political risk and exchange-rate risk are often related, and ultimately affect the normal operation of enterprises in the affected countries. By the end of 2013, the Ukraine crisis had intensified the political risk in Eastern Europe, and the resulting sanctions on Russia affected the crude oil-based commodities market. The global economy was in a turbulent state, and the Russian rouble, Kazakh tenge, South African rand and Chinese yuan (renminbi) experienced huge fluctuations. Turmoil in emerging markets added even more risk to Chinese companies' globalization process.

Political risks are often difficult to predict. When we decide to tap into a market with an unstable political system or an authoritarian state, we need to consider as fully as possible the local political environment, and whether safeguards and emergency action plans can be implemented. Exchange-rate risk can be hedged through financial instruments. Admittedly hedging generates some costs, but given that overseas businesses tend to be relatively bigger in scale, the cost is necessary, especially for companies where there are no natural geographical hedging options. Legal risks are also fairly common in companies that operate globally, and law firms with overseas operations can usually provide comprehensive solutions.

This chapter focuses on the ethical and reputational risks in Chinese enterprises' globalization process. During the process, even when the Chinese firm and the decision-making body of the target company can see eye-to-eye with each other at first, it is still likely that there will be pressures from third parties, including media, government and lobbying groups, society, trades unions, etc. In foreign countries, especially developed countries, it is almost impossible to avoid conflicts and questions from these entities. In managing a target company, its understanding and attitude towards the acquisition determine the results of future operations and integration. The same is true of key employees who need to know whether their interests will be harmed after the acquisition, as well as how their inherent working methodology will be affected. If some employees are not going to be considered in the post-acquisition operation plan, or if their remuneration packages are to be adjusted, it is necessary to understand the trade union's attitude towards the acquisition and any layoff plans. When Chinese enterprises encounter local political elections at a time when they are planning redundancies in their overseas M&As, then stakeholders such as lobby groups can use the media to air their grievances and create complications for the acquisition.

6.1   Balancing stakeholder interests

Many acquisitions fail due to lack of awareness about stakeholder issues. For example, TCL encountered pressure from the unions in Europe which impaired its operations; its layoff plan met with a backlash from unions in France, and TCL could not escape the legal quagmire until 2011. Moreover, in some cases Chinese firms have lost out to foreign companies which made lower offers. In 2010, Huawei attempted to buy Motorola, but lost the bid to Nokia Siemens Networks, which had offered a much lower price than Huawei. Huawei's globalization path, especially its mergers and acquisitions, has been through many tough patches. Besides political resistance, Chinese enterprises must also take into account public relations issues and corporate image.

There has been a prominent increase in protectionism on cross-border trade in the past few years, and Chinese acquisitions have often been rejected for national security reasons, particularly in energy and high-tech industries. The Chinese government has made great efforts in foreign economic and trade negotiations, establishing bilateral trade relationships with many countries and setting up platforms for public diplomacy and investment protection agreements. The government will need to increase its efforts in future to serve as a diplomatic supporter for Chinese enterprises' foreign investment, to reduce trade barriers and protest against national trade protection practices that do not conform to World Trade Organization (WTO) regulations. However, in their globalization process, Chinese enterprises still need to establish a better corporate image and fulfil their social responsibility as international enterprises. China's overseas investments have officially surpassed foreign investments in China. Chinese enterprises' globalization has become the 'new normal', and if the forerunners fail to establish a good image, this would make it more difficult to change other people's impressions about Chinese companies. For example, Chinese corporations are not usually regarded as environmentally friendly.

Do Chinese enterprises pay enough attention to their employees' welfare, career development and corporate culture? Do they actively fulfil their social responsibilities, and do they participate enough in local public welfare and charity events? These are issues that Chinese companies need to take into account, in order to create a good image when they go global. Chinese firms have to consider why some countries are unfriendly towards them. This prejudice is partly due to some Chinese companies' bad practices in earlier overseas business activities. Often the prejudice is not about ethical issues, but is more related to the differences in operating environment between Chinese and foreign enterprises.

Due to differences in national ideologies and political systems, the operating environment in Chinese and foreign enterprises can be quite different. Apart from the political pressures from government bodies, Chinese enterprises also face challenges from trade unions, non-governmental organizations (NGOs), non-profit organizations (NFPs), the media and some social organizations. When Chinese companies go global, it is highly desirable to have in-depth communication with all stakeholders. Taking the following three steps will help:

1. Form a better understanding of the target company. If Chinese companies are confronted by issues that are difficult to tackle, it may be better to call off negotiations.

2. Understand the demands of all stakeholders and use this information to improve acquisition planning, which can increase the success rate of the acquisition.
3. Most importantly, initiate communications with all stakeholders, which will be beneficial for the post-acquisition integration process. If an acquisition goes through, stakeholders are bound to raise issues that the acquiring company needs to face.

Before the acquisition, it is necessary to investigate the interests of all stakeholders, identify potential problems, and then design a system to tackle these issues. The most critical element in this system is mutual benefit and trust. Overseas M&As are not necessarily a zero-sum game. If we can see further and see the bigger picture in the mechanism set up for the acquisition, achieving a win-win situation is not entirely impossible. Companies can set up a mechanism that meets the interests of all stakeholders by considering the following aspects:

1. Global allocation of the value chain and resources.
2. Respect for each other's core interests and spheres of influence.
3. The need to communicate actively with the media and practice corporate responsibilities to establish a positive corporate image.

6.1.1. Global allocation of the value chain and resources

We need to think clearly where the Chinese enterprise should position itself in the value chain before the acquisition, what is the current positioning of the target company and its host country, and whether the M&A can achieve synergy. Global allocation of resources is a matter of following the laws of nature and respecting the facts of resources. For example, where should the R&D centre and the manufacturing and production base be located? If a high-cost production base in Western Europe needs to be transferred to emerging countries such as China or India, how are we to deal with the resistance of trade unions and even the management?

Transferring agricultural production is even more problematic. Due to its climate and topography, China does not have a natural pastoral area. Its winter monsoon climate brings less rain in winter, and if the country is to develop animal husbandry beyond its natural limits, the costs would involve importing animal feed, degeneration of grasslands, etc. This would make the cost of production in China higher than in, say, western Europe or New Zealand, where there are natural farmlands and the climate is mild with plenty of rain; China's environment is relatively poor. Most countries in the world cannot be self-sufficient in every resource. Britain's high latitude is not suitable for planting rice or certain vegetables, so they are mostly imported. Japan and Singapore also lack natural resources, and rely heavily on the global allocation of different produce. Export of abundant resources and import of scarce resources is one of the basic principles of commerce.

6.1.2 Respect for core interests and spheres of influence

Commitment and respect for the scope of business activities is of vital importance for non-wholly-owned acquisitions. It will improve the level of trust between the two parties, which will be mutually beneficial, as well as laying down restrictions on the conduct of both parties after the acquisition. If there is no agreement on these terms before acquisition, leaving it to luck to resolve issues as they occur, this will increase the level of difficulty tremendously. It will also increase distrust between the two parties.

6.1.3 Active communication to establish a positive corporate image

One of the important reasons for analysing risks related to ethical hazards and public opinion in this chapter, is that there is a great difference between the domestic environment in China and the international environment. Domestically in China, companies often respond to questioning from media in a passive manner, and sometimes even more with negative attitudes, such as denying facts, covering up and finding excuses to avoid responsibility. In regions where business culture is more open to public opinion, Chinese enterprises encounter great difficulty in adapting, as they have insufficient experience. Therefore, active and transparent communication with various stakeholders, and sincerely relaying the right message on facts and corresponding solutions, can turn a reputation crisis around and benefit the company by establishing a better corporate image.

As we saw earlier, when Industrial and Commercial Bank of China (ICBC) acquired a 20% stake in South Africa's Standard Bank, it encountered a huge public relations crisis. Now is the time to analyse how ICBC dealt with this crisis.

CASE STUDY:
ICBC ACQUIRES A 20% STAKE IN SOUTH AFRICA'S STANDARD BANK

On 29 October 2007, four days after the announcement of ICBC's investment in Standard Bank Group, Citigroup Global Markets' investment research department released a research report objecting to ICBC's decision to acquire a 20% stake in Standard Bank Group at a price of 136 rand per share. The reasons were outlined as follows:

- Control premium: The 20% stake in Standard Bank Group would hinder the equity acquisition of Standard Bank Group by any other third parties, which means shareholders would lose any future opportunity to control premium; hence shareholders needed to be compensated for this.
- Capital: Standard Bank Group could choose to raise core capital at lower cost instead of by issuing ordinary shares. Even if new shares were issued, warrants should be distributed to all shareholders.
- Negative votes: The 30% premium at 136 rand per share was too low, and shareholders required a price of 161.20 rand per share, or they would vote against the decision.
- Rare value: ICBC needed the infrastructure in South Africa and other regions of Africa. ICBC was also unable to establish its own network, and Standard Bank Group was the only company that could offer both; hence ICBC should pay a higher premium for this due to the rare value it was gaining from this deal.

Millions of South African rand

STANDARD BANK GROUP	2007	2007	2008	2008	2009	2009
	estimated	actual	estimated	actual	estimated	actual
Fiscal year ending 31 December						
Income Statement						
Net interest income	21,794	24,747	25,980	29,448	29,583	31,316
Transaction fees and commissions	14,589	14,511	16,923	17,607	19,462	18,108
Other operating revenues	9,577	10,236	11,119	11,841	12,766	13,404
Total operating revenues	45,960	49,494	54,022	58,896	61,810	62,828
Attributable profit	13,580	16,572	15,541	16,749	17,991	11,996
Balance sheet						
Total assets	1,148,904	1,182,126	1,308,785	1,452,538	1,478,888	1,292,506
Shareholder equity	60,643	68,506	71,424	99,501	83,261	99,369
Return on equity (ROE)	26.90%	24.19%	25.70%	16.83%	25.00%	12.07%
Growth of operating revenue	27.84%	37.67%	17.54%	19.00%	14.42%	6.68%

TABLE 10 STANDARD BANK GROUP'S VALUATION CALCULATED BY CITIBANK, 2007-2009

In overseas M&As, undervaluing companies is rare. If we look carefully at the two financial analysis reports that Citibank released, we can that there is a certain degree of truth in them. The reports' core concept is: Standard Bank Group, as a company with dispersed shareholdings, had good shareholder liquidity. However, ICBC's acquisition of a 20% stake in Standard Bank Group, making it a major shareholder, would negatively affect shareholder liquidity. Large shareholders could directly influence many decisions made by the company, which then creates problems for any future acquisition of Standard Bank Group. Hence, the report suggests that ICBC should pay a higher premium if it wants to buy 20% of Standard Bank Group's shares. Moreover, ICBC is getting rare value in this deal thanks to the unique nature of the Standard Bank Group, and because is difficult for ICBC to find an alternative target, and it cannot easily and rapidly achieve its strategy by establishing branches. When looking at such reports, we need to remove some extraneous political factors.

Table 10 shows Standard Bank Group's valuation calculated by Citibank.

From the contrast between the forecast and actual figures, we can see that the rate of return on assets and the growth rate of operating income are basically aligned with expectations. Revenue growth in 2008 was also consistent with expectations; however, the yield on assets was lower than expected. By 2009, the growth rates of return on assets and operating income were not even half as much as expected. This shows that Citi's expectations from Standard Bank Group were too high, and the stock price was far short of the expected 137 rand (the 2008 financial crisis had affected the growth rate of the index line). The effect on Standard Bank's stock price is shown in Figure 8.

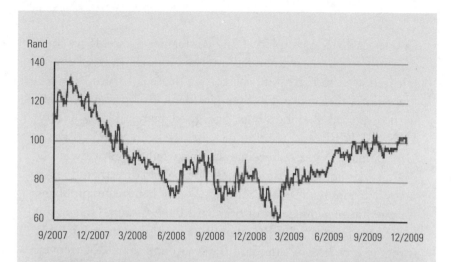

FIGURE 8 STOCK PRICE (RAND) OF STANDARD BANK GROUP, SOUTH AFRICA, SEPT. 2007 - DEC. 2009

The above analysis demonstrates that technically Citibank's analysis was not well founded, and that evaluating in academic terms is much less important than considering how ICBC could persuade its shareholders to vote for the acquisition. In this process, communication with stakeholders plays an important role – it is not enough just to have capital to invest.

When ICBC was suddenly faced with a report like this, there were several strategic options. One was to increase its offer, assuming there was no way to rebut the investors' objections. Another option would be to give up on the deal, if ICBC could not accept the price of 161.2 rand per share and had no other recourse. Jiang Jianqing chose to visit South Africa and communicate with the investors. He gave a speech on the significance of this strategic partnership, and described the future prospects of potential collaboration between ICBC and Standard Bank Group, to an audience of employees and investors. When the chairman of the world's largest bank showed up in front of the investors in South Africa, this drove home to them the importance that ICBC placed on strategic cooperation with Standard Bank Group. Of course, Jiang Jianqing's word alone was not enough – Standard Bank Group also presented some specific and measurable expected synergies at the investors' conference to show that this acquisition was a long-term strategic investment.

Together with Standard Bank Group, ICBC developed a comprehensive communication plan to elaborate the prospects of a win-win cooperation to both internal staff and public shareholders. On 21 November, Jiang Jianqing spoke at the Standard Bank Group's management conference, which was attended by more than 500 managers of Standard Bank Group. Jiang Jianqing emphasized that both banks shared the same vision for globalization in the finance sector, had a common interest in emerging markets, and both cared for the future profitability and shareholder returns of Standard Bank Group. He also expressed his confidence in the management of Standard Bank Group, and said that ICBC would fully support the group. He introduced a strategic cooperation agreement to enhance the confidence of Standard Bank Group's management in this cooperation.

On 23 November, ICBC and Standard Bank Group held an investor conference in Cape Town. Jiang Jianqing; Pan Gongsheng, the then Secretary of the Board of Directors and General Manager of the Department of Strategic Management and Investment Relationships; Jack Maree; and Rob Leith, the then CEO of Standard Bank Group and investment bank business, all publicly spoke at the meeting and answered questions from shareholders. The four were appointed Co-Chairmen and Co-Vice-Chairmen of the Joint Steering Committee of Strategic Cooperation, established by both banks.

Jiang Jianqing explained why ICBC would be a good strategic partner for Standard Bank Group, emphasizing the complementary nature of both banks, the business opportunities and income growth that might come along with strategic cooperation, and ICBC's determination to create value together with existing shareholders of Standard Bank Group. Mali also explained the importance of having ICBC as Standard Bank Group's strategic partner, in view of Standard Bank Group's strategy and the fact that ICBC was a prospective competitive partner.

Leith gave a detailed description of how the bilateral strategic partnership would benefit Standard Bank Group. One of these benefits was the increase in profits of Standard Bank Group by US$40-$60 million in one year and $160-$200 million in three years.[91] The growth would come from five sources:

1. Business and trade between China and Africa
2. Trading and investment banking opportunities in Africa
3. Banking and investment services in Africa for Chinese clients
4. International banking services and investment banking services for Chinese clients
5. Joint global resource funds to invest in mining, metal, oil and gas industries.

On 26 November, Citigroup Global Markets' investment research department released another research report arguing against ICBC's acquisition bid. In addition to reiterating the views of the previous report, the new report also claimed that the premium of 136 rand per share was still too low, even if Standard Bank Group's expected earnings were included.

Finally, on 3 December, Standard Bank Group shareholders voted on the deal. Ninety-five percent of the shareholders voted for ICBC's acquisition of 20% of the shares in the Standard Bank Group for US$5.46 billion. On 24 March 2008, both parties completed the equity and capital transaction. The transaction was marked as the largest foreign investment by a Chinese company at that time, and also the largest foreign direct investment in South Africa.

This is a case study in the importance of communication. Although Citibank's two reports had created something of a crisis for ICBC, Jiang Jianqing promptly communicated with the investors in South Africa about the issue, eventually convincing the shareholders to vote for the acquisition. While the reports caused some obstacles to the acquisition, they also helped to build a rapport between Standard Bank Group and ICBC, and enabled them to complete the acquisition before the financial crisis. This windfall provided Standard Bank Group with sufficient capital to weather the financial crisis. For ICBC, completing the transaction at a predetermined price of 136 rand per share achieved an early strategic advantage in Africa. This cooperation went through rough patches but it finally succeeded for two reasons. First, it succeeded because the transaction did indeed create value for both parties, as shown in the performance improvement of Standard Bank Group promised by its management, which really did serve the best interests of the investors. Secondly, when the chairman of the world's largest commercial bank personally addressed the investors in South Africa, this sincere effort at communication made clear to the investors that the acquisition was a top priority for ICBC, and that they were willing to believe in Standard Bank Group's future with the acquisition.

CASE STUDY:
BIOSTIME AND ISM

It appeared that Biostime's acquisition of ISM (see Chapter 4) was a risk-free deal. However, there were many unknown factors at play after the acquisition, such as getting support from the trade union, convincing the farmers to increase production capacity to meet Biostime's requirements, coping with French media, and increased industry competition.

Of course, cooperation between enterprises demands more than just a paper-based agreement. There were several examples of building trust in the cooperation between Biostime and ISM. Communication with shareholders, media, other clients, and between both companies themselves, surmounted many barriers. As Biostime is a listed company, all its announcements had to follow stock exchange rules. ISM's employees did not yet know anything about this cooperation. It usually takes two years for cows to start producing milk, and in 2015 the EU's milk production quota was about to be scrapped, making the timing rather crucial in 2013. ISM's dairy farmers and management were seriously considering how to sustain market demand after expanding their production capacity. Once the cows started producing milk, if there was not enough market demand, the milk would be wasted. For Biostime and ISM, the most important thing on their agenda then was to persuade the farmers to increase the number of cows.

Following the announcement of a cooperation framework, Biostime's CEO Luo Fei flew to ISM for four meetings: a meeting of farmer representatives (cooperative shareholders), a board meeting, a management meeting and a meeting with the trade union. Thanks to Luo Fei's frank and open attitude and the mutually beneficial nature of the collaboration, all four meetings took place without any major obstacles.

At the meeting of farmer representatives, Luo Fei explained the purpose and prospect of the cooperation with ISM. The farmer representatives questioned Luo Fei at the meeting: "The Chinese are good at bargaining, so will you cut the price of milk once Biostime is in?" Luo Fei said that Biostime was positioned at the higher end of the market, and valued high-quality milk rather than low prices. He promised to sponsor about 20 farmers to visit China each year, and also to send Biostime employees to ISM to study. This personal contact between Luo Fei and the dairy farmers helped build the farmers' confidence, and they later increased their milk production capacity. The contract between ISM and Biostime mentioned cooperation for the next 5 to 15 years, and increasing the capacity would bring long-term and stable economic benefits for the shareholders.

The trade union meeting also passed without many obstacles. ISM's trade union president welcomed Biostime. Biostime's investment would expand ISM's production capacity and create more than 100 jobs in positions such as quality control and product testing, which require technical skillsets and well-educated employees. For a small village in Normandy, creating more than 100 jobs was a big deal.

After the collaboration was announced, a section of the French media questioned ISM's judgement in bringing in a Chinese shareholder, and worried that the local 'jewels' were being 'robbed' by the Chinese. "A Chinese fox is invading the Normandy grassland," claimed one commentator. ISM's director general Daniel Delahaye played an important role in communication with the media.

He repeatedly stressed that the 'jewels' would not be taken away, and as a non-member cooperative shareholder, Biostime could only hold 20% of the shares. They were not entitled to dividend rights, but instead would receive only a low interest income. Delahaye mentioned that this cooperation would expand ISM's share in the Chinese market and thereby create more employment opportunities in France. Cooperative shareholders would increase their income by about €30,000 per person per year. With Delahaye's lobbying and the success of the cooperation project, public opinion in France gradually became positive.

The cooperation between ISM and Biostime also had the potential to affect ISM's other clients. In Europe, these included many well-known brands such as Miso, Nestlé and others. Since these were Biostime's competitors, Biostime's investment in ISM posed a risk to them, especially for companies whose core interest was baby formula. Although Biostime is a major partner for ISM, it takes only about a third of ISM's production, and if the marriage between the two companies resulted in ISM losing its existing clients, this would not be a good deal. So, before ISM signed the cooperation agreement, it requested the approval of its other clients, assuring them that their own formula information would be safe. ISM also reiterated that cooperation with Biostime would improve its production capacity, and Biostime would take 30%-40% of the production after the capacity was increased. The extra capacity could therefore benefit its other clients also. In addition, Luo Fei declared that Biostime had no plans to tap into the overseas market for the time being.

To help its new French partners understand China, Biostime invited ISM's board members to visit. Since many French people have never been to China, this sort of cooperation is invaluable to help them understand the Chinese company better and dispel misconceptions of what the country is like. They visited Biostime retail outlets, talked with Biostime's sales staff, clients and consumers, and all this enhanced their confidence in Biostime and Luo Fei's marketing ability. Delahaye was invited to the annual meeting of Biostime's franchises in Macao, and when he saw the 5,000 participating customers, he could clearly see the potential and vitality of the Chinese market.

Luo Fei was subsequently invited to ISM's 80th anniversary, where Delahaye gave awards to some employees and clients, and the title of 'Chinese Cheese Ambassador' was bestowed on Luo Fei. Interestingly, Luo Fei had never really enjoyed eating cheese before, but after the ceremony he felt honour-bound to eat it, and even came to enjoy it.

6.2   Conclusion

Both the ICBC and Biostime cases involved the core interests of both parties. ICBC handed its business in Africa to the Standard Bank Group, and Standard Bank Group exited other emerging markets apart from Africa. Biostime promised not to access the baby formula information of ISM's other clients, and also made a commitment not to tap into overseas markets for the time being. ISM also promised to provide 30-40% of its expanded production capacity to Biostime. When Chinese companies go global, especially when the target enterprise has relatively greater bargaining power, there must be effort and commitment on common interests from high-level management on both sides – but it also helps to pave the way for future cooperation if the vision is communicated to employees and media, to eliminate reputational risks and assist the post-acquisition operations of the merged business.

Our long-term research shows that internationalization is not necessarily a zero-sum game. If we can design a good framework for overseas mergers and acquisitions, we can work on creating a win-win situation. With China's market size, growth rate and financial environment, if it can incorporate the advanced technology, management experience and branding experience of the West, a win-win situation can be achieved. Success is rooted deeply in mutual benefit and trust, and in the recognition that both parties should strive to maximize economic and social value. We sincerely hope that the image of Chinese enterprises overseas can gradually improve through the globalization process, and that they may have greater awareness of their corporate citizenship and social responsibility.

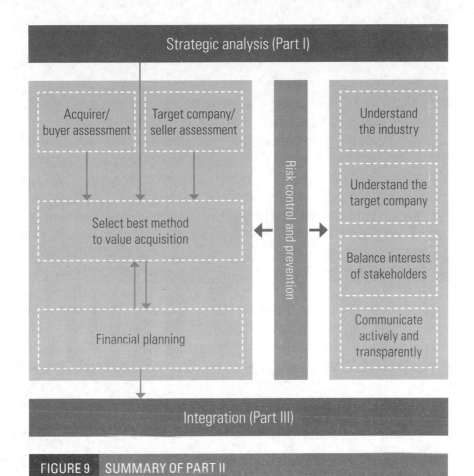

FIGURE 9   SUMMARY OF PART II

PART III
INTEGRATION

CHAPTER 7

INTEGRATION: THE 'LIGHT TOUCH' APPROACH

Many acquisitions around the world fail to achieve their stated objectives, and acquisitions made by Chinese investors are no exceptions. In fact, among M&A consultants the popular '70/70' rule of thumb suggests that 70% of mergers and acquisitions fail to increase shareholder value, and 70% of failures are the result of an inability to integrate the acquired business successfully.[92] Thus, the process of managing an acquired business, which starts as soon as legal documents have been signed, is at least as important as designing a viable strategy (see Chapters 1 and 2), and designing a suitable financial structure for the acquisition deal (see Chapters 3 to 6).

7.1   Classic models of integration

The leading conceptual model guiding post-acquisition management around the world is that of Philippe Haspeslagh and David Jemison.[93] They distinguish two strategic dimensions that are critical for selecting the optimal post-acquisition strategy: organizational autonomy needed by the acquiree, and strategic interdependence between acquirer and acquiree. Based on these two dimensions, they develop a 2 x 2 matrix with four types of post-acquisition strategies: absorption, preservation, symbiosis and shareholding (Figure 10). The absorption model provides the highest degree of integration and the lowest degree of autonomy for the acquired enterprise. The organizational structures, cultures and operations of the parent organization are introduced to the target organization with the aim of achieving a smooth interaction between the two business units. In contrast, the preservation model shows a low degree of integration, so the acquiree enjoys a high level of autonomy. The acquirer barely intervenes in the operations of the acquired company, and allows the acquired unit to develop its own business in its designated markets. The symbiosis model exhibits a high level of integration, but this is achieved by changes in both organizations. Initially, the two parties may maintain their respective operations, culture, etc., and synergies are developed gradually. The shareholding model is suitable for financial investment when there is no intention of achieving strategic or operational synergies between the operations of the two companies.

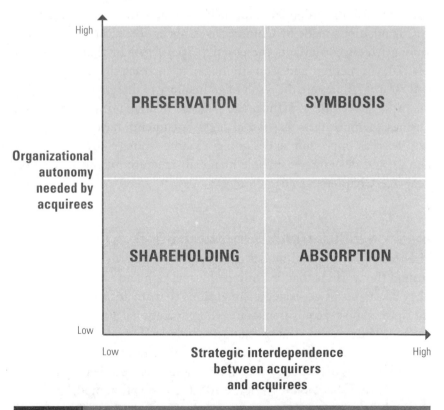

FIGURE 10 MODELS OF POST-ACQUISITION INTEGRATION

Source: Philippe Haspeslagh and David Jemison, *Managing Acquisitions: Creating Value Through Corporate Renewal*. New York: Free Press, 1991. P. 138

During the global M&A waves of the 1980s and 1990s, the quest for new markets has been the leading motive for M&A. In the 2000s, global M&As, notably those led by US multinational companies, have focused on increasing shareholder value by realizing synergies between the two companies, in particular by increasing efficiency and exploiting scale advantages. The appropriate post-acquisition strategy to pursue efficiency gains has typically been the absorption model, which brings together operational resources and minimizes duplication and waste. In the absorption model, the acquirer is leading the acquired company and hence typically replaces the acquiree's leadership team with its own people. The acquiree becomes part of the acquirer, losing almost all its autonomy and adapting to the corporate culture of the acquirer. Representative examples of companies that pursue such a strategy are General Electric and Cisco.

That US companies are more inclined to adopt the absorption model can be seen from the loss of corporate executives after M&As. Already in 1988, a study by James P. Walsh[94] pointed out that in the first year after M&As in the US, about 24% of the executives of the acquired company left; within two years after the M&A, the cumulative executive turnover rate was around 40%; by the fifth year, it reached 59%. By comparison, companies not involved in M&As experienced an average executive turnover rate (including retirement and job-hopping) of 8 to 10% per year. More recent studies find similar patterns. For example, Jeffrey Krug[95] found that the executive turnover rate in acquired companies in the United States after M&A was 36% in the first year, 56% by the second year, and over 70% by the fifth year. To understand the reasons for their departure, Krug interviewed hundreds of executives who had left an acquired company after a merger. His findings suggest that one third of the executives were laid off because the acquirers were replacing the executive team with their own people, while a further third resigned because they foresaw reduced career opportunities in a merged organization now led by people brought in by the acquirer.

As highlighted in Chapters 1 and 2, Chinese and mature Western firms differ considerably in respect of their investment motives. Chinese enterprises conducting cross-border M&As are typically still in the growth stage, and they often acquire mature enterprises to access natural resources, technology or brands. Their own management practices and organizational culture are not (yet) suitable to manage complex operations across multiple countries and locations. Therefore, the absorption model may not be suitable for Chinese enterprises.

7.2   New strategies for emerging markets

Recent studies suggest that many companies in emerging markets adopt an alternative model called 'partnership strategy' instead of the absorption model, and this approach has led to initial successes. This model is close to the symbiosis model, but it places greater emphasis on the partnership between the two sides. For example, Prashant Kale, Harbir Singh and Anand Raman[96] observe that a partnership strategy has been adopted by a wide range of multinationals from emerging economies, including India's Aditya Birla Group, Mahindra Group and Tata Group, Turkey's Hugo group, Brazil's Ambev and China's Neusoft Group. The partnership strategy differs from the absorption model in many critical aspects; Table 11 summarizes the key differences. As the emerging markets situation analyzed by Prashant Kale et al. is pertinent to the challenges faced by Chinese enterprises, the partnership strategy may be more appropriate for them.

	Absorption model	Partnership strategy
Organizational structure	Absorb the acquired enterprise	Keep the acquirees separate
Activities	Integrate core and supporting activities	Selectively coordinate a few key activities
Top executives	Replace	Retain
Autonomy	None/very limited	Near-total
Speed of integration	Rapid	Gradual

TABLE 11   DIFFERENCES BETWEEN PARTNERSHIP STRATEGY AND ABSORPTION MODEL

Source: Prashant Kale, Harbir Singh and Anand P. Raman, "Don't Integrate Your Acquisitions, Partner With Them." *Harvard Business Review* (Dec. 2009).

Our own studies of Chinese MNEs suggest that the post-acquisition strategies of Chinese companies can best be explained by a variant of these conceptual frameworks. Specifically, we suggest focusing on the degree of organizational change taking place in both the acquirer (parent) and acquiree (affiliate) organization. This leads to a 2 x 2 matrix as illustrated in Figure 11 with four types of strategy: 'My Way', 'Your Way', 'Light Touch' and 'Our Way'. The My Way approach envisages the acquirer determining all critical aspects of the acquired firm, similar to the absorption model. This is rare among Chinese acquirers. Your Way may be theoretically interesting when Chinese companies use their financial resources to acquire a company that has superior technological or organizational practices with a view to achieving competitiveness in global markets. However, the approach requires substantive changes in the practices and procedures of the new parent company, which we have rarely seen.

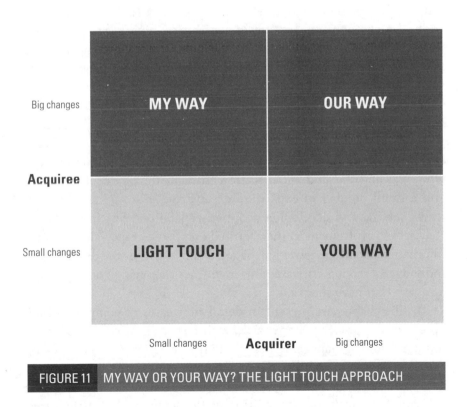

FIGURE 11 MY WAY OR YOUR WAY? THE LIGHT TOUCH APPROACH

Most Chinese acquirers that we have observed pursue the Light Touch strategy. This is well suited for enterprises from emerging economies that acquire firms in developed countries, as the top management teams in developing countries still lack the capabilities in international management, operations and marketing that are required in developed countries. In the longer run, some Chinese investors aim for an Our Way approach, which changes not only the target organization but also the acquirer's own. However, developing an appropriate new organizational structure and culture takes time, so these firms often start with a Light Touch approach that protects the intangible assets of the acquired organization. Thus, as we will see in the next chapter, the path to Our Way tends to go through several stages of integration.

7.3   Four examples of the Light Touch

This chapter presents four cases of acquiring companies that chose a Light Touch approach. In addition to three Chinese cases – AVIC, ICBC and Fosun – we discuss Tata Motors, an Indian company that faced similar challenges, and whose solutions may have inspired many Chinese entrepreneurs.

The essence of the Light Touch approach is to manage acquired capabilities by empowering local decision makers. Recognizing that in the short run, resource transfers and retention are very difficult, investors allow the acquired enterprises to operate independently, while guiding the strategic direction through the board of directors and a small number of expatriate executives. Thus, the emphasis is on preserving and developing acquired capabilities, bearing in mind that active involvement in the acquired company – especially if led by internationally inexperienced managers – might trigger the departure of individuals carrying critical knowledge.[97] As the saying goes, "Beware of assets that have shoes on."

In this chapter we present in detail four cases of companies that opted for a Light Touch approach, with a special focus on aspects of human resource management such as the selection of executives in the acquired company; the balance between authority and control, communication, mutual trust and cultural integration between the two sides; and the acquiree's recognition of the acquirer. We let the cases speak for themselves, before offering our interpretation.

CASE STUDY:
AVIC INTERNATIONAL AND CONTINENTAL MOTORS

China Aviation Technology International Holdings, Ltd (AVIC International) is a large state-owned enterprise, formerly known as China Aviation Technology Import and Export Corporation. Its parent company is China Aviation Industry Corporation. It owns eight listed companies with more than 100,000 employees, assets in excess of 290 billion yuan, and more than 150 overseas business units in over 60 countries. Its core businesses include aviation, trade logistics and high-tech electronics.

Continental Motors was a small American company whose predecessor was established in 1905. It focused on manufacturing aviation piston engines and spare parts as well as related services. Piston engines are used particularly in private and corporate aircraft, while mid-sized and larger planes are normally powered by jet engines. Prior to acquisition by AVIC International, Continental Motors held 44% of the global original equipment manufacturer (OEM) market in piston engines, with 51 distribution centers globally, mainly in North America and Europe. It employed 450 people and achieved sales revenues of US$113 million in 2009. However, the global financial crisis led to a significant decline in the general aviation market in Europe and the US, which significantly affected Continental Motors, which suffered a loss in 2008. At the time, Continental Motors' corporate parent, Teledyne Technologies (Teledyne), also faced financial constraints and decided to put Continental Motors up for sale. In April 2011, AVIC acquired 100% of the equity in Continental Motors from Teledyne.

More than 220,000 general aviation aircraft are operating in the United States today, accounting for 65% of general aviation aircraft globally. The general aviation industry generates more than US$150 billion revenues in the US annually, providing more than 1.265 million jobs. In contrast, China only had 907 general aviation aircraft by the end of 2010, accounting for 0.26% of the global industry. Yet China's civil aviation plan projects that the number of domestic general aviation aircraft will reach 10,000 by 2020, and 15,000 by 2025. Aircraft piston engine manufacturing was essentially non-existent in China, as the engines used there were almost all imported. As AVIC aimed to explore the international market and develop related industries, the acquisition of Continental Motors provided an opportunity to enter the US aviation manufacturing industry, and so strengthen China's domestic aviation business.

RETAINING THE TOP MANAGEMENT TEAM

The original top management team of Continental Motors was made up of six members: the President, four Senior Vice-Presidents (VPs) respectively for Operations, Finance, Technology and Human Resources, as well as the Legal Counsel. President Rhett Ross had worked in the US Navy's submarines for 15 years, and was in charge of engineering and technological management; he then worked as President in Teledyne's energy subsidiary for 7 years. At the end of 2007, Ross was appointed President of Continental Motors. Susan Ames, the Senior VP of Human Resources, started her career by working for the company as a salesperson for many years. As the only female executive in the senior management team, and thanks to her dynamic personality, she also played a vital role in facilitating communication among team members. After Ross had taken over as President, the senior management team had undergone a 'breaking-in period', but by 2009 all members were knowledgeable about the company and the industry. None of the executives held the company's shares; in other words, they were all professional managers.

During the negotiations, President Wu of AVIC International conducted a background check on Continental Motors' executives, and communicated with them at several meetings. He believed in the importance of retaining the acquired management team provided they were suitably qualified:

"We have some principles we follow when acquiring foreign companies. First, the target company should be run by a stable top management team. If the company's executives were to submit their resignation after the acquisition, we would not take it over, as there were no candidates within or outside of AVIC International who would be more fit for the positions. … Second, the executives should identify with our values, ideas and cultural behaviour. Will the target company's corporate culture fit in well with ours?"

After the acquisition, five of the six senior executives continued working at the company, the exception being the Senior VP of Finance, who resigned one year later, stating that he had enjoyed his job at Continental Motors, but his new employer's job offer was irresistible. In addition to company shares and a handsome salary, he saw the prospect of suceeding his new boss, then aged 60, on his retirement. Except for the replacement of the Senior VP of Finance, AVIC added only one executive to Continental Motors' top management team. Ms Tian Shan, Deputy General Manager of the Subcontracting and Manufacturing Division at AVIC, joined Continental Motors as Senior VP of New Business Development, reporting directly to President Ross.

FUSION INSTEAD OF INTEGRATION

AVIC International not only retained Continental Motors' top management team, but also promised not to lay off any employees, to ensure the stability of the company and to keep up morale. President Wu disliked words such as 'integration' or 'control': "Control means you keep yourself away from others. It seems rather rigid. Our culture lays an emphasis on flexibility and fusion."

Under Teledyne's ownership, Continental Motors had been kept under tight control by its owners, especially with respect to cash management. Any cash balance would revert back to Teledyne. After the acquisition, AVIC International gave Continental Motors more autonomy: all major decisions were discussed at the quarterly board of directors (BOD) meeting and AVIC International exerted leadership over Continental Motors through the board, but left the top management team with more freedom in routine operations. Ms Ames, Senior VP of Human Resources, said:

"My decisions are discussed with the entire department to ensure that key personnel are involved. If necessary, I will report to the President. No one tells me that my decision is right or wrong. If there is any doubt, I provide appropriate explanations. My explanations are then accepted. I have complete autonomy."

President Wu regarded AVIC International as an integrated whole, in which each subsidiary was an independent unit. Thus, the parent company had to consider each subsidiary, rather than the other way round. Furthermore, he prohibited bringing the bad habits of state-owned enterprises into any of the overseas-acquired subsidiaries, or conducting inspections for the sake of procedure alone. Thus, AVIC International interfered little in Continental Motors' performance evaluation and incentive system for the top management team, and only made minor adjustments to some indicators. AVIC International also recommended (but did not mandate) the Balanced Scorecard (BSC) system it had put into use. Continental Motors studied the system and decided to adopt it. In the words of Rhett Ross:

"Our old system was focused on manufacturing, so we had to make many adjustments. However, BSC includes all the adjustments we made. It applies to all kinds of businesses, whether engaged in manufacturing, sales or engineering. It's very useful and powerful. ... We would gladly implement it even if it was mandated rather than just recommended, as it was just what we needed."

COMMUNICATION AND MUTUAL TRUST

As the only executive at Continental Motors from AVIC International, apart from her role as Senior VP of New Business Development, Ms Tian had another important responsibility: to facilitate communication between Continental Motors and AVIC, and between the senior management team members. She said:

"I get along well with Continental Motors' top management team members. Before reporting to the headquarters or coming up with some ideas, the members first seek my advice. If their ideas are feasible, they bring them to the BOD meeting. The top management team has no intimate knowledge about business development in the Chinese market. We need to help them contact Chinese companies."

To facilitate coordination, AVIC set up the General Aviation Power Department as a bridge between the parent company, Continental Motors and other airline-related businesses. As head of this new department, Tian also had to help Continental Motors develop the Chinese market. She therefore spent half her time at Continental Motors, and when in Beijing, she would spent every night video-conferencing with Continental Motors' top management team. President Ross described her role:

"It's a tough task to serve as a bridge between two types of cultures and help people from both sides. But she's done it pretty well. ... If one of our employees played the same role at AVIC, things would run even better."

At the same time, Tian helped to improve communications with Continental Motors' top management team. "When they run into difficulties, they often turn to me for help," she said. Ross was seen as a bit of a hard taskmaster, while the other senior executives proved capable, and had their own ideas. Lack of communication thus created friction within the team. In order to alleviate tension, Tian put in tremendous efforts. In one case, Ross had demoted a Senior VP of Technology and cut his salary because he judged him to be inefficient. Without Tian's efforts to mediate, the executive would probably have quit. Upon investigating the situation, Tian found the inefficiency to be due in large part to unreasonable division of work: the VP's responsibilities for new product R&D, production quality control, sales and even after-sales installation did not allow him to focus. Tian suggested that he be left in charge of OEM market development and new technology R&D, a critical area that would bring his strengths into full play. Tian took care to convince Ross that she was not interfering in his work, but trying to offer a helping hand.

President Wu described the relationship between Ross and Tian as follows:

"The American communication style is sometimes too straightforward. And Ross faced difficulties in managing the senior management team on his own. So Tian had to offer her help. ... All in all, what we do is to promote the team's internal communication so that members can learn from each other. A good team should agree to disagree. In spite of our own point of view, we show respect for others. And we need to make the most of our strengths to achieve a common goal."

President Wu presented Ross with a statue of Maitreya, the future Buddha, signalling his hope that Ross could be more flexible and tolerant at work.

For President Wu this approach reflected his leadership vision:

"Many people wonder why we did not replace Continental Motors' General Manager and put in more staff from our side after the acquisition. ... In our eyes, both veterans and newcomers are staff from our side. Besides, whether or not to reshuffle the top management is a matter of trust. If you consider the existing top management team as reliable, you should not doubt their loyalty."

CULTURAL FUSION

Fusion started with strategic planning. Without any mid- or long-term strategic targets, Continental Motors used to draw up a two- or three-year plan. After the acquisition, AVIC International required Continental Motors to make a five-year plan. Furthermore, as three or four key accounts contributed nearly 70% of the company's revenues, Continental Motors had very limited concepts about marketing. AVIC International tried to instil marketing concepts into its top management team. "From my point of view, fusion is created mainly through our culture and ideas. Some major management measures were phased in, instead of being made mandatory," said President Wu.

Ross appreciated AVIC International's strategic acquisition and fusion. He said:

> "Our former parent company regarded us as a cash machine. We were not its core business, so it sold us. But now AVIC International has great expectations for our strategic development. We are working not just for money, but for growth as well. This means we are committed to growth driven by cash. That's the change. We will invest more into new technologies and acquisitions. I think these changes will bring us many benefits."

Thus, for Continental Motors' senior executives an increase in the parent company's share price counted more than the growth of the entire firm or investment in long-term values. AVIC International, in contrast, viewed the acquisition as a strategic investment, paying more attention to the subsidiary's long-term strategy than its short-term cash flow. "Despite having a three-year plan, we put it aside. AVIC required us to draw up a five-year plan geared toward the strategy and vision from both sides. And AVIC offered us a lot of support," said Ross.

To ensure corporate stability and staff morale after the acquisition, AVIC International promised no job cuts. Ross considered this to be too 'kind-hearted': "In the West, a person who performs badly should improve; or else such a person would be fired. If you retain those bad performers, good performers will consider you a weak leader. But AVIC was inclined to retain the staff, regardless of performance." However, he later agreed that in the early acquisition stage, a no-redundancy policy went a long way towards keeping up morale.

Continental Motors employees were also unaccustomed to AVIC International's long-drawn-out meetings to discuss corporate affairs. Susan Ames gave us an example. A mid-level manager had assumed that the meeting he had been called to would end in 15 minutes, but it lasted three hours, and delayed his work.

He complained to her. She asked him whether he had informed the meeting coordinator about his urgent work prior to the meeting; he had not. Ames advised him that he should have informed the meeting coordinator to set his report as the first item on the agenda, as he had some urgent work to deal with – otherwise, he had no right to complain. "So," she continued, "it is important for you to get your ideas across to mid-level managers and staff."

In addition to Ms Tian, AVIC International appointed a junior finance staff member into Continental Motors. Apart from his own job, he helped Tian in her work, and was in charge of receiving visiting AVIC personnel. These dual responsibilities created tensions in the team, as Rhett Ross observed:

> "The Finance Department expected him to perform his duties for finance alone, unaware of the other responsibilities he had to shoulder. His colleagues from the Finance Department thought that he wasn't doing his job well. ... But to be honest, he works very hard. He often picks up official visitors coming in on late-night flights or even during weekends. The staff in the Financial Department, however, cannot understand why he needs to work at nights or weekends."

Local staff found it challenging that they were now part of a company operating across cultures and time zones. As Rhett Ross described the situation: "This does not mean that we need to be 100% Chinese or 100% Western, but that we can be more multicultural." Yet in practice that was not always easy, as Susan Ames observed:

> "We are located in the small city of Mobile [Alabama], and we are not an international company. A large part of my work now is to help our staff address cultural differences. This is the greatest challenge. I give our staff a simple example: the meeting table in China is round, but in the West it is square. This is because Western culture features straightforwardness, while Chinese culture stresses a roundabout way. But these models are only two different approaches."

A SENSE OF IDENTITY

AVIC International's influence on Continental Motors was evident in its working environment. These two companies' logos were placed in the Board Office, the President's Office and other places; photos of senior officials' visits were hung on the walls along the corridors of the office building (a common practice in Chinese organizations); American, Chinese and German flags (AVIC later acquired a German engine company) were placed on senior executives' office tables. "In other words, when you entered the building, you could feel it's your own company," said Tian. AVIC International neither required nor mandated these actions, however, which originated from Continental Motors' sense of belonging and pride.

Changing the company logo reflected Continental Motors' sense of identity with AVIC International and the mutual trust between the two companies. Continental Motors' original logo consisted of V-shaped wings with Teledyne's logo – a maple leaf – in the middle. When designing the new logo, Continental Motors asked AVIC International for advice. However, AVIC declined to meddle in Continental's decision. Continental Motors then sought suggestions from all staff members. After concerted efforts, four designs were shortlisted and submitted to both AVIC International and Continental Motors. The final design featured an eagle soaring high at the centre, which symbolized the United States and echoed the wings in the old design; above the eagle were five golden five-pointed stars, symbolic of star-level service and infused with Chinese elements. Both senior executives and staff at Continental Motors preferred the new design, thinking it more powerful and beautiful than its predecessor.

When the acquisition was first announced, Continental Motors' executives and staff were very concerned that their firm would move to China. Susan Ames recalled: "There were numerous rumours flying about before the acquisition. I kept telling everyone we had a chance to embrace a bright future in a new market." She invited the leaders of the labour union to the acquisition meeting, to convince them that they were in the loop and receiving the same information as everyone else. "The takeover means growth, not a threat," said Ames. "If the company doesn't grow, we will have no jobs. To stay competitive, we need to grow."

Tian's response also provided reassurance: given its present target market in the United States, Continental Motors had no reason to move to China. But she also informed the staff that if its Chinese market grew large enough, the company would set up one or more factories in China. However, they should not worry about any closures. To compete in China, the company would have to trim costs to be more competitive in order to gain more market share, Tian said: "It depends on market forces, and not on any administrative order."

Continental Motors' top management team also realized the importance of continuing to cut costs. After the takeover, they closed their service centre in Long Island, New York because, first, it was a fair way from Mobile and hence costly to manage and, second, due to the market slump, demand in Long Island was too small. Continental Motors gave unionized employees, who made up half the labour force, one more day off per week. Since these employees were paid on an hourly basis, the measure ensured they were still on board during the gloomy economic situation, while the company saved labour costs.

The physical facilities of the 70-year old company were by now showing their age, and needed a facelift. After the acquisition, Continental Motors installed more lights to brighten the offices, brought in new systems to enhance work efficiency, invested in new equipment, introduced new technologies, etc. "Earlier, we never invested in new technologies. Our employees worried about our future. And we had no sense of pride. But what we have done now has increased our staff's confidence and engagement. They are more proud of themselves," said Ross. "In a nutshell, after the takeover, Continental Motors' top management team has put in the utmost efforts. Despite the continued downturn in the market, Continental Motors is faring quite well, with a much higher profit margin," added Tian.

AVIC International was a diversified corporation which mainly focused on foreign trade. It had no manufacturing experience, but was financially strong. When Continental Motors was facing difficulties, AVIC injected capital and waited for the general aviation market to recover, in anticipation of tapping into China's future market potential. Continental Motors' former parent company considered it a 'cash cow', and did not attach much importance to its strategy and marketing. The executive team lacked awareness in this respect, and the company did not develop strategic initiatives. Due to the industry's cyclical downturn, Continental Motors suffered from losses; but it had sound technology and a dependable market, as well as future value-added potential.

AVIC's acquisition of Continental Motors was mainly aimed at its general aircraft piston-engine technology, patents, brands and markets. Continental Motors also had diesel technology, which was felt to be an important future direction for piston-engine development. However, immediately prioritizing the transfer of technical resources would have been problematic, as resources can so easily be lost with the departure of key talents.

The Light Touch partnership strategy works better for a merger of this kind. AVIC International left the operational leadership of the acquired company to the local management team, and provided Continental Motors' executive team with a large degree of authority and autonomy. However, even with this limited direct interference, AVIC International took an active role, developing extensive communication between executives of the two companies, and thereby fostering the development of mutual trust. The influence of AVIC on the operations of Continental Motors came through a combination of governance structures, support for developing the China market, and the presence of one senior AVIC executive 'on the ground'. Ms Tian, as the single Chinese representative in the top management team, had a critical role, and she used soft power effectively to substantially influence not only strategies but, on occasion, operations too. This approach to post-acquisition management was clearly effective: Continental Motors saw a number of strategic initiatives jointly developed, and its financial performance improved. Executives and staff at Continental Motors developed a positive and open mindset regarding cultural differences, and strongly identified with AVIC, which greatly helped the Chinese company to achieve its goal of technology transfer.

CASE STUDY:
ICBC AND STANDARD BANK OF SOUTH AFRICA

As we saw in Chapter 1, Industrial and Commercial Bank of China (ICBC) acquired a 20% stake in South Africa's Standard Bank Group in order to support its customers that were expanding beyond China and needed a banking partner for their overseas activities. Standard Bank was the largest bank in Africa: 1,051 branches in 18 African countries as well as major financial centres in Europe, the Americas and Asia. For more than a decade, Standard Bank had been growing across emerging markets, including Latin America, Asia and Russia. It was looking forward to tapping into the Chinese market, considering China's growing stature and the rapid development in China–Africa trade and investment. Standard Bank established an office in Shanghai and tried to acquire a small bank in China, but found this plan not to be viable.

At the same time, ICBC was hoping to invest in an African bank with a wide presence on the African continent. Standard Bank seemed to satisfy ICBC's requirement. As one of the 'big four' state-owned commercial banks, ICBC pursued global operations through overseas M&As and investments. In terms of business focus, the two banks shared the similar goals. However, ICBC focused mainly on net interest margins, while Standard Bank's advantage was in fee-based corporate and investment banking businesses. Moreover, Standard Banking was one of the biggest providers of precious metals services in the world, a line of business that ICBC intended to enter.

STRATEGIC PARTNERS

ICBC only acquired a 20% stake in Standard Bank, so there were no issues with respect to selecting the executive team, or control and authority. However, ICBC did not simply regard the transaction as a financial investment. Instead, it defined its relationship with Standard Bank as a strategic cooperation based on equity. Before completing the acquisition, the two sides set up a 'Joint Steering Committee on Strategic Cooperation' to guide the cooperation between the two sides. Yang Kaisheng, Governor of ICBC, and Jacko Maree, CEO of Standard Bank Group, acted as Co-Chairmen; Pan Gongsheng, then ICBC's Board Secretary as well as that of the Strategic Management and Investor Relations Department, and Rob Leith, CEO of Standard Bank's Corporate and Investment Banking, served as Vice Co-Chairmen. ICBC's Strategic Management and Investor Relations Department and Standard Bank's Beijing Office were in charge of strategic cooperation.

Following the acquisition of the 20% equity stake, ICBC appointed two non-executive directors to Standard Bank's board. Yang Kaisheng became Standard Bank's Board Vice-Chairman and Non-Executive Director, while Liu Yagan, Deputy GM of ICBC's Strategic Management and Investor Relations Department, also served as a non-executive director.

The Strategic Cooperation Steering Committee and team members on both sides attend an annual strategic cooperation meeting that aims to strengthen mutual trust and cooperation. "At the meeting, we not only draw lessons from the hands-on experience, but also chart a course for future cooperation with a strategic vision," said Zou Xin, Deputy GM of ICBC's Strategic Management and Investor Relations Department. Moreover, ICBC hosted Standard Bank Group's 2013 board meeting in Beijing, to offer its directors an insight into the Chinese bank and China at large.

BOTSWANA POWER STATION PROJECT

As a Botswana government initiative, the 2009 coal-fired Morupule B power station project aimed to boost the country's power generation capacity. One of ICBC's top corporate clients, China National Electric Equipment Corporation (CNEEC), was granted an equipment supply contract for the project. Botswana Power Corporation (BPC) invited bids for a US$825 million financing programme, laying down strict conditions on pula (Botswana currency) financing and hedging as well as on US dollar-denominated export credit. "Some services, such as Botswana pula hedging, were beyond the capability of ICBC and other Chinese banks. Only African banks could handle it; however, few of them had a branch in Botswana," said Shen Min, Deputy GM of ICBC's Special Financing Department.

ICBC and Standard Bank jointly made a successful bid, drawing on ICBC's capital strength and Standard Bank's regional advantages in Africa. ICBC would provide buyer's credit of US$825 million for 20 years; Sinosure and the World Bank would provide a guarantee covering political and commercial risks for 15 and 5 years, respectively; Standard Bank would provide a US$140 million bridge loan, with its global financial market division in London hedging against the exchange and interest rate risks with a currency swap. The deal won three awards in the same year: Africa Power Deal of 2009 by EuroMoney's Project Finance; Africa Power Deal of 2009 by Thomson Reuters' Project Finance International; and Arranger of 2009 by Africa Investor of the Africa Investor Group, an investment consultancy.

The project helped break the dominance of Western banks in financing programmes valued at more than US$500 million in Africa, caused by the limited size and capital of local banks. The backing of ICBC allowed Standard Bank to undertake such a large project, thus gaining a solid foothold in the African finance market. "Given the substantial amount of cross-border financing and the 20-year term, the transaction would have been 'mission impossible' without our strategic cooperation with ICBC," said David Munro, CEO of Standard Bank's Corporate and Investment Banking division.

ICBC and Standard Bank teamed up for many similar projects in Africa. As Wu Bin, general manager of ICBC's International Business Department, explained:

"Acquainted with local laws and regulations, Standard Bank Group clearly knows which projects can generate high earnings or incur substantial risks, offering us a great help. In this sense, our tie-up with SBG has brought us a considerable advantage, as it would be impossible for our branch in Johannesburg to cover the African continent."

GHANA COCOA BEAN PROJECT

Ghana is one of the world's largest cocoa bean producers and exporters. Cocoa beans are harvested once a year. Every year, exporters obtain a one-year pre-export syndicated loan, then purchase the cocoa beans from farmers based on their export orders, paying off the bank loan after export. Initiated in 1993, the syndicated loan rose from US$140 million in 1993 to US$2 billion in 2011/2012. For many years, the syndicated loan had been controlled by a consortium of Western multinational banks.

Jointly with ICBC, Standard Bank Group became a mandated lead arranger for the US$1.5 billion pre-export syndicated loan in the 2010/2011 and 2012/2013 cocoa bean seasons, with other lead arrangers including HSBC and Ghana International Bank. The evolution from a lender to a mandated lead arranger undoubtedly paid dividends for both ICBC and Standard Bank. It was the first time that a Chinese bank had broken into the Ghana market. As a mandated lead arranger, ICBC attached a condition helping Genertec, a Chinese company, to receive a larger share of the cocoa beans' primary market. Previously, Chinese enterprises had sourced cocoa from European and US intermediaries, paying price premiums of around 20%. "The service, which we offered for free, made Genertec more loyal to us," Shen Min pointed out.

Since 2008, ICBC's Special Financing Department has completed 18 joint projects with Standard Bank, issuing loans of US$11.4 billion in total. "Our partnership with Standard Bank Group has made ICBC a local bank in Africa, giving us a considerable competitive edge. We are able to offer more localized services, whether in catering to new needs of existing customers or in tapping into a new market," Shen Min summed up.

CENTRAL BANK OF NIGERIA'S ASSET CUSTODY PROGRAMME

Another example illustrates how the tie-up with Standard Bank benefitted ICBC. In 2011, the Central Bank of Nigeria declared it would convert 5%-10% of the country's foreign exchange reserve into Chinese yuan (equivalent to US$1.6-3.2 billion). The Central

175

Bank of Nigeria entrusted the asset management of these renminbi funds to ICBC.

It is hard to imagine either ICBC or Standard Bank on their own being entrusted with such a large responsibility, given that to manage the fund effectively, knowledge of both the African context and Chinese financial assets is essential. David Munro explained:

"Our partnership with ICBC helped us redefine the proposition we convey to our customers from a product to an event and a process. We are able to enter into a continuous dialogue with customers on what happens in China, how Chinese companies carry out their African programmes, and how Chinese financial institutions bankroll development projects in Africa ... Our negotiation with the Central Bank of Nigeria was a case in point. During the financial crisis of 2009 and 2010, we provided the Central Bank of Nigeria consulting service. When discussing the reserve currency, the Central Bank of Nigeria decided to convert and diversify some foreign exchange reserves in euros and US dollars into Chinese yuan."

PRECIOUS METAL OPERATIONS

Set up in 2009, ICBC's Precious Metal Business Department saw its income surge from 280 million yuan in the first year to 4.4 billion in 2013. ICBC accounted for 50% of the precious metals income of China's four main state-owned commercial banks, handling more than 20% of the trading volume at the Shanghai Gold Exchange. According to the China Gold Association, China's gold production hit 428 tonnes in 2013, while gold consumption amounted to 1,176.4 tonnes. Thus, around two thirds of the gold in China was imported. Domestic supply lagged far behind the soaring demand. "Against this backdrop, it was critical to partner with major precious metals banks worldwide," said Zhao Wenjian, Deputy GM of ICBC's Precious Metal Business Department.

South Africa not only holds the world's largest gold reserve but is also a major producer of platinum and palladium.

Standard Bank's precious metals operations had a long history, dating back to its 1994 acquisition of Ayrton Metals Limited, a UK company dealing in minerals, bulk cargo and structural financial products. In the next decade, Standard Bank acquired related companies, and set up branches or offices in Hong Kong, Shanghai and New York as well as Brazil and Turkey. Thus, Standard Bank had extensive experience in precious metals operations, with a large customer base and an established business model.

ICBC's Precious Metal Business Department cooperated with Standard Bank in its physical gold business in three ways. It sold physical gold from Standard Bank at the Shanghai Gold Exchange, it processed gold from Standard Bank into value-added investment or collectable items (such as gold coins and bullion), and it provided gold-related financing, leasing and inter-bank lending. Thus, for example, a gold mining company could sell future contracts on their expected output of gold to manage risk and stabilize cash flows. "By virtue of Standard Bank Group's rich experience and insights into market trends, we can gear our products toward customer needs," said Zhao Wenjian.

A milestone in the cooperation between the two banks is a joint venture which is under way at the time of writing: ICBC is to take a 60% stake in Standard Bank London's commodity, currency and capital transactions, while Standard Bank Group is to maintain its 40% stake. Sim Tshabalala, Co-Chairman of Standard Bank Group, said:

> "Given a higher capital requirement, we badly need the trading volume. Apart from our expertise, we boast advanced equipment, and excellent risk management skills and capable personnel, while ICBC can bring us the required trading volume. Thus, our tie-up with ICBC will be 'a marriage made in heaven'."

Simon Ridley, Financial Director of Standard Bank Group, also noted that the partnership would elevate the relationship between the two banks to new heights.

SHARING HUMAN RESOURCES

Along with the boom in China-Africa trade and China's investment in Africa, an increasing number of Chinese people were working in Africa. To deliver better services to these customers, Standard Bank planned to recruit Chinese employees at its branches in South Africa, Tanzania, Kenya and Congo. ICBC comprehensively supported Standard Bank Group in this. Wang Wenbin, Chief Representative of ICBC's Africa Office, said:

"Ben Kruger [Executive Director of Standard Bank Group] mentioned that Standard Bank Group was looking to employ Chinese employees in six to seven African countries. They needed to not only speak Chinese well, but also know about Chinese culture and the way Chinese people do business, as well as both banks' product lines and processes. ICBC's Africa Office itself was not sufficiently staffed. My advice was that he should not act hastily as employment involves a lot of legal issues. We are carrying out a pilot programme for sharing human resources in Ghana."

ICBC's Africa office sent one employee to Standard Bank of Ghana to handle local Chinese companies. The employee signed a job contract with Standard Bank of Ghana. While maintaining his original job contract, ICBC's Africa office gave him an option to return to ICBC, and guaranteed that his salary at Standard Bank of Ghana would not be lower than what he was receiving at ICBC, to alleviate any worries over such a transfer.

However, local staff at Standard Bank of Ghana argued that it was inequitable for the employee from ICBC to receive a higher salary than they did. ICBC and Standard Bank of Ghana discussed this issue. Wang Wenbin described the challenge:

"When we proposed providing the employee with a private car and housing allowance, Standard Bank of Ghana flatly refused on the grounds that even its local staff were not entitled to these benefits. After talking with me, Ben Kruger finally gave his consent. To take forward the HR cooperation, Standard Bank of Ghana was ready to foot the bill."

CULTURAL INTEGRATION

ICBC and Standard Bank Group addressed their differences in social and corporate culture in a cooperative manner. For example, the two banks were poles apart in their perception of credit. As a traditional commercial bank, ICBC mainly derives its income from net interest margins. Due to the huge cost of foreign capital, ICBC was inexperienced in 'expanding out', and was inclined towards risk aversion or matching risks and ROI. On the other hand, as an investment bank, Standard Bank derived a higher share of its revenues from fee-based business. Thus, inclined towards high-risk investments, Standard Bank strove to achieve the greatest return with the least amount of capital.

In consequence, ICBC's views diverged from those of Standard Bank Group on lending, percentage of contributions, and allocation of income from intermediary business. After assessing the long-term cooperation prospects and consolidated income on both sides, ICBC was neither inclined to nor capable of clearly allocating profit for each business. Shen Min described these differences:

"We may obtain less profit from this project, but more from the next one; and vice versa. It is the long-term consolidated income that matters most. ... Standard Bank Group has put in place an efficient risk–return ratio assessment system. If the system shows it is unwise to provide loans for a certain project on account of meagre earnings, SBG will choose to charge the service fee only, leaving ICBC to provide funds. We have every reason to believe that Standard Bank Group, which is recommending the project, is confident on risk control, even if its investment is just a fraction."

ICBC continued to try to persuade Standard Bank that capital investment should match earnings for both banks. Despite ICBC's larger size and stronger lending ability, it was a bounden duty for

Standard Bank Group to invest funds in projects; otherwise, ICBC would think that Standard Bank feared an excessive risk. After a period of adjustment, Standard Bank did come around to ICBC's point of view, and tried to align its percentage of contributions with ICBC's.

In view of its own inclination towards risk-aversion, ICBC required Standard Bank to allocate a higher percentage of funds to high-risk projects in Africa. "If Standard Bank failed to make a certain percentage of investment, we wouldn't undertake the project on our own. They agreed with me on this issue," said Shen Min. At the outset, Standard Bank insisted on charging a large chunk of income from intermediary business. Later on, they adjusted and allocated income based on a percentage of contributions, as ICBC also took on other tasks while issuing loans.

INFORMATION SYSTEMS INTEGRATION

The cooperation between the two banks also extends to IT. ICBC and Standard Bank connected the core banking systems in 18 African countries, and conducted long-term cooperation in cash management and international settlements. In 2012, ICBC developed a mobile banking system for Standard Bank. "In two months, we developed the Windows phone banking system. They were highly satisfied with the quality and efficiency," said Ma Yan, deputy general manager of ICBC's IT department. Interested in ICBC's credit card business, Standard Bank Group's credit card team visited ICBC's credit card centre and exchanged ideas about relevant technology and operations. As a further aspect of cooperation, these IT projects helped build mutual trust.

The two banks also differed considerably in their use of IT. Whether in data mining or product coverage, ICBC's independently developed IT system was way ahead of its rivals in the industry. Compared with ICBC's centralized and standardized IT system, Standard Bank's fragmented systems were yet to be fully integrated. Each of its subsidiaries or operational units had adopted its own system and engaged its own service providers. At the same time, Africa was lagging behind other continents in IT, such that Standard

Bank was less motivated to upgrade its IT systems, while heavily outsourcing IT services.

Yet there were also positives to Standard Bank's approach, as Ma Yan observed:

> "Standard Bank's rigorous IT project assessment and decision process provided us with a great deal of inspiration. Our IT process is not as rigorous or complicated, but more efficient, thanks to the remarkable progress of the innovation-driven IT industry in China. In theory, their IT system is more scientific, but it cannot keep pace with the burgeoning financial industry in China."

Owing to these differences in IT culture, ICBC's staff felt that their cooperation with Standard Bank Group was making little headway in IT application, while Standard Bank's employees complained that ICBC exerted too much pressure on them. However, after extensive personal contact, IT staff on both sides gradually became more accustomed to each other's working styles.

DIFFERENT CONCEPTS OF HIERARCHY

The organizations also different in their implicit cultural values, such as the understanding of organizational hierarchies. Ben Kruger, Co-CEO of Standard Bank Group, cited two examples that shed light on differences in the hierarchy concept. The first was about meetings:

> "At a meeting with ICBC, Chairman Jiang Jianqing and I sat at the head of the table, while the others were seated around us; he and I talked to them at great length, while the executives from ICBC didn't voice their opinion until they were invited to do so. At our own meeting, you would not know which participant in the room is a superior and who is a junior, as everyone present can freely speak their mind."

Kruger's second example relates to communication within the hierarchy. Kruger directly telephoned an ICBC employee who had played a pivotal role in a transaction or put forward a unique proposal for Standard Bank Group's IT solution. This approach was rebuked by ICBC's staff who complained that Kruger should have talked with its executives first. "These examples show we should handle these issues more from a cultural perspective to ensure we do not do anything wrong," said Ben Kruger. Indeed, in Chinese organizations lateral communication across different units is often frowned upon as heads of units view it as undermining their authority.

Thanks to the efforts of both sides, these cultural differences did not adversely affect the cooperation. Ben Kruger said:

> "ICBC's staff are capable, diligent and ready to discuss with us. Cultural differences do exist. We also make efforts to learn more about the Chinese language and culture. We need to be more prudent in 'saving face' and addressing hierarchy. We have spent much time learning how to interact with the Chinese company without offending its staff. We think all these considerations are quite important."

Before its investment in Standard Bank, ICBC had already had more than ten years of international experience and had established nearly a hundred overseas branches. It had strong capability in managing and running overseas banking businesses, as well as financial strength. By following existing customers who were entering African markets, to provide them with the value-added services that they needed, ICBC could further enhance its relationship with them.

Standard Bank's executive team had rich management experience, including partnerships around the world, as well as excellent management and operation models. It was in good financial condition, and with ICBC's investment just before the global financial crisis, Standard Bank was able to pull through the years of crisis relatively smoothly. As the largest bank in South Africa, as well as in Africa as a whole, Standard Bank had a strong customer base, extensive expertise and experience in investment banking, and a world-leading precious metals business.

The strategic cooperation with ICBC gave full play to its potential in adding value. Standard Bank's expertise and customer relationships in Africa would have been difficult to transfer, but the partnership approach made it accessible to ICBC.

The limited overlap of the core business along with strategic synergies in specific areas (and the fact that ICBC only acquired a 20% stake in Standard Bank) made the Light Touch the obvious choice for managing the relationship. The two partners attached great importance to communication, mutual trust and cultural integration, and on that basis cooperated on on numerous projects that created win–win opportunities for both sides. In particular, ICBC had established client relationships with major Chinese businesses, along with access to financial resources in China, while Standard Bank contributed its local expertise across Africa.

This model was effective: Standard Bank Group treated their cultural differences with a positive attitude and identified with ICBC, and also attached great importance to their cooperation. Although ICBC only held a 20% stake in Standard Bank, and only two seats on its board of directors, its impact was much bigger than a 20%-shareholder would normally have.

CASE STUDY: FOSUN AND CLUB MED

Headquartered in Shanghai, investment company Fosun Group was a conglomerate aiming to become a leading global business and focusing on China's economic strength (see Chapter 2). Fosun Group's parent company, Fosun International, has been listed on the Hong Kong Stock Exchange since 2007. In 2016, Fosun International reported total assets of 487 billion yuan and total revenues of 74 billion. Fosun has 17 offices in 12 countries and regions, with 55,800 employees.

Club Méditerranée SA, commonly known as Club Med, was founded in France in 1950, and is famous for its 'all-in holiday' resorts and its 'gentle organizers' (G.Os.). G.O.s act as instructors and helpers at the resort, helping guests arrange their schedules, creating a friendly atmosphere to make guests feel genuinely welcome.

Initially developed for France's domestic market, Club Med soon expanded internationally and, since 2004, has repositioned itself from low- and mid-range to high-end markets. However, the global financial crisis severely affected Club Med's business, leading to a loss of nearly €53 million in 2009, and its stock price fell to a record low of €12.60. Yet, while markets in Europe and the United States were shrinking, the Asian market picked up with fast-growing profits, and Club Med decided to develop the Chinese market.

Club Med had explored China as early as 2003. At that time, their main operations were focused on the company's overseas resorts. In 2009, Club Med negotiated separate strategic cooperation in China with Hainan Airlines Group and CYTS Tours, but did not reach any agreement for various reasons (including lack of maturity of the 'all-inclusive vacation' model in China). Fosun noticed Club Med's interest in the Chinese market and, in 2010, obtained a 7.6% stake in Club Med, investing 210 million yuan, which was its first overseas investment.

In the second half of 2010, Club Med launched its first Chinese project, Sun Mountain Yabuli. By 2011, Club Med saw 41% more guests from China at its global properties. The number increased another 30% in 2012, and the resort operator's total earnings in China increased by 33% year on year.

In 2013, Fosun and Club Med decided to work together to launch Joyview, a short excursion programme targeting first- and second-tier Chinese cities. For this purpose, Fosun desired to increase its holdings in Club Med. In May 2013, in association with France's AXA Private Equity, Fosun bid on a first-round takeover offer for Club Med at the price of €17.5 per share. A minority shareholder of Club Med objected to the low price and managed to delay the process. In August 2014, the Italian tycoon Andrea Bonomi joined a bidding war, and announced his offer for Club Med at a price of €21 per share. The take-over battle raged for several months under close media scrutiny, and eventually, after eight rounds of bidding, in February 2015, Fosun bought a 98% stake in Club Med at a price of €24.6 per share for a total investment of €958 million.

In an interview with Reuters[98], Henri Giscard d'Estaing, CEO of Club Med, expressed his happiness to have a "stable and powerful shareholder" like Fosun. "It is we who wanted to have a Chinese partner, because we anticipate that China will become the number one tourism market, and it would not have been wise to go at it alone," he said. "The takeover battle slowed us down. The good news is that we are catching up."

ORGANIZATIONAL INTEGRATION AND GOVERNANCE

After the takeover, Fosun executives – Guo Guangchang, Fosun Group's Chairman, Qian Jiannong, Fosun Group's Vice President and Directing President of the Tourism and Commercial Group, and Xu Binbing, Managing Director of the Tourism and Commercial Group – joined Club Med's board of directors, which has five members in all. Qian Jiannong also joined the Global Strategy Committee. Fosun executives are now involved in setting targets and evaluating performance, while Fosun's capital department works with Club Med in handling critical financial negotiations with banks, and Fosun's internal audit team conducts annual internal audits of two or three of Club Med's business units. Beyond these governance processes, the executive management team has remained largely autonomous.

In the post-merger integration, Fosun laid great emphasis on 'coordination'. Fosun sent only two staff members (one from Fosun Group and one hired locally) to Club Med's headquarters to collect information and to coordinate and communicate between the two organizations. Club Med's original executive team remains substantially unchanged, apart from the merger of the marketing and digital promotions departments, which were headed by a newly appointed VP. The merger of these two departments greatly improved the degree of digital marketing at Club Med. On the other hand, the CEO of Club Med became Fosun's global partner.

In addition to its group headquarters in Paris, Club Med has three other headquarters: one for the core area (France, Belgium and Switzerland), a regional headquarters for Europe and Africa, and an operating headquarters. After the takeover, Club Med streamlined its Parisian staff and eliminated redundant stores, salespeople and some call centres which did not reflect digital marketing trends.[99] A total of 210 employees were laid off, while more than 100 new jobs were created. Facing pressure from the labour unions and the French government as a result of this adjustment, Fosun prioritized effective dialogue with both. In addition, Fosun took the initiative in communicating with local media, and hired a local PR firm to coordinate media relations. As a result of tactful and positive PR, the local media coverage of the matter was at worst neutral, and at best somewhat favourable. The adjustment was expected to save Club Med about €5.5 million per year.

PERFORMANCE GOALS FOR TOP MANAGEMENT

Club Med's original incentives system did not provide effective motivation for the management team: the management held options at an exercise price of €30 to €40, while the stock price had been just less than €30 before 2008; hence the options were meaningless. After the acquisition, Fosun introduced a new incentive mechanism for the management team. A total of 120 Club Med executives and managers were self-financed into an equity incentive programme, and many of them have invested the amount of their annual salary, while the CEO and CFO have put in €2 million.

In terms of setting performance goals and evaluation, all of Club Med's management indicators are divided into two categories: the company's financial performance, and individual performance corresponding to various management positions. The company's financial performance has four major indicators: earnings before interest, taxes, depreciation and amortization (EBITDA), free cash flow, revenue, and net profit. Executive pay has become heavily performance-based. The CEO, for example, would receive a bonus as high as their annual salary in case of 100% achievement of performance targets. If performance rates reached 80% to 100%, bonuses would be adjusted as appropriate;

less than 80% indicates that no bonus would be given. In case of performance in excess of the set target, the maximum bonus could reach 175% of annual salary. For the CFO, payment of a bonus equivalent to 80% of annual salary would be considered if 100% of the performance target is achieved, while VPs and directors of business units are paid at a ratio of 50%, and so on.

OPERATIONAL REFORM

After studying Club Med's business operating system, Fosun initiated reforms in two key areas. First, Club Med's procurement costs had been excessively high and had to be optimized. For example, when Club Med purchased uniforms for their resort staff, they went through European brokers to contact middlemen in China, who finally bought the uniforms from a Bangladeshi supplier. After the reform, the purchasing cost of uniforms was reduced by 55%, as Fosun's trading subsidiary, Yuyuan Tourist Mart, bought them directly from Chinese suppliers.

Second, Club Med's pricing system was too inflexible. For more than a year, they applied the same price worldwide. This suited French travellers' tendency to plan their holidays a year ahead of schedule, but such a pricing system can lead to a loss of customers and diminish profits during peak seasons. Thus, Fosun hired Boston Consulting Group (BCG) to help develop an optimized pricing system. The new system is more flexible, and uses different pricing strategies based on the preferences of customers in different regions. For example, in North America, pricing is adjusted on a quarterly basis, with additional price reviews before major holidays; while in China, pricing is adjusted on a monthly basis. Club Med increased its revenues by tens of millions of euros with the new pricing system.

SYNERGIES: NEW RESORTS

Fosun helped Club Med to develop its resort business in China with networks, resources and real estate. Since 2011, Club Med has added five new resorts in China at the following locations: Yabuli (northeast China); Guilin, a south Chinese city known for its dramatic landscape of limestone karst hills; Dong'ao Island (a tropical island in Zhuhai, South China); Sanya (the southernmost city on Hainan Island); and Beidahu (a downhill ski resort located outside the city of Jilin in the northeastern province of Jilin). None of these were new constructions: all were existing projects selected for Club Med by Fosun. Yabuli Resort, for example, was originally established as China's first ice-and-snow centre. However, it suffered from a major disadvantage of geographical location: it took three and a half hours by car to reach Yabuli from the nearest large city, Harbin. In extreme winter weather, snow and ice would add another two hours; temperatures may drop to -20°C. Business was poor under the original owner. However, after Club Med took over the operations, the business revived. Occupancy rates soon exceeded 40%. Beidahu Resort in Jilin Province opened for business at the end of 2016, by which time it had pre-sold 60% of its rooms for the coming year. Occupancy in the first week of trial operations exceeded 95%.

Fosun and Club Med both invested to strengthen Club Med as a ski resort brand. The plan was to further integrate existing ski resorts worldwide – partly through the closure of smaller, low-end resorts and their replacement with large-scale, high-end ones – as well as to build new ski resorts in greenfield areas. For example, Fosun helped Club Med build a ski resort with more than 400 rooms within the Tomamu Resort of Hokkaido, Japan. The Tomamu Resort was invested in by Yuyuan Tourist Mart, a subsidiary of Fosun. The resort was scheduled to open by the end of 2017. Samoëns Ski Resort in Grand Massif, France, also due to open in late 2017, offers a grand 360-degree view of the Alps and is only an 80-minute drive from Geneva Airport.

SYNERGIES: DEVELOPING THE CHINESE MARKET

Before its acquisition by Fosun, Club Med was heavily dependent on the European market, from which it derived 70% of its revenues. With the support of Fosun, Club Med has been able to further diversify and stabilize its revenue sources. Three types of initiatives stand out:

1. In China, the marketing strategy shifted from individual travellers to corporate key accounts. Fosun recommended accumulating key accounts, by means such as exhibitions and conferences. In addition, they introduced some key clients to Club Med, such as the Zhejiang Provincial Chamber of Commerce, the Chinese Entrepreneurs Association and other organizations. With these initiatives, and the aforementioned new resorts, China became the second-largest market for Club Med.

2. Club Med created new opportunities for transcontinental travellers while increasing year-round occupancy rates at its resorts. For example, Chinese tourists usually avoid travelling to the island province of Hainan in the summer, due to its hot weather. Yet, for European tourists, summer is the perfect season for beach and resort vacations. Therefore, Club Med used its global sales channels to guide more European tourists to Sanya. On the other hand, Club Med's two ski resorts in China and the one resort in Hokkaido, Japan, attract more Australian ski enthusiasts. As of the end of 2016, Australian visitors at Club Med's Asian ski resorts had increased by 173% from 2011. "The tourism industry is becoming more and more globalized; and because of the seasonal nature of tourism, the global layout helps reduce the seasonal impact of tourism," Qian Jiannong pointed out.

3. Cooperation between Thomas Cook (a leisure travel group from the UK) and Club Med created opportunities to grow the European customer base. In 2015, Fosun acquired a 5% stake in Thomas Cook, later increased to 11%. Then Fosun set up a joint venture in China with Thomas Cook, with a share ratio of 51% to 49%. Thomas Cook is the world's oldest travel agency, serving more than 20 million customers a year. Club Med complements Thomas Cook, especially in customer composition: Club Med leads the market in French-speaking areas of Europe, but is relatively weak

in Germany, the UK and the Nordic countries. At the same time, Thomas Cook serves these countries and regions with its extensive sales network and customer base. The cooperation between the two companies enables customers to book trips to Club Med via Thomas Cook's branches.

REORGANIZING THE FOSUN GROUP

In 2016, Fosun set up a Tourism and Culture Group that included all the tourism and cultural assets of the Fosun group, including Club Med, Thomas Cook, and Fosun's assets and resources in its Hotels and Scenic Investment Management Company, its Performing Arts Company (still under development), and its City Mini Club and online travel agency platform. The CEO of Club Med was named Vice-Chairman of the new group, and Club Med's CFO is a member of the group's executive team as well.

The Tourism and Culture Group brought major projects together under the one umbrella of the Fosun Group, enabling the concentration of operations such as government affairs, land auctions, project bidding and so on. Enhanced internal cooperation between the group's affiliated businesses was to generate new business opportunities. Club Med's Tomamu Ski Resort, which is supported by Yuyuan Tourist Mart, is an example of such synergies.

Fosun's Tourism and Culture Group has also launched a talent-training programme. In collaboration with the Shanghai Institute of Tourism (SITSH), two classes of students are enrolled in a cooperative education programme with Club Med. After graduation, students sponsored by Club Med will work as G.Os or village leaders at Club Med resorts.

CULTURAL FUSION

In order to promote cultural fusion, Fosun has introduced a series of activities and initiatives. For example, in its early phases, Club Med was an energetically entrepreneurial organization, creating the 'all-inclusive' model, and was the first company to invest in resorts in the then-unfamiliar tourist destinations of Cancún, Bali and other places. However, in the process of business growth, the spirit of entrepreneurship gradually vanished. Fosun hopes to revive entrepreneurship at Club Med by initiating various cultural activities.

Club Med had well-established processes of international transfer for their G.Os, partly due to the seasonality of resort business that requires manpower to be deployed when needed. Moreover, transfers across resorts provided a variety of experience and practice for G.Os. New initiatives were launched to encourage regional teams to facilitate mobility and transfers, while promoting collaboration among functional sections across regional borders. For example, Club Med China's Director of Finance knows the financial situation of the entire company, whether the headquarters finance department is conducting financial restructuring or other measures, and hence can judge how best to cooperate with them in China.

Fosun's corporate culture values 'positive initiative', 'accommodation' and 'self-closed loops'. That is, upon encountering a problem, employees are expected to take the initiative to understand the problem, use all accessible resources of the company to solve the problem, and promote collaborative development. Club Med's units, however, act autonomously, like the Chinese saying, 'only clearing away the snow in front of one's own door'. This has actually led to some odd situations: for example, when Greater China had an IT problem, they asked the France IT headquarters for help – though as a matter of fact, in special areas such as IT or digital marketing, China is more advanced than France. As Fosun corporate culture has been introduced since the acquisition, Club Med China's employees are not only encouraged to solve these kinds of problems on their own, but also to share the experience with their French colleagues.

Fosun Group is an investment company focusing on China's economic strength, and concentrated in the principal investment areas of 'big consumption' and 'big finance'; whereas Club Med is a tourism business that suffered business losses as a result of the global financial crisis. Both revenue and profits fell dramatically in Europe – Club Med's main market – and the United States, while at the same time the market rebounded strongly in Asia, especially in China. The two sides had complementary needs, and the pairing also suited Fosun's strategy of "China's dynamic grafting of global resources". Fosun took a Light Touch approach to integration. It maintained Club Med's original executive team and provided them with a high level of autonomy in daily operations. The integration process emphasized coordination, and there were operational reforms in only two key operational aspects: procurement and pricing.

Fosun saw itself as a supporter and facilitator, providing all kinds of backing and resources to Club Med, including capital, real estate, market and customers. It integrated the resources of different businesses within the Fosun group by establishing the Tourism and Culture Group, which was expected to generate further synergies for Club Med. Thus, despite limited direct engagement in the leadership of Club Med, Fosun contributed in multiple ways to helping Club Med to turn around its business onto a profitable growth path by 2016.

CASE STUDY:
TATA MOTORS AND JAGUAR LAND ROVER

The final case study of this chapter concerns an Indian company rather than a Chinese one. However, in studying this company, Tata Motors, we found many similarities to the challenges and operational solutions developed by Chinese companies. Thus, arguably, the acquisition of Britain's Jaguar Land Rover (JLR) by Tata Motors represents a prototypical example of the Light Touch model of post-acquisition management. Before telling the story, however, we should acknowledge one important difference. The cultural differences between the UK and India – or at least between the business elites of these two countries – are substantially less than those that Chinese investors face in most of their overseas ventures. This is because of the historical heritage and legal system that these two countries share, not to mention the many Indian business leaders with a British education.

Tata Motors is a subsidiary of the diversified Indian conglomerate Tata Group. Jamsetji Tata founded Tata in 1868. The company inherited the founder's spirit of charity, and has long been one of India's most respected enterprises. The Tata Group operates in seven major business segments: engineering machinery, materials, information technology, services, energy, consumer products and chemicals. Its main subsidiaries include Tata Steel, Tata Motors, Indian Hotels and Tata Power. It has over 100 subsidiaries in 80 countries, of which 32 are listed companies.

Tata Motors was founded in 1945 and grew into India's largest automobile company. Tata Motors is also one of the world's top heavy and medium-sized truck manufacturers, and the world's fourth-largest heavy and medium-sized bus manufacturer. In 1998, Tata Motors entered the field of passenger cars, and is currently ranked second in the Indian market. The best-known models are its independently developed and designed Indica and Indigo, as well as the world's cheapest car, the Nano. In 2007, prior to the acquisition of JLR, Tata Motors' sales were US$7.2 billion, and the company had 22,000 employees.

Established in 1922, Jaguar was originally a motorcycle sidecar manufacturer. The brand became known especially for the superior performance of its racing cars. In 1960, Jaguar was incorporated into the British Motor Corporation, and it went through several ownership changes until it was acquired by Ford in 1989. However, Jaguar did not make a profit from the time it was acquired by Ford.

Land Rover was founded in 1945, and was mainly known for its rugged four-wheel-drive vehicles. In 1966, Land Rover was acquired by the Leyland Motor Group, and after several ownership changes it too was acquired by Ford in the year 2000. In 2002, Ford merged Jaguar and Land Rover to create Jaguar Land Rover (JLR).

Tata Motors acquired JLR in 2008 when Ford was facing financial difficulties due to the global downturn. Since Jaguar and Land Rover were both famous high-end British automobile brands, while Tata Motors was a low-end manufacturer from India, the media and investment banks universally expressed concern as to how two of Britain's most iconic brands would survive and develop under the management of an Indian company.

THE ACQUIRER'S POSITIONING

Prior to the official acquisition of JLR, Tata Motors made three commitments:

1. Jaguar and Land Rover would maintain their British brand identities and be manufactured in Britain.

2. There would be no layoffs for three years, and agreements with the trade unions would be kept with respect to employee compensation packages, including pensions and outsourcing terms. In exchange, JLR employees accepted a 25% cut in their wages.

3. Until 2011, JLR would continue its original business plans, which included the launch of some new vehicles, while lowering the dependence on developed markets (which accounted for 80% of JLR revenue at that time) by increasing sales revenues from emerging markets.

Although it had acquired a 100% stake in JLR, Tata Motors viewed itself as more of a strategic investor. It did not seek synergies as the product portfolios and target markets of the two companies were totally different, which meant that they neither shared any parts nor had overlapping staff positions. The original JLR top management team remained, and Tata Motors only sent one executive, its CFO, to JLR. Ralf D. Speth, then CEO of JLR, spoke highly of the new CFO: "He is a very senior and experienced manager … With his experience, he helped to train our organization to become independent, especially in the years 2008, 2009 and 2010 … He is very cultivated, nice, refined and wise. He trained our finance managers very well."

Tata Motors' positioning as a strategic investor was reflected in aspects such as human and financial resource management. JLR set up a five-member supervisory board, with Tata Motors' chairman as its chair and three further members from Tata Motors. The top management team held official meetings with the supervisory board four or five times per year. Tata Motors' top executives devoted time to JLR. Ravi Kant, Vice-Chairman and Managing Director of Tata Motors, visited JLR twice every month, staying three to four days each time. Ratan Tata, Chairman of the Tata Group, visited JLR regularly, attending meetings and even visiting clients with JLR's top management team.

Tata Motors did not take any dividends from JLR for the first three or four years. Instead, it made a huge investment into JLR, injecting £500 million in the first year, followed by £1 billion, £2 billion, and £3.5 billion in the following years. Even after JLR had repaid all of its debt in 2011, Tata Motors still kept most of JLR's profits in the company, and only took a small amount of dividend. "If you compare our dividends with our competitive car companies, we pay very little. That gives us the opportunity to invest more in the future," commented Speth.

TURNAROUND EFFORTS

Tata Motors supported several major measures to help turn JLR around. In the first months, Tata Motors established a cash flow management system at JLR, hired financial services company KPMG to manage the system, and sent people from its finance department to direct the process, to ensure the company's liquidity.

The second measure was cost reduction. Tata Motors brought in consulting firm Roland Berger to formulate an aggressive cost reduction proposal. Roland Berger had done similar cost reduction projects for numerous European and Japanese companies, and it would have been difficult for JLR to reject the plan by such a prestigious consulting company. "It was a proposal that involved an extremely large cost reduction plan, which shocked the company at that point of time. There was huge reluctance. However, we explained to them, and the company gradually started to implement it," recalled Ravi Kant. In fact, Tata Motors was drawing on its own experience 14 years earlier, when it had incurred losses and then become profitable again after two years of a radical cost-reduction plan. However, such a plan could not be executed by external agents; it had to be driven internally. Tata Motors helped set up about ten cross-department teams within JLR to push the plan ahead, and these teams reviewed progress twice a month. Thanks to this plan, it took JLR only six to seven months to achieve the turnaround target and reach the break-even point.

Tata Motors helped JLR to implement these two initiatives by establishing a rigorous evaluation–feedback system. Kant focused on leading the top-tier management team of 10-15 people, while trans-level meetings and informal 'town hall' meetings were held every six months. The evaluation–feedback system aimed to pass on the message that the management team needed to be held accountable for the company's performance and that the company needed to rely on itself for the future.

THE FACILITATORS

"We said, 'Look at this. It is your company. It is your destiny. How can you take it forward? We are the facilitators.'" Kant's words were at the core of Tata Motors' approach in integrating JLR. This approach had helped Tata Motors to turn around South Korea's Daewoo Commercial Vehicles, which it had acquired in 2004. Tata Motors gave JLR's top management team a high degree of autonomy in terms of operating the company. Tata Motors motivated the management team with both long-term incentives (phantom shares linked to Tata Motors' performance) and short-term incentives (performance bonuses linked to key performance indicators). The Transformation Office, which continually monitored the progress of the company's transformation process, consisted of people from both JLR and Tata Motors.

The leadership team of the Tata group trusted the JLR management team, offered them extensive support and maintained regular communication. The top teams of both companies visited each other on a regular basis. JLR's CEO noted:

"Mr Cyrus Mistry [Chairman of Tata Group, 2012-2016] trusts that we can deliver. This changes behaviour. We have to take over responsibility of ownership. And the responsibility from the leadership team goes down to the lower ranks. It also changes the culture. It means you have to think the unthinkable. ... We have a very close relationship with the Tata Group. And it helps a lot... There is transparency between us, across the entire hierarchy. With this kind of active transparency, we can save a lot of time, and we have a very fast decision-making process."

The approach worked. It raised the JLR team's self-esteem, which had been low during the unsuccessful years of Ford ownership. Says Speth:

"All of a sudden, we got the freedom to decide our future. We clearly recognized that there was no way we could get over one billion pounds every year from Tata. We had to define our mission and strategy. We had to move a little bit faster to do both, restructuring and preparing for additional growth. We also had to communicate in the right way to involve the people behind us."

Tata Motors' successful turnaround efforts also made JLR employees realize that the organization's interests coincided with their own. Both Jaguar and Land Rover had a complicated M&A history, so JLR employees had reasonable concerns regarding Tata Motors' acquisition. Ravi Kant acknowledged this:

"You work in a certain company. You like the brands and products, but there is a huge amount of uncertainty. It can be very annoying and brings about uncertainty and unpredictability to your career. Therefore, people can take the view that doing anything is useless, as anyway the company is going to be bought by somebody, and that they will also soon be gone. Many people had the same view of Tata's acquisition. We needed to find ways to remove these views, and enable the majority of people in the organization to eventually realize that what is good for the company is also good for them."

RESULTS OF INTEGRATION

Six years after being acquired, JLR doubled its output from 200,000 to 400,000 cars, and more than tripled its revenue from £6 billion to £19.5 billion, with employees increasing from 16,000 to 32,000. It was rated one of the best employers for college graduates in the UK by *The Guardian* newspaper. CEO Speth attributed JLR's success to Tata Motors' management philosophy: long-term orientation, trust, mistake tolerance, entrepreneurial spirit, and strong cultural values for employees and society. "Mr Ratan Tata made it happen, and made further investment so that JLR could survive. Without Tata, JLR would not exist any more," he said. Not only the management team but employees across the company felt grateful to Tata for having trusted their abilities and guided their efforts.

Tata Motors' core car business is low-end economy cars; its parent company Tata Group has strong financial resources, and has a strong sense of social responsibility; Tata Motors' top team has rich experience not only in management but also in post-acquisition integration. In its due diligence before acquiring JLR, Tata Motors found that JLR had quality problems, but had been rapidly improving, with a strong pipeline of new products in development. It had a strong foundation in automotive engineering and design, which could enable the development of new products; it had a network of loyal dealers; and the Jaguar and Land Rover brands were powerful. In other words, despite suffering losses for a long time, JLR had intrinsic assets, with potential to add value.

Tata was aware of two primary limitations of its own: it was a company from a developing country acquiring a company from a developed country; and it was a low-end car company buying a high-end car company. Therefore, it needed to rely on reputable external third parties to gain credibility among the acquired businesses, which was why it hired KPMG and Roland Berger to help develop turnaround plans. Tata Motors had successfully acquired and integrated South Korea's Daewoo Commercial Vehicles, so it expected to replicate this experience. The model used to manage Daewoo Commercial Vehicles and JRL corresponds to what we call the Light Touch partnership strategy. Tata Motors positioned itself as a 'facilitator' and a 'strategic investor' from the outset. It retained JLR's identity and brands as well as its executive team, who were given great autonomy. It maintained active communication with the team.

Compared with the Chinese enterprises discussed in this chapter, Tata has been more directly involved in the acquired business, notably by establishing strong governance and incentive schemes, and by introducing actionable strategic plans to address the core concerns of the company – specifically cash-flow management and cost reduction. But Tata stayed out of operational management. Ultimately, Tata Motors enabled JLR's own leadership team to turn JLR around.

7.4   Conclusion

Many Chinese companies conducting cross-border mergers and acquisitions face similar challenges to those addressed by Tata Motors, in that they have significant gaps in their own capabilities – notably international management capabilities. These gaps make it more challenging to acquire a company in a developed country. Intangible assets such as technology and brand, that are difficult to transfer once acquired, could easily be lost if key talents leave the company. The Light Touch approach offers a solution to this challenge. It allows the acquirer to keep the acquired company localized, while respecting its corporate culture and supporting its managerial talent.

If the acquired company has a certain degree of management ability, with a great potential for adding value, then the Light Touch partnership strategy may be the most suitable approach to integration. On the other hand, when the acquired company is in urgent need of strategic change, lacks a competent management team, or is an incomplete organization (as in carve-outs of business units from existing organizations), then the Light Touch is likely to prove insufficient.

From the point of view of human resources, the essentials of the Light Touch cooperation model include:

- retaining the original executive team of the acquired company
- maintaining the independence of the acquired company
- giving a great degree of autonomy to the executive team
- emphasizing the need to build communication and mutual trust
- paying attention to cultural integration between the two parties.

However, our case studies also show that even without direct involvement in the acquired firm's management team, Light Touch acquirers can shape the acquired company through 'soft power', provided that managers at the interface between the two organizations are culturally sensitive and ready to act as bridge builders.

CHAPTER 8

VIA TRIAL AND ERROR TO 'OUR WAY'

The Light Touch approach is suitable for many of the cross-border acquisitions undertaken by Chinese investors in recent years, but not for all. If the acquired company is too weak, or if the acquirer envisages the realization of major operational synergies, then a more active involvement may be necessary. Thus, some Chinese investors by design or necessity have developed an Our Way approach to integrating their historical operations with newly acquired ones. Due to the relative novelty of cross-border acquisitions for Chinese businesses, such an integration has often evolved over several stages of trial and error.

8.1   Stages of integration

This chapter explores two companies that have already gone through multiple phases in their post-acquisition integration, with some initiatives being more successful than others. The first case explores how Four Dimensions tried to integrate its British joint-venture partner, while the second case investigates Lenovo's integration approaches at different stages. The discussion considers aspects such as selecting the executive team of the acquired company, maintaining a balance between authority and control, establishing communication and mutual trust between the two sides, integration of both parties' cultures, and the acquired company's identification with the acquirer.

CASE STUDY:
FOUR DIMENSIONS AND JOHNSON SECURITY

FIRST STAGE

As discussed in Chapter 1, Four Dimensions, a Chinese manufacturer of security vehicles, first established a joint venture with Britain's Johnson Security, and later gradually acquired all of its shares. Initially, the executives of Four Dimensions-Johnson Industries Group (FDJI) were mainly from Four Dimensions. Most of them were also its founding members, who had started the company with CEO Wang Yan, and had been working for the company for eight to ten years. The position of HR Director remained vacant for a long time as the company did not place a high value on HR management. The founder-management team was very loyal to the company, but had its limitations. For example, in 2001 the Board of Directors suggested bringing in Johnson's advanced technology, management philosophy and information system to improve FDJI's productivity and management, but they faced a lot of resistance by some senior executives who feared that such a change would impair their personal interests. Consequently, the proposed change was not fruitful. The company had no other choice but to restructure the top management. As it was difficult to identify the right people, FDJI experienced frequent change in its management team. In spite of continuous business growth, FDJI failed to build a stable and effective management team, and lacked people able to lead Johnson's post-acquisition integration.

When Four Dimensions acquired Johnson in 2007, Johnson's General Manager resigned. Wang Yan then assigned two Chinese executive directors to handle HR and finance, and production and operations, respectively. One of them was a management consultant, the first Chief Representative of Roland Berger China and founder of Bexcel Management Consultants, who later became Vice-President of Capgemini. The other was a senior professional manager who had worked at General Motors for a decade, overseeing its supply chain. However, the two Chinese appointees found it difficult to communicate with Johnson's management team. The former believed in the philosophy "I am here to tell you what to do," whereas the latter felt: "You don't know anything about Johnson. How can you tell us what to do?"

Most of Johnson's British employees resisted the acquisition by Four Dimensions as they did not trust the company. "The Chinese will learn everything that we know. And when they are finished, they will get rid of us and transfer everything to China," said a British employee, probably representing thie views of many of his colleagues at the time.

During the strategic planning process, a major disagreement emerged. Four Dimensions wanted Johnson to improve its financial situation as soon as possible, whereas Johnson's executive team insisted that they needed more time to achieve Four Dimensions' goals. For example, Johnson used a time-rate salary system, whereas Wang wanted Johnson to change to a piece-rate system. He proposed that 90% of Johnson employees' total salaries be fixed, and the remaining 10% be a variable component based on performance. This proposal was strongly opposed by Johnson's executive team. Johnson's HR manager Peter Harwood said:

> Mr Wang Yan believed that as long as we told employees "from today on we will use a piece-rate salary system – 90% is fixed, 10% is variable," it would be alright. But we can't do things this way in the UK. We have to first communicate and negotiate with employees. Only when they agree, can we do it. It will be a time-consuming and difficult negotiation, but Mr Wang didn't understand it. He thought, "I am the owner of the company, so why can't I do it?"

As the disputes between Four Dimensions and Johnson's top management escalated, several of Johnson's senior executives resigned. Four Dimensions had to recall its two executive directors. In summing up the experience from the acquisition, Wang Yan said:

"The first year after an acquisition, especially the first three months, have a great impact on its success. But we made a lot of mistakes in the first three months. In this stage, communication between the two sides is very important. There should be a well-designed plan to communicate with executives and employees of the acquired company. We should give them a bright future and win their trust."

SECOND STAGE

In October 2007, Wang Yan appointed Johnson's Technical Director, John Field, as Acting General Manager. He had worked at Johnson for more than three decades. At the same time, Yan Zhuohui was dispatched to Johnson to head the integration process. An MBA graduate from Oxford, Yan had previously worked at Procter & Gamble as a Production and Supply Chain Manager, and had also led an enterprise resource planning (ERP) project at Deloitte Consulting. Unlike the previous two executive directors, Yan did not become directly involved in Johnson's daily management, but was focused on providing its General Manager with advice on the integration, and on facilitating the connections and communication between Four Dimensions and Johnson.

In May 2008, Four Dimensions established a management committee at Johnson, which consisted of Dr Lin, Yan Zhuohui, the newly appointed Finance Director, the Operations Director and the incumbent Sales and HR Directors. Dr Lin, a Johnson partner in the UK, was a Philippine-Chinese and a former professor at Oxford University; he had two years' experience in a consulting company and could speak Chinese.

As the integration progressed, Wang Yan further recognized the cultural differences between the two sides, and realized that many measures that are effective in China do not apply in the UK. In particular, respect for the acquired company and its employees is very important to the Chinese. Four Dimensions hired HR consulting firm Hewitt in the UK, who helped Wang Yan to communicate with the British employees, partly to express respect for Johnson and its employees, but also to convey a sense of crisis to them. Four Dimensions had been doing its best to defuse the negative emotions felt by the British employees – for example, Four Dimensions had not laid off anyone at Johnson, retaining all employees who wished to stay. However, Johnson's employees in the UK remained sceptical about the real intentions of the Chinese company and the Chinese managers.

Two issues contributed to the frequent changes in Johnson's top management team. First, the two parties disagreed on the company's strategic orientation. Four Dimensions expected Johnson to achieve rapid growth in terms of sales and profitability, and also wanted to rapidly relocate its manufacturing facilities to China, while Johnson thought these strategies were too aggressive, insisting that fast growth must be based on bigger investment in facilities and workforce. Secondly, Johnson had been founded as a family business, and though it had come to be managed by professional managers, many founding members remained in the company and clung to the established ways of doing things – and were thus resistant to Four Dimensions' initiatives for change.

In October 2009, Lü Wenhua joined Four Dimensions as President, and was given great authority by Wang Yan in multiple areas, including finance, HR and administration. Four Dimensions decided to take an indirect approach to managing Johnson – namely, weakening the role of Johnson's General Manager by having Johnson's functional departments managed by the corresponding departments of Four Dimensions; for example, Johnson's Operations Director would report to Four Dimensions' VP of Operations. In the meantime, Johnson changed its General Manager twice. Mike Euson, who finally took on the role in 2011, had worked at Johnson for 16 years, gradually climbing up the corporate ladder from engineer to director, VP and then General Manager in charge of both sales and operations.

THIRD STAGE

Wang Yan realized early on that the cash-in-transit (CIT) vehicle industry was technology-driven and labour-intensive, and that a combination of a British brand with production in China could result in success. During the initial period with Johnson, Wang Yan and Lü Wenhua gradually clarified their thinking on what should be actually manufactured in China, and how to effectively combine that with the British brand. Lü explained: "CIT vehicles are highly localized products. Every country has different requirements. Nevertheless, some general components are standardized, so they can be manufactured in China and shipped to the UK for customized assembly." In other words, Johnson should remain responsible for product design, assembly, sales and sample production, while FDJI in China took care of the production of standardized components. All finished products would be sold under the Johnson brand.

With this strategy, FDJI and Johnson maintained a kind of supplier–customer relationship. However, as independent subsidiaries under Four Dimensions, they sometimes ran into trouble with mutual collaboration and coordination. To address this problem, Four Dimensions reformed its organizational structure and management model in early 2013, separating its departments into CIT vehicle and ambulance divisions (Four Dimensions had acquired the German ambulance manufacturer KFB in 2009). The CIT vehicle division was headquartered in the UK with Euson as General Manager of the division, managing FDJI's production of standardized components in China as well as Johnson's engineering designs, assembly and sample production in the UK.

Rather than tightly controlling Johnson as before, this time Wang Yan and Lü Wenhua granted more autonomy to Euson, and took a hands-off approach to his daily work. Euson's management team at the time was composed of 13 members: 11 British and 2 Chinese nationals. The procurement and production of FDJI were headed by Chinese executives.

Four Dimensions managed Johnson through performance evaluations, and at the same time it established a new incentive system. In the new system, Euson was entitled to an additional allowance and performance-based bonus; if he performed well, his total compensation package could increase by more than 30%.

In addition, Euson and his management team were entitled to stock incentives worth up to 10% of the equity.

With a clearly defined strategy, an organizational structure aligned with corporate strategy, and a competent top management team, Four Dimensions now stepped onto the fast track of growth. CIT vehicles marketed under the Johnson brand captured 70%-80% of the British market, while Four Dimensions products were exported to the Middle East, and orders from Spanish and French customers started coming in large volume.

Encouraged by the greater autonomy, attractive incentives and an effective 'British brand + made-in-China' strategy, Euson became more focused on his new role. He argued:

> "Our advantage lies in the mutual support and collaboration between our British and Chinese operations. It has created a remarkable synergy. Furthermore, we have sharp insights into the markets of different countries. ... My job is to build a management team, articulate our corporate strategy and promote teamwork to do things right."

Wang attributed his previous idea of always using Chinese executives to manage Johnson to the 'Chinese complex', saying: "A Chinese company may be inclined to replace the management team of the company acquired with Chinese executives. But if you want to build an international business, you'd better abandon this idea." He regretted that he had not retained Johnson's original executive team:

> "What do you want to get by acquiring a company? Its technology, brand, channels or markets? You should know that all these are built upon its management team. If you acquire the company but dismiss its existing management team, you may get nothing that you want. Therefore, you must respect the systems and management team of the target company."

From establishing a joint venture with Johnson in 1997 to wholly owning Johnson in 2007, Four Dimensions had been unable to establish a stable and mature executive team, and had no experience in managing overseas subsidiaries. The domestic CIT vehicle business was dominated by strong incumbents, and as a private enterprise, Four Dimensions could not compete in this industry. Compared with British manufacturing companies, the biggest advantage of Chinese counterparts was labour costs. Johnson's production costs were 5% to 10% higher than its local competitors. After FDJI took over the production of standardized components, Johnson's production costs dropped to 5% to 10% lower than its local competitors.

Four Dimensions' integration process was a long-drawn-out procedure that lasted seven years and passed through three stages. Due to Wang Yan's 'Chinese complex', Four Dimensions adopted the My Way integration approach in the first stage, although it did not have the ability to implement this approach, which resulted in resistance in the acquired company from top to bottom, and this stalled the integration process. In the second stage, Four Dimensions attempted to take an indirect route. Although it appointed a British national as Johnson's general manager, it tried to weaken his role by establishing functional reporting lines to VPs based in China. The result was frequent changes in general managers, and Wang Yan was unable to set up a stable executive team. In the third stage, with an increasingly clear strategy, Wang Yan recognized the true value of the acquisition, and Four Dimensions took an Our Way model by authorizing the British business unit to oversee the entire CIT vehicle division, including the China business, and by establishing an effective incentive mechanism.

CASE STUDY:
LENOVO AND IBM

Lenovo's acquisition of IBM's personal computer business is probably the most widely discussed acquisition of a major American business by a Chinese suitor. Thus, few words of introduction are necessary, and this discussion will focus on the several stages in the integration of IBM's PC business, to explore the logical cause and effect.

FIRST STAGE

In May 2005, Lenovo announced the acquisition of IBM's global PC business. Steve Ward, former Senior VP of IBM and General Manager of IBM Personal Systems division, became Lenovo's new CEO, and Yang Yuanqing, former Vice-Chairman of Lenovo, President and CEO, became Lenovo's new Chairman of the Board. Ward had worked at IBM for 26 years, and previously served as General Manager of IBM ThinkPad. Among the 13 top executives of the Lenovo Group, 6 were from IBM, including the CEO, global COO, CMO and head of product development.

Qiao Jian, Lenovo's Senior VP, recalled:

"At that time IBM had around 10,000 employees, and Lenovo had pretty much the same, basically 50/50, but among all of Lenovo's senior management team members, there was no one who had international management experience. Besides, among the top 20 or the top 100 management team members, only two or three people could speak English. Under such circumstances, how should we move forward? Our initial strategy was to 'maintain stability', to protect the business as much as possible without letting it be affected. The first CEO, Steve Ward, managed people in a polite way, and managed businesses in an orderly manner, and thus retained the customers and employees."

From May to September that year, Lenovo adopted a parallel organization model in which Lenovo International (the former IBM PC business division) and Lenovo China were both operating as per their original business model; the two organizations shared financial, legal, HR and other functions, while business functions such as supply chain, product, production and sales operated independently. Lenovo International did not change its management team. Its working methods and processes, staff salaries and benefits remained the same; nearly all 10,000 employees were retained, and the 20 executive team members signed one- to three-year contracts with Lenovo.

To promote cultural integration between Lenovo and IBM, Lenovo put forward a three-word principle: 'Honesty, Respect, Compromise'. Yang Yuanqing interpreted this principle as:

"Firstly, people should be honest with each other. If we have any problem, we should put it on the table and talk about it openly; secondly, we should show respect, and we should not think one's own past culture is the best, instead we should first of all respect each other's culture, and then decide whose is better; the third is to compromise, for if we all insist on our own views, problems might emerge in the end."

According to Lenovo's first-quarter earnings report released in August 2005, Lenovo Group and the IBM PC business were both profitable, but Lenovo was also facing an embarrassing situation: its China business was feeding its global business, and its net profit margin fell from 5% before the acquisition to 2%.

SECOND STAGE

As Qiao Jian explained:

"In this phase, Lenovo conducted comprehensive integration, including integration of organizations and people, as well as integration of brands, product lines and management systems. The integration of the management system included that of the salary structure, as they were different previously."

In October 2005, the two systems formally merged. Lenovo's plan was to establish a unified global management platform and command centre, sharing resources like R&D and supply chain, so as to reduce costs and improve efficiency. Of the two brands, Lenovo would target small and medium-sized companies as well as consumers, while the ThinkPad brand would target high-end customers.

In December, William Amelio succeeded Ward as CEO. Amelio had worked at IBM for 18 years and had also served as Senior VP of Dell and as President for its Asia Pacific and Japan operations. Amelio introduced eight executives from Dell to senior positions at Lenovo Global. The Lenovo executive team became a 'multinational force' consisting of people from Lenovo, IBM and Dell.

As Qiao Jian recalled:

"Dell's culture is making decisions quickly, doing things decisively, willing to make changes, and being performance-oriented and cost-oriented. After Amelio became the CEO, he carried out three major layoffs, restructured the organization, replaced the management team, greatly reduced the supply chain costs, and divided the regions again. I think a very big advantage was that it made everyone (including Lenovo people and IBM people) realize that we had to change. Only through change can we move on."

In order to improve the global supply chain management, Amelio made some personnel adjustments: Liu Jun, Senior VP for Global Supply Chain, was replaced by Amelio's old subordinate Jerry Smith; Guo Minglei and Song Hong, two VPs of Lenovo in charge of global supply chain, also left for personal reasons. By March 2008, there were only six original Lenovo people in the top team of 23 executives. In this phase, Lenovo transferred its R&D and manufacturing from high-cost to low-cost areas, and laid off more than 2,000 employees in two years, which was 5% of all the employees.

During that period, Lenovo also carried out cultural integration. They started 'cultural cocktail' activities so that everyone had a better understanding of the differences between Chinese and Western culture. They also established a global integration and diversification office to promote Lenovo's new 'global culture'. Based on honesty and respect, Lenovo added the new values of winning and the pursuit-of-performance orientation.

During the fiscal year 2007-2008, Lenovo's performance declined, with a net profit of US$460 million, including a one-time gain of US$65 million from selling the loss-making Lenovo Mobile.

"Lenovo successfully completed the post-acquisition integration of IBM PC business. The acquisition is a success," said Yang Yuanqing.

THIRD STAGE

In 2008, the financial crisis caused a major downturn in the commercial market for computers; however, the consumer market was relatively less affected. As Lenovo's overseas business was primarily in the commercial market, the company saw a significant decline in business. In early 2009, Yang Yuanqing resumed the position of Lenovo's CEO, and Liu Chuanzhi acted as Chairman. In the international executive team of nine people, five were Chinese and four were foreigners. Lenovo also set up an eight-strong executive committee, with the Chinese and foreign sides taking four positions each. They jointly took responsibility for the Group's operations.

In January 2009, the Lenovo Group announced a further layoff of 2,500 people, accounting for 11% of its employees. At the same time, Lenovo announced a strategic adjustment plan: on the customer side, it changed from IBM PC's original key accounts based on relationship, to the former Lenovo's personal and small and medium-sized customers; with respect to business regions, it turned more and more from mature markets to emerging markets. A new 'Two Fists Strategy' envisaged the ThinkPad product group as the 'left fist', targeting mature markets and commercial key accounts, and consolidated its market while strengthening profitability so as to ensure profit maximization. It took the Idea product group as the 'right fist' to target emerging markets and consumers, not aiming to be profitable in the early period, but to focus on capturing market share and to gain market awareness.

In April 2010, Lenovo released a mobile Internet strategy, and launched its first generation of mobile Internet terminal products to handle the impact of mobile Internet on personal computers. In April 2012, Lenovo released a 'PC+' strategy: Lenovo would launch a terminal product covering four product categories – smartphone, tablet PC, personal computer and smart TV. By integrating with

Lenovo Leyun services, it realized its transition from a traditional personal computer industry leader to a PC+ field leader.

In this phase, Lenovo was committed to building a culture of 'ownership', from a '4P' to a '5P' culture:

1. **Plan**: Think before promising.
2. **Perform**: All promises should be realized.
3. **Prioritize**: Corporate interests first.
4. **Practice**: Make progress every day, every year.
5. **Pioneer**: Dare to be the world's first and encourage innovation.

During the fiscal year 2012-2013, the sales of Lenovo Group were US$33.873 billion, a year-on-year increase of 15%, and its net profit was $635 million, a year-on-year increase of 34%. Lenovo still maintained the world's second position among personal computer manufacturers. Its global sales of smartphones rose by 3.7 times, occupying the second place in the domestic market.

Lenovo was one of the most recognized computer brands in China, with a broad retail network and low-cost and efficient procurement, production and distribution channels. However, before the acquision of IBM's PC business, the firm had no international experience. However, Lenovo was strong financially. During 1994-2000, Lenovo's average annual turnover and profit both grew by more than 80%, with a market share of more than 30%. In the year prior to the acquisition (2004), its net profit was HK$120 million.

After acquisition by Denovo, the competitive edge of IBM's PC business was much stronger compared with other competitors in the Chinese market such as Dell and Hewlett-Packard. The two companies complemented each other remarkably both in business and in geography, and the growth potential was huge. If the scale was expanded, IBM's PC business would be in a stronger position to control the supply chain of the PC industry. In 2003, the IBM PC unit generated revenues of US$11.56 billion, accounting for 10% of IBM's total revenue, with a loss of $118 million. However, IBM had a strong value proposition, as it was the world's top high-end corporate computer brand, with a strong advantage in corporate customers and in global sales and service networks. But IBM's technology, brand and sales channel resources could easily be lost with the departure of key talent, and could not easily be transferred on a large scale.

Lenovo's post-acquisition integration process was divided into three stages, as the arrangement of its executive team turned from appointing the executives of the acquired company, to introducing outside executives, and then returning to the Yang and Liu partnership. The first stage was the stabilization phase – to stabilize the team, customers and related stakeholders. Lenovo had few executives experienced in international management, so it appointed IBM's Steve Ward as the CEO. This was followed by the integration phase: Lenovo introduced William Amelio and the Dell team. The third stage was the development stage. Over the three years of integration and learning, Lenovo's own executive team gradually gained the ability to manage international business. Yang Yuanqing returned as the CEO, and there are now an equal number of Chinese and foreign executives in the top executive team.

8.2   Conclusion

The complexity of post-acquisition management implies that the ideal model of integration may not be found immediately, especially if the acquiring organization has limited prior experience in managing M&As. The Four Dimensions–Johnson and Lenovo cases illustrate that due to the complexity of post-acquisition integration, regardless of management capability, financial strength and ability to enhance value after acquisition, integration often has to go through several stages, after comprehensively taking into account the situation of both sides and the macro market environment. Four Dimensions initially used the My Way approach, which took a wrong turn; it gradually transitioned to the Our Way approach, which brought the company onto the right track. Lenovo changed from Light Touch to Your Way and then to Our Way, according to its own organizational capabilities and development needs. Lenovo's approach to managing and integrating IBM's PC business is largely seen as successful, and an inspiration to other Chinese entrepreneurs with ambitions to build a globally competitive company.

Light Touch, Our Way, My Way, Your Way… whatever way a Chinese company adopts, there must be a degree of organizational change both in the company itself and in the affiliate it has acquired. There are many factors that could influence the decision whether to change the critical aspects of the affiliate: these include how closely the parent company wishes to control the affiliate, whether the parent's strategy is to build global standardized systems within the group or keep the affiliates localized, etc. Even if the acquiring firm decides that the affiliate needs extensive changes, it must still consider whether it has the capabilities to maintain the affiliate's operation and customer bases, especially in the case of companies from developing countries in the early stages of post-merger integration.

But the most important factor of all is the company's strategy and motivation for undertaking M&As. For those companies that hope to expand in terms of size or market share, organizational changes such as layoffs and reducing overlap businesses are essential. If the aim is to acquire tangible assets such as advanced technologies, brands and/ or capabilities, then the priority must be to retain existing talent and facilitate the transfer of these assets; this implies a minimal degree of organizational change in the acquired company. The wide-ranging case studies we present in this book make it clear that Chinese companies' post-merger integration strategies play a crucial role in supporting their globalization strategy.

NOTES AND FURTHER READING

1   Ministry of Commerce of People's Republic of China, National Bureau of Statistics of People's Republic of China, State Administration of Foreign Exchange, "2012 Statistical Bulletin of China's Outward Foreign Direct Investment," China Statistics Press, 2013, accessed 22 Nov. 2017

2   J.P. Beijing, "What is China's belt and road initiative?", The Economist (15 May 2017); https://www.economist.com/blogs/economist-explains/2017/05/economist-explains-11, accessed 17 Nov. 2017.

3   中国经济网——《经济日报》,【学思践悟·十九大】坚持对外开放基本国策 促进"一带一路"国际合作, 2 Nov. 2017; http://views.ce.cn/view/ent/201711/02/t20171102_26730922.shtml, accessed 22 Nov. 2017.

4   2016 *Statistical Bulletin* of China's Outward Foreign Direct Investment.

5   Jack Sidders and Vinicy Chan, "China's $246 Billion Foreign Buying Spree Is Unraveling, *Bloomberg Markets* (11 May 2017; https://www.bloomberg.com/news/articles/2017-05-10/china-s-246-billion-takeover-spree-is-crumbling-as-sellers-balk, accessed 17 Nov. 2017.

6   Greenfield investment is a form of FDI where a parent company creates a new business from scratch (literally on an undeveloped or 'greenfield' site in the host country) that it fully owns.

7   2016 *Statistical Bulletin* of China's Outward Foreign Direct Investment.

8   2016 *Statistical Bulletin* of China's Outward Foreign Direct Investment.

9   2016 *Statistical Bulletin* of China's Outward Foreign Direct Investment.

10 2012 *Statistical Bulletin* of China's Outward Foreign Direct Investment.

11 2016 *Statistical Bulletin* of China's Outward Foreign Direct Investment.

12 ChinaGoAbroad,《中国企业国际化报告2014》节选—中国企业海外投资走向"高端路线"; http://www.chinagoabroad.com/zh/article/17845, accessed 18 Nov. 2017.

13 The Economist Intelligence Unit, 2013, 中国海外投资指数报告, http://graphics.eiu.com/assets/images/public/China_going_global/China_Going_Global_Chinese_version.pdf; accessed 19 Nov. 2017.

14 *OECD World Investment Report 2017*, Annex, table 2: FDI outflows, by region and economy, 1990-2016.

15 *OECD World Investment Report 2017*, Annex, table 04: FDI outward stock, by region and economy, 1990-2016.

16 Ibid.

17 Reconnecting Asia, "Belt and Road at China's 19th Party Congress - Quotes and Quotas," Reconnecting Asia, Last modified October 26, 2017, https://reconnectingasia.csis.org/analysis/entries/belt-and-road-19th-party-congress/, accessed 22 Nov. 2017.

18 中国经济网《经济日报》,【学思践悟·十九大】坚持对外开放基本国策促进"一带一路"国际合作, 2 Nov. 2017; http://views.ce.cn/view/ent/201711/02/t20171102_26730922.shtml, accessed 22 Nov. 2017.

19 Brookings University – Future Development, "China's Belt and Road Initiative", 22 Sept. 2017; https://www.brookings.edu/blog/future-development/2017/09/22/future-development-reads-chinas-belt-and-road-initiative/, accessed 22 Nov. 2017.

20 中国经济网《经济日报》,【学思践悟 · 十九大】坚持对外开放基本国策 促进 "一带一路" 国际合作, 2 November, 2017; http://views.ce.cn/view/ent/201711/02/t20171102_26730922.shtml, accessed 22 November, 2017.

21 中国自由贸易区服务网,http://fta.mofcom.gov.cn

22 The model was originally proposed in J. H. Dunning, "Towards an Eclectic Theory of International Production," *Journal of International Business Studies* 11(1) (1980): 9-31. The most comprehensive development and application of the model is contained in the textbook by J. H. Dunning and S. M. Lundan, "Multinational Enterprises and the Global Economy", 2nd edn. (Cheltenham: Elgar, 2008).

23 On the debate on ownership advantages and emerging-economy MNEs, see for example A. M. Rugman, "Theoretical Aspects of MNEs from Emerging Economics" in R. Ramamurti and J. V. Singh (eds), *Emerging Multinationals in Emerging Markets* (New York: Cambridge University Press, 2009), 42-63; R. Ramamurti, "What Is Really Different About Emerging Market Multinationals?" *Global Strategy Journal* 2(1) (2012): 41-47; A. Verbeke and L. Kano. "The New Internalization Theory and Multinational Enterprises from Emerging Economies: A Business History Perspective," *Business History Review* 89(3) (2016): 415-455; Klaus E. Meyer, "Catch-Up and Leapfrogging: Emerging Economy Multinational Enterprises on the Global Stage," *International Journal of Economics of Business* (forthcoming).

24 The internationalization process model was originally proposed by Johanson and Vahlne in 1977, and periodically updated by the same authors over the next 40 years. For the most recent debate over the merits and limitations of the model, see the debate in *Journal of International Business Studies,* Vol.48 (2017).

25 On the application of the internationalization process model to emerging-economy MNEs see S. Young, C. H. Huang and M. McDermott, "Internationalization and Competitive Catch-Up Processes: Case Study Evidence on Chinese Multinational Enterprises," *Management International Review* 36 (1996): 295-314; K. E. Meyer and Thaijongrak Ornjira., "The Dynamics of Emerging Economy MNEs: How the Internationalization Process Model Can Guide Future Research," *Asia Pacific Journal of Management, Vol 30, Issue 4* (2013): p1125-1153; Klaus E. Meyer, "Process Perspectives on the Growth of Emerging Economy Multinationals" in A. Cuervo-Cazurra and R. Ramamurti, (eds), *Understanding Multinationals from Emerging Markets* (Cambridge: Cambridge University Press, 2014): 169-194; P. Hertenstein, D. Sutherland and J. Anderson, "Internationalization Within Networks: Exploring the Relationship Between Inward and Outward FDI in China's Auto Components Industry, *Asia Pacific Journal of Management* 34(1) (2017): 69-96.

26 Leslie Hook, "China's Wanda to Buy AMC for $2.6bn," *Financial Times* (21 May 2012); https://www.ft.com/content/752013e8-a2fc-11e1-826a-00144feabdc0, accessed 22 November, 2017.

27 Scott Mendelson, "Box Office: 'The Great Wall' Targeted American and Chinese Audiences but Pleased Neither," *Forbes* Media and Entertainment (23 Febraury, 2017); https://www.forbes.com/sites/scottmendelson/2017/02/23/box-office-the-great-wall-targeted-american-and-chinese-audiences-but-pleased-neither/#5571308f2e23 accessed 22 November, 2017.

28 "Latest News: Wang Jianlin Gives Open Lecture at Oxford to Decrypt Wanda's Globalization," Wanda Group Official Website (24 February, 2016); https://www.wanda-group.com/2016/latest_0224/1125.html, accessed 22 November, 2017. Additional sources for case study updates: Josh Nobel and Gabriel Wildau, "Dalian Wanda Changes Property Strategy after IPO," *Financial Times* (15 January, 2015), https://www.ft.com/content/cda49dc0-9c98-11e4-a730-00144feabdc0, accessed 22 November, 2017; "Corporate Profile," Wanda Group Official Website, https://www.wanda-group.com/corporate/, accessed 22 November, 2017.

29 中国行业研究，"间断两年后中国企业重返非洲采矿业，"中国行业研究，(8 February, 2014); http://www.chinairn.com/news/20140208/163909507.html, accessed 23 November, 2017.

30 Sources: "MagIndustries taken over by China's Evergreen" *National Post* (20 April 2011); "Potash price hammered as Russians may flood market", *CBC News* (30 July 2013); "MagIndustries Corp reveals evidence that subsidiaries allegedly paid major bribes in Republic of Congo", *National Post* (17 June 2015); "The MagIndustries Investigation: Another example of RCMP's investigation into CFPOA violations arising out of overseas corruption," www.osler.com, (18 June 2015) accessed 27 November, 2015.

31 The quote is obtained from field research conducted by the Center for Globalization of Chinese Companies. ChinaCases.org, accesssed 27 November, 2017.

32 Ibid.

33 Freda Wan, "China's Food Security, 2.0 and Beyond," *Forbes Asia* (21 May, 2014), https://www.forbes.com/sites/fredawan/2014/05/21/china-food-security/#3367449829ba, accessed 22 November, 2017; Whitney McFerron, "China Ending its One-Child Policy Offers a Boost to Dairy Demand," *Bloomberg* (29 October, 2015), https://www.bloomberg.com/news/articles/2015-10-29/china-ending-one-child-policy-offers-boost-to-world-dairy-demand, accessed 22 November, 2017; Chalida Ekvitthayavechnukul, "Bright Food-Backed Synlait Milk buys Auckland-Based Dairy Firm for $39.8m," *Deal Street Asia* (2 June 2017), https://www.dealstreetasia.com/stories/bright-food-synlait-milk-purchase-39-8m-74142/, accessed 22 November, 2017; Mote Chan，"中国乳业的下一个10年：品类战争时代," *Sohu News* (7 October, 2017), http://www.sohu.com/a/196234607_313170, accessed 23 November, 2017.

34 Chervon, "Chinese Manufacturer Chervon Acquires Skil Brand from Bosch," *ChinaGoAbroad* (2 September, 2016), http://www.chinagoabroad.com/en/recent_transaction/chinese-manufacturer-chervon-acquires-skil-brand-from-bosch, accessed 17 November, 2017.

35 人民网，"新华视点:中国手机出口10亿部 换不来1%利润?，"人民网 (23 October, 2012); http://finance.people.com.cn/n/2012/1023/c70846-19361076-1.html, accessed 27 November, 2017.

36 工业品营销研究院，"【行业分析】迷茫的中国制造，未来之路在何方？"工业品营销研究院，(1 August, 2014), http://www.china-imsc.com/yanjiu_info_377_1588.html, accessed 27 November, 2017.

37 网易新闻，"中国职工受教育水平较低，高素质技术人才匮乏，"中国新闻网, (March 2013) http://news.163.com/13/0307/16/8PCL41RN00014JB6.html, accessed November 22, 2017; 163 News, "Chinese workers had mostly low level of education; China lacked highly-educated workers," China News.

38 刘梅，"揭开中国消费者的面纱，"钛媒体, (26 April, 2013); http://www.tmtpost.com/498353.html, accessed 27 November, 2017.

39 Center for Globalization of Chinese Companies, "ICBC and Standard Bank Case", ChinaCases.org, accessed 22 November, 2017.

40 Jerin Mathew, "China's ICBC to Bolster London Trading Operations Via $770m Deal with Standard Bank," *International Business Times* (30 January, 2014); http://www.ibtimes.co.uk/chinas-icbc-bolster-london-trading-operations-via-770m-deal-standard-bank-1434406, accessed 18 November, 2017.

41 Andrew England, "ICBC Buys Stake in Standard Bank's UK Business," *Financial Times* (2 February, 2015); https://www.ft.com/content/b4c8903c-aade-11e4-91d2-00144feab7de, accessed 22 November, 2017.

42 "Biostime Agrees to Finance French Infant Formula Plant Expansion," *Dairy Reporter* (4 July 2013); https://www.dairyreporter.com/Article/2013/07/05/Biostime-agrees-to-finance-French-infant-formula-plant-expansion, accessed 17 November, 2017.

43 Ibid.

44 Wang Zhuoqiong, "Biostime Swallows Swisse Wellness Group," *China Daily* (19 September, 2015); http://www.chinadaily.com.cn/bizchina/2015-09/19/content_21923805.htm, accessed 21 November, 2017.

45 Elisa Nessl, "Chinese Nutrition Firm Biostime Chooses Geneva to Go International," *Switzerland Global Enterprise* (10 May, 2017); https://www.s-ge.com/en/article/news/chinese-nutrition-firm-biostime-chooses-geneva-go-international, accessed 17 November, 2017.

46 Ashlee Clark Thompson, "It's Official: GE Appliances Belongs to Haier," *CNET* (6 June, 2016); https://www.cnet.com/news/its-official-ge-appliances-belongs-to-haier/, accessed 22 November, 2017.

47 Xie Yu, "Haier Bought GE Appliances for US$5.6 Billion. Now it's Working on Fixing it," *South China Morning Post*, (23 October, 2017); http://www.scmp.com/business/companies/article/2116486/chinas-haier-has-plan-help-continue-turnaround-ge-appliances, accessed 23 November, 2017.

48 Associate Press, "Haier Boss Looks Far Beyond Appliances," *abc News* (30 March, 2017); http://abcnews.go.com/amp/International/wireStory/haier-boss-appliances-46457320, accessed 23 November, 2017.

49 Xie Yu, "Haier Bought GE Appliances for US$5.6 Billion. Now it's Working on Fixing it," *South China Morning Post* (23 Oct. 2017); http://www.scmp.com/business/companies/article/2116486/chinas-haier-has-plan-help-continue-turnaround-ge-appliances, accessed 23 November, 2017.

50 魏方舟，"华为发布2015年年报，全球销售额3950亿，海外收入58%，"白鲸出海, April 2016, http://www.baijingapp.com/article/5141, accessed 23 November, 2017 Wei Fangzhou, "Huawei distributed 2015 annual report; the company generated 395 billion in revenue, out of which 58% were from overseas market," Bai Jing Chu Ha.

51 腾讯科技，"鹰的重生 TCL国际化征途中的革新与蜕变，"腾讯网，(11 October, 2007); http://tech.qq.com/a/20071011/000195.htm, accessed 27 November, 2017.

52 刘佳，"一个感动中石化的法国人，"新浪专栏，(20 May, 2013); http://finance.sina.com.cn/column/international/20130520/084415517843.shtml, accessed 27 November, 2017.

53 Reuters, "Fosun Finally Set to Win US$4.3 Billion Takeover Battle for Club Med," *South China Morning Post* (5 January, 2015); http://www.scmp.com/business/companies/article/1674111/fosun-finally-set-win-us43bln-takeover-battle-club-med, accessed 21 November, 2017.

54 中国国际经济合作学会，"复星海外模式分析：要做的改变将远不仅是走出一场风波这么简单，"中国国际经济合作学会，2016年; http://cafiec.mofcom.gov.cn/article/tongjipeixun/201607/20160701366946.shtml, accessed 14 April, 2017.

55 Tom Levitt, "China Seeks Safety in US Meat Giant Smithfield," *Chinadialogue* (6 March, 2013); https://www.chinadialogue.net/blog/6066-China-seeks-safety-in-US-meat-giant-Smithfield/en, accessed 17 November, 2017.

56 Steve Schaefer, "Pork Pact: China's Shuanghui Will Pay $4.7B for Smithfield Foods," *Forbes* (29 May, 2013); https://www.forbes.com/sites/steveschaefer/2013/05/29/pork-pact-chinas-shuanghui-will-pay-4-7b-for-smithfield-foods/#71b7320f348f, accessed 22 November,2017.

57 Daisuke Harashima, "China's pork giant WH expanding presence in US," *Nikkei Asian Review* (16 December, 2016); https://asia.nikkei.com/Business/Companies/China-s-pork-giant-WH-expanding-presence-in-US, accessed 22 November, 2017.

58 Daisuke Harashima, "China's Pork Giant Wh Expanding Presence in US," *Nikkei Asian Review* (16 December, 2016); https://asia.nikkei.com/Business/Companies/China-s-pork-giant-WH-expanding-presence-in-US, accessed 17 November, 2017.

59 Smithfield Foods, "Smithfield Foods Completes Acquisition of Pini Group's Packaged Meats Companies," *Nasdaq GlobeNewswire* (1 June, 2017); https://globenewswire.com/news-release/2017/06/01/1005318/0/en/Smithfield-Foods-Completes-Acquisition-of-Pini-Group-s-Packaged-Meats-Companies.html, accessed 17 Nov. 2017; "Chinas WH Group to Buy Romanian Meat Producers in Europe Push," *Reuters* (26 September, 2017); https://www.reuters.com/article/us-wh-group-romania-acquisitions/chinas-wh-group-to-buy-romanian-meat-producers-in-europe-push-idUSKCN1C102A, accessed 18 November, 2017.

60 张奕，"三一重工收购德国大象案例探讨，"现代商贸工业，2012年第8期，91-92页 Zhang Yi, "Sanyi acquired Putzmeister case analysis", Volume 8, 2013, Pages 91-92

61 Ibid.

62 Caroline Copley, "As China Shops for German Firms, One Early Example Reassures," *Reuters – Technology News* (3 June, 2016); https://www.reuters.com/article/us-putzmeister-sany-insight/as-china-shops-for-german-firms-one-early-example-reassures-idUSKCN0YO2IA, accessed 18 November, 2017.

63 张奕，"三一重工收购德国大象案例探讨，"现代商贸工业，2012年第8期，91-92页 Zhang Yi, "Sanyi acquired Putzmeister case analysis", Volume 8, 2013, Pages 91-92

64 搜狐新闻，"收购沃尔沃5年后，吉利竟成杀气腾腾的国车黑马，"搜狐新闻， (June 19, 2015); http://www.sohu.com/a/19428889_132355, Sohu News, "Geely became a leading vehicle manufacturer in China five years after its acquisition of Volvo," Sohu News.

65 搜狐新闻，"收购沃尔沃5年后，吉利竟成杀气腾腾的国车黑马，"搜狐新闻，Last modified June 19, 2015, http://www.sohu.com/a/19428889_132355 Sohu News, "Geely became a leading vehicle manufacturer in China five years after its acquisition of Volvo," Sohu News.

66 Lyu Chang , "Geely Acquires British Electric Startup Emerald," *China Daily Europe* (4 March, 2014); http://europe.chinadaily.com.cn/china/2014-03/04/content_17319391.htm, accessed 18 November, 2017.

67 Wu Yiyao, "Geely Swoops on Stake in Saxo Bank," *China Daily* (9 May, 2017); http://www.chinadaily.com.cn/business/motoring/2017-05/09/content_29258944.htm, accessed 18 November, 2017.

68 丁远，张华，董梁，"联想系列案例———世纪之交的选择，"中欧国际工商学院案例库， Last modified 2012. Yuan Ding, Hua Zhang, Liang Dong, "Lenovo - Case A," ChinaCases.org.

69 Ibid.

70 Ibid.

71   Ibid.

72   Ma Si, "Lenovo Acquires NEC Stake in Joint Venture," *City of Beijing* (6 July, 2016); http://www.chinadaily.com.cn/beijing/2016-07/06/content_26006775.htm, accessed 19 November, 2017.

73   丁远，张华，董梁，"联想系列案例———世纪之交的选择，" 中欧国际工商学院案例库, Last modified 2012. Yuan Ding, Hua Zhang, Liang Dong, "Lenovo - Case A," ChinaCases.org.

74   For a review of this literature see Klaus E. Meyer, "What Is Strategic Asset Seeking FDI?" *Multinational Business Review* 23 (1) (2015): 57-66.

75   Yang Jing and Wu Jing, "The end of the wheel," *Caixin Weekly* (formerly *New Century*) 20 (26 May, 2014); http://magazine.caixin.com/2014-05-23/100681385.html

76   Li Dong Sheng, CEO of TCL, was selected as the 'CCTV 2004 China Economic Person of the Year'. He said in his acceptance speech: "If we want to be a super power country, we have to have our own international companies, our generation has to embrace the challenge and get our hands dirty and become the first to test the water."

77   "Pledge announcement on the right of holding shares of Rotary Vortex Ltd., by Henan Shuanghui Investment Development Limited." Shuanghui Development's holding company pledged all its non-tradable shares in Shuanghui Development, and promised the future profit dividend to secure Shuanghui International's offshore bank loans (used to purchase Smithfield).

78   For more on WH Group's capital story, see "WH Group," *Caixin New Century* and "鼎辉是与非," *21ˢᵗ Century Economic Report*.

79   "Newbridge Investment: King of Buyout Funds," *The Economic Observer* (7 May 2010)

80   "Lenovo's Capital Inheritance," *Talent* (December, 2010)

81   "Lenovo's Global Approach," *Sanlian Life Weekly* (September, 2010)

82   "Lenovo's Capital Inheritance," *Talent* (December, 2010)

83   Yang Yuanqing, "No Funding Gap Available for Three Major Investment Institutions to Join Lenovo," *Sohu IT* (31 March, 2005)

84   "Legend of Lenovo: How to Gain Value Through Overseas Acquisitions," *Chinese Entrepreneur* (17 November, 2007)

85   "Yang Yuan Qing's Lenovo to the World," *Chinese Entrepreneur* (17 November, 2007)

86   "Lenovo's Capital Inheritance," *Talent* (December, 2010).

87   Ibid.

88   Ibid.

89   Ibid.

90   The case was supported by Professor Zhang Hua of the Finance Department at CEIBS.

91   "We failed to deliver our promises," admits David Munro, current CEO of a corporate and investment banking firm under Standard Bank Group, '… In the first year, profit contributed by the strategic cooperation was around US$10 million … Now, looking back on what happened then, I think we may have had no choice."

92 This rule probably originates from Jack Prouty, a partner at the US consulting firm Step-Change Management, and former partner at KPMG Global Mergers and Acquisitions.

93 *Managing Acquisitions: Creating Value Through Corporate Renewal.* (New York: Free Press, 1991).

94 "Top Management Turnover Following Mergers and Acquisitions." *Strategic Management Journal* 9 (1988): 173-81.

95 *Mergers and Acquisitions: Turmoil in Top Management Teams.* (New York: Business Expert Press, 2009).

96 "Don't Integrate Your Acquisitions, Partner With Them." *Harvard Business Review* (Dec. 2009): See also P. Kale and Harbir Singh, "Characteristics of Emerging Market Mergers and Acquisitions" in David Faulkner, Satu Teerikangas and Richard J. Joseph (eds), *The Handbook of Mergers and Acquisitions.* (Oxford: Oxford University Press, 2012).

97 For a further discussion of the challenges of talent management and human resource development in Chinese MNEs see Klaus E. Meyer and Katherine R. Xin, "Managing Talent in Emerging Economy Multinationals: Integrating Strategic Management and Human Resource Management," *International Journal of Human Resource Management* (2018, advance online).

98 Dominique Vidalon, Pascale Denis, "Club Med back on expansion path with China's Fosun - CEO" *Reuters* (8 June, 2016); http://www.reuters.com/article/clubmed-fosun-idUSL8N18U3LE, accessed 17 November, 2017.

99 The Club had 56% of customers booking via a tablet or smartphone.

25TH

LID
ANNIVERSARY

Sharing knowledge since 1993

- 1993 Madrid
- 2008 Mexico DF and Monterrey
- 2010 London
- 2011 New York and Buenos Aires
- 2012 Bogotá
- 2014 Shanghai